D1564272

GOVERNANCE

for

The Two-Year College

RICHARD C. RICHARDSON, JR.
Northampton County Area Community College

CLYDE E. BLOCKER
Harrisburg Area Community College

LOUIS W. BENDER
Florida State University

Prentice-Hall, Inc., Englewood Cliffs, New Jersey

to

Patricia B. Richardson

Janne S. Blocker

Elizabeth N. Bender

ISBN–0–13–360677–5

Library of Congress Catalog Card Number 70–39061

10 9 8 7 6 5 4 3 2 1

PRINTED IN THE UNITED STATES OF AMERICA

*Prentice-Hall International, Inc., London
Prentice-Hall of Australia, Pty. Ltd., Sydney
Prentice-Hall of Canada, Ltd., Toronto
Prentice-Hall of India Private Limited, New Delhi
Prentice-Hall of Japan, Inc., Tokyo*

Contents

part two   THE THEORY

part three   THE ORGANIZATION

Foreword

The community college developed with elements of both secondary school and university structures incorporated in it. From the secondary schools it inherited a focus on the teaching-learning process, primary interest in students, and an administrative structure that saw the president (principal) at the top of a chain of command. Faculty ranking systems, an emphasis on subject matter specialization, and major curriculum emphases came from the universities.

Much of the history of the community college has centered around its attempts to reconcile the anomalies in structure and functioning that resulted from the disparities in its heritage. The early community colleges developed with autocratic leaders making all the major decisions in a context of rigid bureaucracy, secrecy, and an attitude of "If you don't like it, you can leave!" However, the twin developments of faculty militancy and student unrest in the 1960s forced a redefinition of community college administration. The autocrat became as outmoded as the hickory stick and today's college administrator operates in a sphere of compromise and reconciliation between contending forces.

This book is written by three men of vast practical experience in managing community colleges. They know the value—nay, the necessity

—of administrative structures and relationships that mitigate conflicts. Recognizing that state and national legislation, professional associations, accrediting and licensing agencies, and the predilections of local governing boards are frequently at odds, they present a picture of administration that is uniquely qualified to live with contending forces. And they offer indispensible, comprehensive advice on how to handle these relationships. Refusing to hide behind platitudes and vague recommendations, they offer concrete suggestions for reconciling the frequently conflicting demands of the various legally constituted, voluntary, and quasi-legal forces that impinge upon college management.

The book is for presidents, aspiring presidents, graduate students, and others who wish to learn philosophies and techniques of effective administration. It accepts the institution itself as the point of attention and assumes that the administrator's responsibility is to insure institutional perpetuity. And within this framework it holds that the best possible result for an administrator is "a feeling that a just compromise among conflicting interests has been effected." The administrator who accepts these premises will find much of value in these pages.

Here are concepts of administration for the modern educational institution. The authors argue for a participant model in order to obtain optimal satisfaction, effectiveness, and communication both within the institution and between the institution and its various constituencies. They emphasize that the community college must not maintain a top-down bureaucracy, that all the people within it have to be recognized as having needs and desires that the institution—in order to remain viable—must satisfy. And one of the ways those needs can be satisfied best is by offering all parties—students and faculty members, as well as administrators—a full share of responsibility in making institutional decisions.

This view of administration as a participatory process will not be palatable to the bureaucrats, young and old, who insist on knowing who reports to whom and who see the president at the top of the pyramid. The administrator who maintains his position of authority by withholding information and manipulating subordinates especially will be bemused by statements such as "painful as the process of revelation may be, the consequences of attempting to continue a policy of secrecy are apt to be even more drastic." The person whose satisfaction with his job demands a corps of sycophants gains no sympathy in these well-documented pages. However, this book is not directed toward the autocrat. It is for a new generation of educational leaders who will take the community college into an era in which all people within the institution are well aware of what it is about.

ARTHUR M. COHEN
Associate Professor in Higher Education,
University of California, Los Angeles

Preface

Crisis management in American higher education has become common-place. The advent of confrontation tactics combined with the develop-ment of power groups seeking to manipulate public opinion has contributed to the emergence of a series of issues with which our colleges have frequently been ill prepared to cope. The consequences of ineffec-tive responses are only too evident in the loss of public confidence as well as in the increasing number of symptoms of institutional malaise.

During the past decade the two-year college has grown from a relatively insignificant segment of higher education to a principal source of educa-tional opportunity for millions of students. This period of unparalleled growth has resulted in the development of large complex institutions susceptible to the same problems of internal rigidity, conflict, and lack of coherent direction that have plagued many four-year colleges and universities. An examinaton of the ineffectiveness of many of our re-sponses to the conditions of growth and the challenges of change leads inescapably to the conclusion that we must reappraise our administrative and governance procedures in search of viable alternatives to traditional practices that have become outmoded.

In part, our problems can be related to the peculiar dichotomy that has existed between theory and practice in the field of educational administration. Practitioners have given limited attention to administrative theory as evidenced by the literature of practitioners which, replete with homilies and personal experiences, may be said to constitute the folklore of administration. The danger of separating theory from practice is evident in the structural rigor mortis that has so impaired the functioning of many of our institutions. Good theory and good practice are inextricably interwoven. To observe that a practice works without knowing why leads to the blind observance of tradition. By the same token, saying that a practice ought to work when it obviously doesn't is contrary to common sense. An understanding of the situational determinants of effective practice contributes to an ability to initiate change when new variables occur.

The purpose of this book is to combine theory and practice to suggest a viable alternative to traditional practices of college administration and governance. The alternative we suggest is the participative model which has as its goal the development of cooperative relationships among all members of the college community as opposed to confrontation, which seems increasingly to be an inevitable concomitant of the more traditional bureaucratic model. While our focus is clearly upon the institution, we have endeavored to identify and suggest methods of adjusting to the rapidly growing array of external forces that shape institutional environment and those who interact within it.

We suggest the existence of three major internal constituencies requiring two separate procedures for interaction. Given the existence of a workable consensus sustained by common values and norms, the bureaucratic administrative structure remains the most efficient procedure for accomplishing coordination. In the absence of such a consensus, new values must evolve through the structure of governance that operates to protect the interests of all three constituencies while at the same time providing the means of effective interaction through which equitable and, hence, workable compromises may evolve. The structure of governance offers the power relationships of interdependency as an alternative to the power conflicts induced by the inappropriate use of the authority of the structure of administration.

The concepts discussed in this volume are the product of interactions between students, faculty, administrators, and trustees. While it would be impossible to acknowledge all of the contributors, a heavy debt is owed to the faculties, staffs, trustees, and students of the institutions with which the authors have worked. Without their contributions this would simply be one more book about subjective perceptions of practical experiences or an additional compilation of the residue of scholarly thought. Thanks to their contributions these ideas have been tested and evaluated. Their proper application does have the capability of creating a more effective environment for human development along with a level of achievement necessary to restore public confidence and trust in our institutions.

It is not easy to implement the ideas contained in this book. If the situation were not so very critical and the alternatives so sterile we would be inclined to advise the reader to proceed with the participative approach at his own peril. Most of us must unlearn behaviors that our entire experience with the existing system of education has fostered before we can begin to learn the behaviors this system demands. It is not easy to substitute the active involvement and accountability demanded by the participative model for the comfortable passivity and mediocre performance standards to which we have been accustomed. The rewards, however, are as great as the sacrifice demanded. Within the participative model everyone is expected to grow, change, and develop. An institution is so much more exciting and inspiring when everyone feels the fulfillment of being a contributing member.

The writers gratefully acknowledge the significant assistance in the development of this manuscript provided by Mrs. Ruth Brewer, Mrs. Jo Eslinger, and Mrs. Betty Bender.

RICHARD C. RICHARDSON, JR.
CLYDE E. BLOCKER
LOUIS W. BENDER

part I

THE
CONTEXT

one

National and Regional Influences

To understand an organization, we must analyze its internal structure as well as its relationship to the system within which it functions. While it is not possible to separate the two in actuality, for our purposes it will be helpful to begin by focusing attention upon the general environment before undertaking an analysis of internal functioning of the two-year college.

The concept of a model or system is a useful tool for social analysis. A system is an aggregate of things, parts, or people forming an organized complex whole. It is made up of distinct elements which are directly or indirectly related to all other elements. Any change in the position or behavior of a particular element induces change in varying degrees in all other elements of the system. The ultimate components of a social system are the individuals within it.

Organizations are essentially subsystems within a total socio-political-economic system. They interact and this interaction stimulates changes in relationships between organizations as well as changes within each organization. Every organization has a hierarchy of values and functions which rarely totally agrees with that of any other. In higher education this can be demonstrated by comparing the institutionalized values of complex universities with those of public comprehensive community colleges (6:118–122).*

THE LANGUAGE OF SYSTEMS

To understand the dynamics of the social system as it relates to the two-year college, as well as the intricacies of internal structure and function within the individual institution, we must first consider the concept of systems and some of the processes of systems analysis. The first characteristic is that of the hierarchy of systems (18:85–86). Moving from a macrosystem to a microsystem in higher education we can identify a wide range of influences which impinge upon the individual college. At the periphery would be the U. S. Office of Education and its subsystems, followed by state departments of education or other legally constituted state agencies at a more proximate level. As one moves toward the institution, additional subsystems can be observed, including local governmental units and less formal organizations within the political and social structure.

The principle of subsystems applies to four-year colleges as well as to most two-year colleges organized with three primary subsystems—students, faculty, and administration.

Another concept essential to understanding of systems has been defined by Timms:

> A central feature of man-made systems of all types is the effort in their design to effect control of the interrelationships of system elements so as to *regulate the final output of the system* (18:98).

Such control takes place through feedback loops. Feedback loops, whether they be singular or multiple at any point in time, tend to shift the goal-seeking activities of the organization, change the operating channels or the feedback loops themselves, and induce changes in the subsystems within the organization through the feedback of new internal data.

The concept of a feedback loop represents an effort to overcome a basic problem in the analysis of the interaction of an organization with the larger universe. The dilemma is clearly defined by Buckley in his statement concerning the difficulty of making the

---

* References are identified by numbers in parentheses throughout the text. The number preceding the colon refers to publication, listed by number, in the references at the end of the chapter; the number following the colon refers to pages in the cited text.

. . . abrupt leap from dyadic and small group processes to "institutions," along with an assumption of non-problematic structural maintenance and stability founded on normative consensus, legitimate authority, common values, internalization of roles via socialization, and the like (3:127).

The problem is essentially that of trying to define and describe a particular organization in a highly complex and differentiated intercommunications matrix. No organization is "free floating" in an undifferentiated universe. Rather, it is subjected to and interacts with an array of external forces.

The utilization of simultaneous complex transactions enables the system or subsystem to develop a communications network which provides for the free flow of (1) historical information, (2) information from the environment, and (3) information about the organization itself (7: 198). Clearly any organization functions within an historical context. It needs to be familiar with and to utilize information relative to antecedent events in its own history and in the community. In addition, an organization needs a constant flow of information from the environment in order to stimulate effective responses and to counteract the natural tendency to drift away from reality. (See Figure 1.1.)

THE POLITICAL SYSTEM

A truism too often ignored by educators says that colleges exist in a political system. Within this grand design social demands, such as access to higher education or urban problems, are converted into issues requiring the attention of the government and the electorate. In order to understand the internal dynamics of an organization, it is necessary to understand the external forces to which the organization must respond (8:1–84).

The total societal environment can be viewed as being comprised of four systems: (1) ecological, (2) biological, (3) individual, and (4) so-

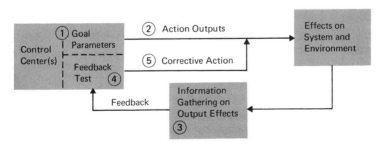

FIG. 1.1 FEEDBACK CONTROL OF GOAL FORMULATION AND SEEKING
Source: From *Sociology and Modern Systems Theory* by Walter Buckley. Copyright © 1967 by Prentice-Hall, Inc., and reprinted by permission.

cial. The explicit content of each system and the sum of their various interactions make up the total environment, which creates demands for political action through a process of information feedback; such demands are converted into specific outputs, such as legislative enactments or decisions by administrative agencies. The political process is the avenue for the conversion of needs into governmental responses or solutions to problems.

An essential element of any political system is the competition for available resources. Higher education is only one element among many competing for political attention and support. In the political arena the most pervasive competitors are defense, welfare, transportation, and public schools. Each of these sectors has legitimate demands for support, and each competes with the other in attempting to set forth the strongest possible case for its needs. The situation is complicated further by higher education's variety of demands, which are neither clear nor consistent. As a result, its appeals for support may seem to be contradictory at times.

For purposes of our analysis, we will divide the external influences affecting organizational behavior within the two-year colleges into three broad categories: national and regional, state, and local. The press from each of these levels generates both directions and restraints upon the organization. The expectations of society have far-reaching effects upon behavior patterns within individual colleges. The intermix of external press and institutional adaptation shape the college into varying configurations at different points in time.

THE TWO-YEAR COLLEGE IN THE NATIONAL SCENE

As we examine influences from the national perspective we are immediately confronted with three complications: (1) confusion as to national goals and lack of clearly defined expectations for higher education, (2) rapidly changing and vacillating leadership on the national level, and (3) the late arrival of the two-year college as a national priority.

Confusion over national goals is self-evident. Domestic programs enunciated and implemented by Presidents Kennedy and Johnson to better the human condition have become a shambles, partly as a result of military commitments abroad. Efforts to find viable solutions to urban problems have been stymied by rural and suburban oriented members of Congress and state legislatures. National policies have been formulated on a crisis-to-crisis basis rather than upon clearly stated long-range national goals. Although there is sharp disagreement as to future emphases upon social problems, trends having an impact upon higher education are becoming apparent as evidenced in the statement of Clark Kerr:

New national attention is being turned from the fields to the streets, from affluence to poverty, from white Protestants to minorities, from growth to welfare, from suppressing nature to designing the urban ecology. Higher education will not be far behind. It has followed in turn religion, industrialization, and national power—always with a lag, but it has followed the nation and it will do so again—some campuses more than others and, as always, some not at all (11:251).

Popular expectations of higher education are equally confused. Viewed from the national level, one can discern an array of expectations which will generate conflicts between society and community colleges, but perhaps ultimately induce institutional changes of significant magnitude.

There has been an almost endless succession of committees, commissions, task forces, and self-appointed critics suggesting fundamental redefinitions of the roles of higher education (17, 14, 16). The issues raised of direct import to two-year colleges indicate a wide range of concerns. First, what services should these colleges perform which will meet the general requirement of an educated citizenry? Second, who will provide financial support and in what proportion of the total cost? Third, should community colleges be agents of social change or should they confine themselves to the transmission of culture and the vocational preparation of students? Fourth, who will determine the educational objectives of colleges and what will they be? Fifth, how much flexibility is necessary for higher education to respond effectively to changing social needs? And last, to whom will professionals be accountable for economy and effectiveness of educational programs?

The rampant confusion in the public mind relative to what higher education should be and what it should do, coupled with accelerating problems of fiscal support, has encouraged colleges to appeal to national and state governments for policy direction and financial support. It is apparent that the dilemma confronting higher education, particularly the community college, is the magnetic pull toward centralized bureaucratic control on the state and national levels.

In 1962 Morrison and Martorana observed the predominate trend of that time to be the "recognition of a partnership of the state, the locality, and the students sharing in current operational costs, and of the state and locality sharing costs for capital construction of the public two-year colleges" (13:32). Within a decade, however, the executive director of the American Association of Junior Colleges, Edmund J. Gleazer, had perceived a very different shift in the locus of support and power from the local to the state level. As he approached the completion of his national study of community colleges in 1971, Gleazer observed:

In a search for some relief from steeply mounting property taxes the trail leads to the state capitol. More money from the state seems almost inevitably related to a greater demand for accountability by the state in the use of these funds. Thus, state level boards are created. They call upon local institutions to present ten-year building and program plans; then they ask for justification of the addition of any new programs. Soon the issue develops, "Who calls the shots?" Students and faculty are calling for more decisions to be made locally and the community calls for greater responsiveness by the colleges. Whether state systems or multi-campus districts, questions are being asked about the sensitivity and responsiveness of the institution to the varied needs of the communities. Although a degree of local autonomy seems called for to enhance the development of the college community itself and the relationship of the college with the community it serves, trends toward increased power at the state level are clearly evident. Hence, another dilemma (9).

Congressional action, however well intended, has contributed to the general confusion by passing piecemeal and erratic legislation for higher education. Congressional appraisal of needs has always been fragmented, with the result that there is no unified and sound national policy structure and no reliable and consistent funding program. As a result of unpredictable policy and funding shifts on the part of the national administration in Congress, federal funds are euphemistically called "soft money," and it is indeed an adventurous administrator who attempts to build long-range program commitments upon these sources of revenue.

U.S. Office of Education

The U.S. Office of Education is an anomaly. In the federalist system where education is specifically assigned to the states, USOE's policy-formulating responsibility is virtually nonexistent. Although a department of the Executive Branch, it is particularly vulnerable to congressional intervention, and consistent policy and funding activities are virtually precluded because of categorical appropriations from Congress.

Additional problems encountered by USOE grow out of its attempts to serve all levels of education, from preschool training through graduate and professional levels. As a large bureaucracy, it tends to fulfill the prophecy that a bureaucracy will gradually displace its original purposes by tasks and activities directed toward its continued existence and growth. A tendency for bureaus to perpetuate their own interests has made it difficult for two-year colleges to find officials receptive to the articulation of their needs. Between 1966 and 1971 no bureau within the Office had specific responsibilities for such institutions.

The fragmentation of federal programs has made it exceedingly difficult for a college to know where to turn for appropriate information and guidance when seeking federal support. Even the bureaus within the USOE often represent fragmented programs; repeated internal reorganizations, a concomitant of each new national administration, create even further confusion. In spite of all the Office's efforts, dissatisfaction over the lack of clear leadership has been evidenced by the Nixon administration as well as by educational leaders.

Approximately one-third of all federal funds for education are distributed through categorical grants. While this method gives USOE powerful leverage to make institutions develop explicit programs tailored to national priorities, many disadvantages are inherent in the system. "Grantsmanship" within institutions has developed its own unique bureaucracy. Programs are often initiated in order to "win" a federal grant which commits the college to directions and resource allocations inconsistent and sometimes in conflict with its original goals.

USOE has also been plagued by sporadic and unpredictable congressional appropriations. The Office of Education is frequently confronted with twelfth-hour legislation and appropriations made by Congress. The use of these funds requires the development of guidelines and regulations within an unreasonably short period of time. The Office has been forced to address itself to problems requiring twenty years of research and development, with fiscal resources restricted to capriciously timed one-year appropriations. This is in sharp contrast to planning and funding available to such agencies as the National Aeronautics and Space Administration, the Atomic Energy Commission, and the Department of Defense.

Other Agencies

Many federal agencies are responsible for programs having a direct bearing upon the two-year college. The Labor Department is responsible for institutional compliance with the Civil Rights Act of 1964, which requires fair employment practices when federal funds are used for building construction. This department also supervises antidiscrimination requirements for hiring practices of colleges, as they might reflect discrimination on the basis of sex or race.

The Commerce Department through the Small Business Administration provides funding for a number of educational programs given by community colleges. In addition, programs can be funded through the departments of Defense, Agriculture, and Labor.

NATIONAL PROFESSIONAL ORGANIZATIONS

National professional organizations of the greatest importance to two-year colleges include: the American Association of Junior Colleges, the American Council on Education, and the American Association for

Higher Education. The American Association of Junior Colleges is generally accepted as the national spokesman for two-year colleges. It evolved first as a forum for private colleges, but during the last twenty years has shifted its attention to the interests of public institutions as well. Its efforts have been directed toward developing better understanding and support of the nature, purpose, and missions of public and private two-year colleges (2).

Community colleges were the last type of institution to arrive on the national scene. Prior to 1960, most public two-year colleges were submerged in public school systems, lacking identity, clarity of purpose, and political potency. The confluence of three forces in the 1960s stimulated the rapid development of AAJC and its member institutions. They were (1) strong executive leadership in the Association, (2) legal recognition of community colleges as a part of higher education by most state legislatures, and (3) stimulation of interest in community colleges in major universities by the W. K. Kellogg Foundation.

The contributions of AAJC to the development of community colleges have been immense. The Association has been the primary communication link between individual institutions and the federal establishment. It has also assisted many states in the planning and development of new colleges or statewide systems. Other important contributions include funding for the development of paramedical programs and assistance to developing institutions.

In sum, AAJC has attempted to represent two-year colleges and their various constituencies at the national level. It has provided material assistance in improving communications between the federal establishment, state directors of community college systems, and university professors involved in the preparation of professional personnel.

The American Council on Education and the American Association for Higher Education are both made up of virtually all elements of higher education. The most important contributions are their services as communicators of the needs and activities of higher education to government, business, and industry. They also perform an important function in the dissemination of information among their membership.

Three groups compete as spokesmen for professionals in higher education: the American Association of University Professors, the National Education Association, and the American Federation of Teachers. The AAUP has traditionally focused upon the academic setting of the institution. Its guidelines for academic freedom of faculty and rights and freedoms of students are valuable resources for all institutions in the development of policies and procedures. The role of the AAUP in fostering a positive academic climate has been clouded as faculty members have turned to the organization to support welfare demands. In 1968, Davis wrote:

Although not committed to collective bargaining as the most desirable means for exerting the faculty influence in institutional government, the A.A.U.P. has recognized that in certain situations collective bargaining may achieve some goals of a college or university faculty. It has thus authorized its chapters, after consultation with the A.A.U.P.'s general secretary, to exercise their discretion on whether or not to seek collective bargaining status (5:12).

The National Education Association has clearly shifted its goals and priorities with continuing growth and changing conditions. The advent of the American Federation of Teachers, with its willingness to represent faculty in seeking improved salary and fringe benefits, influenced the NEA to change its original role centered upon professional improvement to that of a welfare-centered organization. The myth that faculty as professionals would not resort to strike tactics for the resolution of disagreements has been shattered as large numbers of young faculty questioned the sanctity of "service to mankind" as sufficient reward for teachers. Communities began to discover this historic assumption would not satisfy contemporary faculty who compared their economic status with the gains achieved by nonprofessional and professional groups through collective action.

Labor unions early perceived that the administrative structure of educational institutions placed the chief administrator between faculty and policy board in such a way that faculty often felt unrepresented or at the mercy of the chief administrator's ability to promote their interests. It was only a matter of time before faculty began to recognize the importance of organized power for the achievement of economic benefits. Arthur F. Corey, in an analysis of the development of professional negotiations for teachers observed, "Tyranny in modern times begins by exploiting the unorganized mass and then uses this instrument to destroy all other organizations. The strongest guarantee against authoritarianism is the presence in society of many strong, voluntary organizations" (4: 332).

Jean R. Kennelly defensively justified this trend by insisting that, "Because an organization borrows a union technique, it does not follow that the organization becomes a union . . ." (10:89). Nevertheless, it is clear that the acceptance of salary remuneration and fringe benefits offered by the board of trustees as secondary to the privilege of serving a professional calling has ended. No longer can administrators expect to intimidate faculty on the basis of professional conduct and service to mankind ethics.

ACCREDITATION

Institutional accreditation is an extremely pervasive and important influence on colleges and universities. By nature of their voluntary membership, accrediting agencies are dependent upon the continuing support and participation of member colleges. Thus, on occasion, changing circumstances in member institutions, necessitate change within the accreditation structure. In other instances, the institution is forced to adapt as a consequence of accreditation and its relationship to third-party issues.

The accreditation process answers four fundamental questions. They are (1) "What are you trying to do?" The institution is expected to enunciate its purpose, mission, and objectives. (2) "Do you have the necessary resources to accomplish that?" Visitation teams see how well the institution's human, physical, and economic resources have been made available and organized to perform the task. (3) "Are you in fact doing what you say you are doing?" This question can only be answered by examining the institution's graduates. Accrediting agencies typically have not considered visiting and evaluating an institution until at least one class graduates and a follow-up study on it has been completed. At one time a minimum of five to seven years was involved from the founding of an institution until its consideration for candidacy. More recently pressures from federal agencies using recognition by regional accrediting agencies as a prerequisite for federal funds have forced changes in the duration and type of intermediate stages through which institutions must pass before accreditation is granted. (4) "Is there reasonable assurance of perpetuity of the institution?" This question has frequently been the basis of recommendations designed to remove questionable management practices or to overcome detrimental political interference.

By understanding these four basic questions, the administrator can assess the value of institutional accreditation as well as appropriate uses of the process to strengthen his institution. Accreditation provides an important opportunity for self-improvement or for protection from debilitating external or internal forces. The study period during which an institution examines itself in the light of criteria outlined by the accrediting agency can identify areas which need to be upgraded. Committees of faculty, administrative staff, students, and community members often stimulate corrective efforts as examining previous practices reveal deficiencies.

Accreditation can become a highly charged issue within the institution and within the sponsoring community. It must be thoroughly understood and planned for so that advantages materialize and dangers are avoided. Failure to assess the constituents' level of readiness for or belief in the results of an evaluation can be disastrous. When an institution, particularly a developing one, assumes recognition is automatic and fails to prepare its community for any other eventuality, loss of faith in the institution and its administration can result.

A second major consideration confronting the two-year college is the accreditation of programs. Professional accrediting represents a complex problem because of the expense and many different agencies involved.

Program accreditation is an outgrowth of the efforts of individuals in a given field to professionalize their calling, sometimes in the interest of assuring quality services to the public; other times as a means of controlling admission of those who would enter the profession. Two-year colleges, because of their paraprofessional and technician career programs, have experienced increasing pressures from different professional accrediting associations to conform to criteria prescribed by practitioners of the various fields. Some colleges have discovered interrelated dependencies which force them to make internal adjustments in order to initiate and maintain such occupational programs.

The federal Allied Health Act and many state licensing boards for nursing have required or recommended that associate degree nursing programs meet the National League for Nursing specifications. Criteria established initially were based upon traditional diploma school and baccalaureate programs and required completely unrealistic staffing and laboratory experiences. As institutions exerted pressure on this organization, modifications relaxed requirements unrelated to qualitative aspects of associate degree programs.

Another disadvantage of professional accreditation has been its tendency to establish unrealistically high requirements for some programs. Requirements for selected technical curricula set by the Engineering Council for Professional Development have been so rigorous that students meeting their prerequisites are tempted to proceed toward a baccalaureate degree in engineering rather than pursue an associate degree. As a consequence, often fewer students enroll in ECPD approved programs resulting in extremely high costs per student. In addition, such standards encourage some faculty to emphasize college parallel curricula at the expense of occupational programs.

To reduce the proliferation of professional accrediting agencies, the National Commission on Accrediting was formed by several hundred institutional members, the six regional accrediting associations, the American Association of Junior Colleges, and several other national organizations of institutions. The Commission has stabilized the situation by fostering a reexamination of policies, procedures, and practices. Many two-year colleges turn to this organization when considering program accreditation.

INFLUENCES OF FOUNDATIONS AND PHILANTHROPIC ORGANIZATIONS

A variety of national foundations and philanthropic organizations have contributed to the development of community colleges by demonstrating an increasing interest in their evolving role. While support by such foundations is sometimes directed toward national organizations or institutions peripheral to the local community college, indirect services and benefits have nonetheless resulted. In other cases, through direct grants, foundations have supported various activities of local colleges.

The W. K. Kellogg Foundation has been prominent among those philanthropic organizations interested in and committed to strengthening the two-year college. This foundation made substantial grants to ten leading universities throughout the nation from 1960 until 1971 for the establishment or expansion of community college leadership training programs which produced a cadre of well-prepared administrators. The same Foundation contributed to the growth of continuing education centers in universities and two-year colleges, setting the stage for vigorous demands upon Congress and state legislatures to provide for continuing education programs (1).

At the beginning of the 1970s, the W. K. Kellogg Foundation shifted its emphasis from training administrators for two-year colleges to supporting curriculum development and leadership training in health occupations. Concurrently, it gave new attention to the growing phenomenon of state coordination or control of two-year colleges.

The American Association of Junior Colleges has been materially strengthened through continuing grants from the W. K. Kellogg Foundation. Throughout the 1960s substantial sums were awarded to AAJC to develop occupational education programs by means of inservice training activities, new program identification, and curriculum design and development. In 1971, another grant made to AAJC provided for a three-year project to pursue international education as a possible dimension of the community college.

The Carnegie Corporation is another foundation that has earned a reputation for supporting studies, investigations, and research in higher education. In the mid-sixties a grant to study student personnel programs had major impact upon the improvement of this area of service. The Carnegie Corporation has provided significant assistance to studies assessing the potential contribution of two-year colleges to the solution of many complex domestic problems. Task force reports released in 1970 and 1971 called for national and state legislation to expand and strengthen community colleges throughout the country, especially those serving urban centers.

The Danforth Foundation and the Ford Foundation have also been interested in and supportive to community college programs preparing faculty to teach in career programs, and improving educational opportunities for the disadvantaged. Foundations and philanthropies are important nongovernmental influences serving as deterrents to overcentralization and political manipulation. Several foundation grants have supported research to anticipate the consequences of greater state involvement in the everyday operations of the community college. Through sponsorship of the W. K. Kellogg Foundation and the Carnegie Commission on Higher Education, more was written in 1971 on state responsibilities, involvement, and coordination and control than had been written during the previous decade.

OTHER NATIONAL INFLUENCES

Congressional interest in the community college mushroomed at the end of the 1960s when Senator Harrison A. Williams introduced a bill envisioned by him as the Community College Act of 1969. Senator Williams gave testimony to document the fact two-year colleges had not received their fair share of funds under federal legislation passed during the sixties. While the Williams bill did not become law, it was to be the beginning of repeated pressures within and upon Congress to give support to comprehensive postsecondary institutions serving the local community.

Other forces are at work to carry this objective forward. The Education Commission of the States is one of these. Created as a consequence of James B. Conant's book, *Shaping Educational Policy,* wherein he proposed a nationwide educational policy to bring order out of the chaos of the nation's variety of higher education institutions, the Education Commission of the States became a reality through grants of the Carnegie and Danforth Foundations. Political and educational leaders of several states realized that the political process must be used if the citizenry of contemporary America is to be adequately served. As observed by Wendell H. Pierce, Executive Director of the Education Commission of the States, "The uniqueness of an organization bringing together politicians and educators to strengthen education frightened many. Experience has shown that close association of these two usually competitive forces, away from the heat of state conflicts, is effective and instructive for both" (15:335). Thus, forces at the local and state levels are brought together at the national level in an attempt to solve problems transcending local jurisdictions but which have not been successfully resolved in the past through the interaction of public, college, and internal constituencies.

In addition to the Education Commission of the States, a variety of voluntary regional bodies are designed to encourage coordination and cooperation among institutions; at the same time they guard against the possibility of centralized control resulting from national influences on higher education. Among these may be included the Southern Regional Education Board (SREB) in 1948, the Western Interstate Compact for

Higher Education (WICHE) in 1951, and the New England Board of Higher Education (NEBHE) in 1956, all of which have grown in scope, magnitude, and function as the complexities of higher education have been recognized. These agencies, interestingly enough, have evolved more in response to gubernatorial direction than as a result of the leadership of educational administrators (12).

They have been able to attract highly talented professionals and have wide latitude in their range of activities. Kroepsch observed, "When interpreted liberally there is probably no functional area of cooperation in the field of education beyond high school that is denied these agencies by their charter" (12:36). While they do not have coercive powers, they do have strong leverage through their relationship with legislatures.

WICHE in particular has grown from a regional organization coordinating roles among western states to one providing national leadership in the development of models for management information systems and program planning budgeting systems. This project, funded by the U.S. Office of Education, is envisioned to assist individual states in synchronizing with or becoming elements of a national structure eventually feeding into the U.S. Office of Education. Not only have WICHE functions expanded, but its membership and participation have also increased. A significant number of eastern states have become financially committed, participating as members of the compact. Kroepsch concludes:

> In the years ahead, WICHE will continue— (1) to seek new ways to increase educational opportunity for western youth in all fields, (2) to assist colleges to improve their academic programs and the institutional management, (3) to aid in the expansion of the supply of specialized manpower—including the development of new programs for continuing education, (4) to help our institutions and agencies respond to the changing economic, social, and educational needs of the region, (5) to keep state officials and the general public informed about the needs in higher education in the West. The future is full of challenge. WICHE approaches it cooperatively—and with confidence (12:38).

The full impact of WICHE upon the internal direction of two-year colleges has not yet been determined. It is apparent, however, that its taxonomy of terms and informational collecting procedures, if adopted by the U.S. Office of Education, will provide direction and possible restraint to every college. Some view this prospect with alarm, seeing a danger of standardization press upon the internal flexibility of the institution. We believe some symmetry can materially aid the institution and its administration.

The Southern Regional Board represents another body which began with the purpose of coordinating services and expanding opportunities among cooperating states with a commitment toward economy of resources for all member institutions, regardless of administrative boundaries. This board has moved more and more toward active leadership in the direction of planning and programming institutions, including efforts to maximize a commitment to humanitarian needs. Individual institutions seeking to identify their role will find a wealth of research material available as a result of the efforts of these regional bodies. Several provide professional development activities as well.

The recent development of educational information and retrieval centers has made available information to all of higher education. The ERIC center for junior colleges, located at the University of California, Los Angeles, is concerned with all aspects of two-year colleges. It provides a facility for the collection, coordination, and dissemination of materials of interest to those responsible for administration, teaching, and counseling in community colleges. The staff of ERIC also generates original research studies and other publications of value to the field.

SUMMARY

It has been our purpose in this chapter to provide a framework within which the complex array of external forces acting upon the two-year college may be examined and related to internal pressures and responses, the latter to be examined in subsequent chapters. The concept of a system provides the basic framework for our analysis. Each element of a system both affects and is affected by other elements. Within the larger sociopolitical system can be found in descending order of magnitude and proximity a series of subsystems comprised of elements which attempt to maintain themselves through the continuing process of stimulus and response. The feedback loop represents the mechanism through which the complex transactions occur.

In addition to the concept of system, we have examined national and regional influences which shape and in turn are shaped by two-year colleges. Our review included administrative and legislative influences, national professional organizations, accrediting associations, foundations and philanthropic organizations as well as coordinating commissions and compacts. While we have not attempted to deal with the totality of national forces with which the institution and its leadership must contend, those influences impinging most directly upon and having the greatest potential for future direction have been analyzed.

REFERENCES

1. ALFORD, HAROLD J., *Continuing Education in Action*. New York: John Wiley, 1968.
2. BRICK, MICHAEL, *Forum and Focus for the Junior College Movement*. New

York: Bureau of Publications, Teachers College, Columbia University Press, 1964.

3. BUCKLEY, WALTER, *Sociology and Modern Systems Theory.* Englewood Cliffs, N. J.: Prentice-Hall, 1967.

4. COREY, ARTHUR F., "Educational Power and the Teaching Profession," *Phi Delta Kappan*, 49:331–34 (February 1968).

5. DAVIS, BERTRAM H., "The AAUP and the JC," *Junior College Journal*, 39:11,15–16 (December 1968).

6. DECHERT, CHARLES R., "Integration and Change in Political and International Systems," in *Positive Feedback: A General Systems Approach to Positive/Negative Feedback in Mutual Causality,* ed. John H. Milsum. New York: Pergamon, 1968.

7. DEUTSCH, KARL W., "Mechanism, Teleology, and Mind," *Philosophy and Phenomenological Research*, 12:185–222, 1951.

8. EASTON, DAVID, *A Systems Analysis of Political Life.* New York: John Wiley, 1965.

9. GLEAZER, EDMUND J., Director, Project Focus, an interview in Bethlehem, Pa., May 1971.

10. KENNELLY, JEAN R., "Collective Bargaining in the Community College," *Educational Record,* 52:87–92 (Winter 1971).

11. KERR, CLARK, "New Challenges to the College and University," *Agenda for the Nation,* ed. Kermit Gordon. Washington, D. C.: The Brookings Institution, 1968.

12. KROEPSCH, ROBERT H., "Regional Cooperation in Higher Education," *Compact,* 4:35–38 (April 1970).

13. MORRISON, D. G. and S. V. MARTORANA, State Formulas for the *Support of Public Two-Year Colleges,* Bulletin 1962 No. 14. Washington, D. C.: U. S. Department of HEW, OE 57004.

14. *Open-Door Colleges: Policies for Community Colleges.* New York: McGraw-Hill, 1970.

15. PIERCE, WENDELL H., "The Politics of Education," *Phi Delta Kappan,* 49:335–36 (February 1968).

16. *Report of the Commission on Tests.* New York: College Entrance Examination Board, 1971.

17. *Report on Higher Education.* Washington, D. C.: USOE, 1971.

18. TIMMS, HOWARD L., *Introduction to Operations Management.* Homewood, Ill.: Richard D. Irwin, 1967.

two

State

Influences

More and more changes within two-year colleges are initiated at the state level. Legal foundations established by the state legislature define explicitly in most states both the purpose of the institution and its organizational structure. Broad parameters of daily operation are commonly set forth in legislative regulations. State funding patterns also have a marked effect upon the institution.

State laws should ideally define the nature and intent of the two-year college and its relationship to other segments of higher education, and then give colleges the freedom to plan and implement their educational programs. In many instances, however, legislative power has mushroomed beyond laws explicitly defining a college's mission to include control over organizational structure and procedural activities of administration, faculty, and students. In addition, such laws usually grant intermediary governmental bodies the jurisdiction and power to set regulations and rules for the operation of the individual institution.

Some states have developed systems of community colleges governed and administered at the state level. Policies are formulated with the entire state viewed as a community, and the multicollege system functioning as a single large unit. Community colleges of a few states are governed and administered through the state university system, with the board of trustees of the parent institution establishing policies for the colleges. At the opposite end of the spectrum are states where community colleges are viewed as autonomous with respect to overall direction and operation, although some state control exists.

State regulations range from highly detailed, prescriptive rules and requirements to those which are primarily philosophical in nature. The posture of the statewide policy-making body can be identified by the specificity encompassed. New York and Florida, while encouraging local determination by a local board of trustees, have developed detailed and inclusive regulations covering even the specifics of day-to-day operation. Similar regulations are found in the more centralized statewide systems of Virginia and Minnesota. Yet among the centralized state systems, Colorado and Massachusetts have had generally broad definitions and permissive regulations (13).

A more immediate intermeshing between the two-year college and external influences exists at the state level than at the national. Paradoxically, while state influence is more direct, long-range statewide goals are nonetheless ambiguous. The absence of precise national goals is balanced in part by national priorities which emerge as a consequence of national or international crisis. The brevity of a governor's tenure combined with short terms for legislatures inhibit the states from developing long-range priorities to the same degree possible in a more stable national setting. State legislative and executive branches have further compounded this difficulty with power struggles for primacy in allocating resources. In evaluating state influences, therefore, it is necessary to consider political processes to understand the impact that this feedback loop may have on the internal structure and direction of two-year colleges.

DIRECTIONAL INFLUENCES

The contextual framework within which the local institution must operate as a consequence of state-level actions can be divided into two classifications. The first, and by far the more complex, is directional influences which directly or indirectly shape the aims of the institution. These influences answer such fundamental questions as whether the two-year colleges of a given state will be open-door comprehensive institutions or limited in some aspect of admissions or programming, or whether they will be solely responsible for all postsecondary education of less than baccalaureate level, or will be one of many institutional arrangements, i.e., technical institutes, area vocational centers, branch campuses. Directional influences also determine whether the institution will be the community resource for adult education, continuing education, and community services, or whether all or part of these programs will be sponsored by other institutions.

The Legislature

Political scientists have identified a variety of trends in the development of the legislative branch of state government. As more complex problems confronted legislatures, it was necessary to extend their sessions. The more information required to decide issues necessitated a staff of legislative assistants. Some states now provide a staff, either to strengthen the legislative position over the executive or to overcome some of the impediments that may be deliberately or inadvertently placed between the legislature and its information sources.

Higher education is only one of many competing social needs. The legislature through the cycle of the feedback loop has inputs from many directions. The political process is naturally one of confrontation and trade-off, as different interests are represented by individual legislators who respond to pressures from their constituencies. Thus in the overall situation higher education may have a relatively low priority.

An analysis of proposed legislative bills introduced in various state legislatures can provide two-year colleges with information on trends taking place within the state, even where statewide goals are absent. At the beginning of the 1970s, it was increasingly clear that legislatures had moved away from placing large amounts of money in graduate education and research within the state universities. In the past, most universities used the prestige of research and graduate education as the avenue to national or international recognition.

Life-styles of students, the increasing costs of all public services, and the loss of confidence in scientific endeavors to resolve humanitarian problems redirected concerns of state legislatures to other areas. Some of the specific directions include:

1. Public responsibility for tuition-free higher education has been replaced by the attitude that the student add his resources to that of the taxpayer.

Reactions of private colleges and economy-minded taxpayers have encouraged legislators to place a larger proportion of the cost of education on the student.

As these shifts occur, the community college can expect to obtain less public support for free tuition, and an increase in the number of students who would formerly have attended state colleges and universities

but who must now look to the community college as a less costly alternative. This trend will be particularly apparent among young people from
lower- and middle-class families.

2. Shifts of procedural responsibilities from local institutions to state agencies
    can be seen in the growing tendency of legislatures to designate ad-
    ministrative agencies with authority over personnel, facility construction,
    and purchasing.

These shifts have been a consequence of implied problems of accountability, as well as occasional abuses at the institutional level. Although much concern has been expressed by the academic community,
increasing jurisdiction passes from the hands of the local institution to
the state as legislatures attempt either to economize or to force greater
similarity among institutions.

3. Past concepts that higher education is a neutral agent in the solution of
    social problems has been replaced by a feeling that higher education has
    a specific responsibility to contribute actively to the solution of problems
    of society, as change agents.

Community colleges have become strategic potential facilitators of
social change, particularly when viewed as flexible and responsive to social needs. The challenge to the administration and faculty of the community college to maintain flexibility and adaptiveness is obvious.

The Executive Branch

A dilemma confronts state governors who find it more and more difficult to establish their own priorities or programs for their administration. Most newly elected governors assume office with a myriad of crises
plaguing the state, and an incessant demand from the general public
for more services. Conversely, public funds are usually already committed to existing programs and services mandated by previous executive
and legislative action.

Many of the budgetary requirements of state government are built-in
obligations which absorb the major portion of the annual operating
budget. These, combined with inflationary forces, make it necessary for
a new governor to direct his first efforts toward maintaining equilibrium
between spending and fiscal resources. However strong the new governor's wish to develop and implement new programs, he must first deal
with inherited problems and, more often than not, budgetary deficits.
His problems are complicated by the continuing fiscal demands of existing programs and services, and the lethargy of a large bureaucracy committed to maintaining the status quo. Bureaucratic inertia makes it
virtually impossible to change the direction of existing programs or initiate new ones in a short period of time.

The governor affects the momentum of the individual college primarily through shifts of program priorities and budgetary allocations. If two-year colleges are viewed as less prestigious and less politically potent than other colleges and universities, they will frequently be given a lower priority in the state budget and appropriations recommendations for the legislature. The early struggle of two-year colleges for recognition within the established order of higher education has passed in most states. Governors want to be reelected and accomplish this by providing popularly accepted services to the people. The broad base of service of community colleges is a political reality which few politicians can ignore (11:19–22).

Coordination of Higher Education

In order to bring about greater efficiency and economy of programs and services within higher education, statewide coordination of institutions has become a matter of concern in many states. Governors and state legislators have been motivated to establish formal statewide coordinating agencies in order to bring some rationality and order to higher education. These officials have a vested interest in the effective and economical delivery of higher education to all of the people of the state. They also feel compelled to consider program priorities in terms of social and economic rather than institutional needs.

Glenny noted the trend toward greater state-level coordination resulting from external pressures:

> The new coordination did not arise out of foresight by educators but from demands of legislators and governmental agencies for more efficient use of public monies. They wanted to eliminate wasteful duplication of programs resulting from competition among state institutions, to facilitate realistic and scientific budget requests, and to establish the rationale for developing new institutions and campuses (5:87).

In most states, community colleges have had the most to gain and the least to lose through state coordination. Public community colleges never enjoyed the degree of autonomy found in public and private colleges and universities. Further, as junior members of the educational enterprise, community colleges have been strengthened by the creation of state-level coordinating boards who can get the attention of both the executive and legislative branches.

Most state legislatures, when enacting laws creating coordinating boards, mandate that the boards undertake or develop a master plan of long-range programs and budget planning for higher education covering five, ten, or even twenty years. Master plans, while frequently less than viable enforcements of cooperation and coordination among institutions of higher education, have generally fostered the growth and development of two-year colleges, counteracting many of the competing forces of other segments of institutions including state colleges as well as politically entrenched state universities.

Only twenty states had state coordinating agencies in 1959. In 1969, forty-eight of the fifty states had developed some type of statewide coordination or control. Berdahl's study confirmed the widespread trend toward statewide coordinating boards having either advisory or regulatory powers. His analysis of relationships is revealed in Table 2.1 and the accompanying explanations.

It can be observed from Berdahl's table and definitions that voluntary efforts to coordinate higher education, usually favored by state universities, peaked in the 1950s and then declined markedly, while the

TABLE 2.1 NUMBER OF STATES IN EACH CATEGORY OF COORDINATING AGENCY (1:34–35)

CATEGORY	1939	1949	1959	1964	1969
I. *No state agency*	33	28	17	11	2
II. *Voluntary association*	0	3	7	4	2
IIIa. *Coordinating board*	1	1	2	3	2
IIIb. *Coordinating board*	0	0	3	8	11
IIIc. *Coordinating board*	1	2	5	7	14
IV. *Consolidated governing board*	15	16	16	17	19

Note: The categories are as follows:
I. No state agency
II. Voluntary association
IIIa. Coordinating board; institutional majority; advisory powers
IIIb. Coordinating board; public majority; advisory powers
IIIc. Coordinating board; public majority; regulatory powers
IV. Consolidated governing board

I. States which have neither a single coordinating agency created by statute nor a voluntary association performing a significant statewide coordinating function.
II. States in which voluntary statewide coordination is performed by the institutions themselves operating with some degree of formality.
III. States which have a statewide coordinating board created by statute but not superseding institutional or segmental governing boards. This category is divided into the following subtypes:
   a. A board composed in the majority of institutional representatives and having essentially advisory powers.
   b. A board composed entirely or in the majority of public members and having essentially advisory powers.
   c. A board composed entirely or in the majority of public members and having regulatory powers in certain areas without, however, having governing responsibility for the institutions under its jurisdiction.
IV. States which have a single governing board, whether functioning as the governing body for the only public senior institution in the state or as a consolidated governing board for multiple institutions, with no local or segmental governing bodies. (1:18–19)

number of states with governing boards increased only slightly. Concern for institutional autonomy has counteracted trends for greater coordination, creating in many institutions a reaction against the principle of long-range planning designed for statewide coordination of a system or even subsystems. James L. Miller, Jr. observed, that while universities and colleges resist outside control of any sort, they can and do support coordinating boards on specific issues of policy which appear beneficial to an institution (7:27).

Direct governmental control over higher education is clearly evident when fiscal and program retrenchment become necessary. The delicate partnership of government and college is subjected to its greatest stress at this point.

> Coordination may mean one thing when the agency first attempts to bring order among the state institutions and a different thing when a system has been established, cooperative attitudes developed, and certain procedures routinized (4:61).

Coordination of Two-Year Colleges

Coordination or control of two-year colleges has been formally stipulated in forty-three states. In many instances, responsibility is vested in an existing board or agency responsible for all public colleges and universities. Recent studies show an increase in mandated coordination and control of public two-year institutions at the state level as a concomitant of increased state financial support. Further, legislatures have tended to charge these agencies with specific responsibilities for planning, budget review, and approval.

Wattenbarger and Sakaguchi reported thirteen states have a state-level board primarily responsible for serving community colleges. Those included were Arizona, California, Colorado, Connecticut, Delaware, Illinois, Maryland, Massachusetts, Minnesota, Mississippi, Virginia, Washington, and Wyoming. Five other states operated their public two-year colleges through the state university system, with the board of trustees of each university serving in the capacity of a state-level board for the colleges. They were Alaska, Hawaii, Kentucky, Nevada, and New York. (Puerto Rico is also in this category.) A state-level board with responsibility for all public institutions of higher education including the community colleges was functioning in Arkansas, Georgia, New Mexico, New Jersey, Ohio, Oklahoma, South Carolina, Texas, Utah, West Virginia, and Wisconsin.

In addition, fourteen states reported a state board of education with extended responsibility over community colleges including Alabama, Florida, Idaho, Iowa, Kansas, Louisiana, Michigan, Missouri, Montana, North Carolina, Oregon, Pennsylvania, Rhode Island, and Tennessee (14).

Wattenbarger and Sakaguchi classified the functions of the different boards according to analysis of the principle activities and authority ascribed to them. They observed that eight performed governing functions; twelve performed governing-coordinating functions; and twenty-three performed coordinating functions only (See Table 2.2).

TABLE 2.2   DISTRIBUTION OF STATE LEVEL BOARDS, BY TYPE AND FUNCTION (14:37)

| | | FUNCTIONS | | |
TYPE OF BOARD	GOVERNING	GOVERNING-COORDINATING	COORDINATING	TOTAL
Board for CJC only	3	5	5	13
Board of Higher Education	3	0	8	11
University System Board	1	4	0	5
Board of Education	1	3	10	14
Total	8	12	23	43

Wattenbarger and Sakaguchi concluded, ". . . patterns of governance, as reflected by provisions for a state-level board, do not seem to evolve from a logical and rationally planned solution to the consideration of the changing requirements of the institutions" (14:17).

One difficulty inherent in statewide coordination or control is the ability to maintain a balance between state and local needs and interests. Consistency in policy application throughout a system has much to recommend it; however, detailed prescriptive policies and procedures from the state level can inhibit or even preclude required institutional adjustments to local needs. The state governing board can also be used by administrators as a convenient way to avoid making difficult decisions. Appeals to a remote group by administrators, faculty, or students has eroded self-determination on many campuses.

The governing-coordinating agencies have somewhat less responsibility and authority over the internal affairs of their constituent institutions than is true for the governing boards. Wattenbarger and Sakaguchi, in classifying this group, observed that the governing-coordinating board and its administrative agency place primary emphasis upon the development of statewide plans for facility and program requirements, development of criteria for the establishment of new institutions, development of budget recommendations for the governor and legislature or both, and secondary emphasis in those areas described previously as the major concern of governing bodies.

One of the dilemmas confronting governing-coordinating boards is the power needed to maintain compliance by all colleges. The temptation of the agency to seek conformity through coercion rather than persuasion makes the delicate balance precarious. For example, in one state a two-year college indicated in its catalogue that certain courses would meet state teacher certification requirements. Such courses are typically offered during the third and fourth years of state colleges and universities. A corrective measure proposed to the state board was a regulation for a common catalogue, course numbering system, and course syllabus. It is obvious an act by one two-year institution could impose restrictions upon all similar units in the system.

Coordinating agencies have the least authority and responsibility. They depend primarily upon the power of persuasion or influence to induce behavioral changes in individual colleges. They tend to delegate most authority for policy and procedure to the individual units, leaving such matters as personnel policies, regulation of student life, and other professional matters in the hands of local authorities (14:31–33).

Judicial

Among less frequently considered state-level directional influences have been the rulings of courts and interpretations by offices of the attorney general. State statutes, regulations, and administrative edicts increasingly are being subjected to judicial examination as taxpayers, faculty, students, administrators, or others challenge their validity or constitutionality. Nearly every state two-year college system has been affected significantly by rulings of the state supreme court or by local courts on issues dealing with internal and external matters. *In loco parentis* issues have not been as immediate or complex for community colleges as for residential colleges and universities; however, significant rulings have affected membership on the board of trustees, authority for local taxation, and the power of eminent domain.

Brubacher observed that the courts as never before are applying the principles of the First, Fifth, and Fourteenth Amendments to the transactions of higher education institutions. The due process clause in the First and Fourteenth Amendments has been applied to the rights of students, faculty, and taxpayers as well (3).

Courts have begun to move away from the earlier position that educational institutions as instruments of government are immune from suits. State laws and court decisions place greater and greater pressures upon the institution to protect itself from any type of liability. Other rulings create the need to reexamine profit-making activities even when the profits are intended to perpetuate the institution (2:159–60).

An important resource for the local college on matters of state statutes, particularly newly enacted laws, is the state attorney general. These interpretations are particularly helpful in matters over which a state agency will need to rule.

Other Governmental Agencies

Other governmental agencies contribute to the directional influences upon the purposes and programs of the community college. The state vocational education agency and its board represent particularly important ones. Their jurisdiction over the allocation of funds for occupational education programs, and often adult education and continuing education as well, places them in a strategic position for shaping priorities for community colleges. Unfortunately, in some states the relationship between these bodies and two-year colleges has been tenuous. Historic frictions between protagonists and antagonists of the vocational versus academic debates seemingly continue to poison the minds and motives of men who purport to be committed to the service of the student who ultimately pays the price by having less than desirable educational opportunities. Such tragic custom seems to be waning, however.

Licensing boards represent another directional determinant for the community college, by being involved in operations such as staffing, certification, examination, and of course requirements. Requirements may become so burdensome as to discourage an institution from operating even a needed program.

Nongovernmental Organizations

A host of statewide organizations and bodies represent various publics whose activities and actions can contribute to the shaping of the community college when they take positions on proposed legislation affecting such institutions, or when they use the media to influence sentiment. The state chamber of commerce, the economy league, the manufacturers association, state labor unions, and statewide service associations all have taken positions which influenced legislative actions on community college issues. Political parties at the state level have also exercised similar influence, particularly when gubernatorial candidates in the development of their political platforms have seen fit to include or exclude a plank directed toward the development of a strong community college system.

A final group of organizations deserving comment is the voluntary state educational bodies. Positions taken by statewide professional organizations for administrators, trustees, school directors, faculty, or students frequently give direction to efforts creating statutory or regulatory provisions designed to influence the mission or programs of the two-year college.

OPERATIONAL INFLUENCES

In addition to the directional forces previously discussed, a second major classification of state-level influences may be identified. Operational influences are those which impinge upon the day-to-day activities of the college by prescribing procedures which establish the parameters within which internal operations must occur. Requirements for reports add to the workload of faculty and administrative staffs carrying the potential for generating conflicts and tensions, particularly when reports or other requirements are not perceived as germane to the institution's mission.

Erosion in the role and scope of decision-making by the college administrator can be a consequence of state-level intervention. The Newman report observed that governors and legislators "are assuming a much more active role in campus affairs" as it becomes more important politically to prevent "embarrassing incidents" which have frequently placed presidents and board members in "roles as public defenders of their points of view and/or apologists for campus incidents." The report concludes, "Political safety, rather than academic leadership, becomes the priority" (9:25).

Commenting further on the dilemma confronting college presidents, the same report observes:

> Sandwiched between faculty and students (who have bases of support beyond the campus) on the one hand, and tiers of system administrators and interventionist-minded state officials on the other, the president of a system campus is becoming less and less able to carry his own case to the press, is less and less able to build a supportive constituency for the particular institution he heads. Thus, his role has become one of the most difficult in higher education (9:26).

The Legislature

Legislatures have enacted laws dealing with internal procedural activities of the institution, sometimes as a consequence of overt solicitation by one or more of the college's constituents and at other times as a response to a perceived unwillingness or inability on the part of the institution to act. In an effort to realize economy and to extend existing resources, legislatures have turned to organizational control strategies as well as to different concepts of funding. Alternate control strategies can be seen in the number of statutes which assign to state agencies responsibility for monitoring purchasing, employment, building, and programming at the local level. Changes in funding concepts can be seen in the new statutes imposing additional student fees, prescribing minimum teaching loads for faculty, requiring new forms of planning such as a program-planning-budgeting system, and shifting from scholarship grants to student loan assistance programs.

The Executive Branch

Gubernatorial directives aimed at reducing spending because of lagging tax revenues or political strategies not infrequently have strange results. Flat rate reductions of expenditures of state funds is quite common. More often than not, such decisions are made by budget officers whose training, experience, and understanding of the intricacies of college operation are either limited or nonexistent. Such decisions can cut or eliminate travel funds, decrease student enrollments, or delay the use of a building for the want of furniture and equipment.

Administrators are familiar with the axiom that in order to enjoy an adequate flow of fiscal support from the state it is necessary to demonstate growth and expansion. The traditional philosophy of state budgeting is to classify activities into three categories: maintaining existing programs, expanding existing programs, and introducing new programs. Most often when resources are severely limited, both expansion and new programs are cut.

Expanding programs under normal circumstances are those most favored by the legislature and executive for they convey an aura of success. New programs, however, carry the liability of being unproved, hence potentially embarrassing if unsuccessful. They also represent added costs, thus budget cutters are most likely to trim new programs without really listening to the rationale set forth by the institution.

In some states, budget cutting is accomplished by directing each program agency to cut a certain percentage of its overall budget. It is most effective when state officials then meet with college representatives and work out a strategy for accomplishing the necessary reductions. Under such an approach, each institution understands the reasons for its required reductions and can through delegated responsibility make the necessary adjustments in priorities on the basis of knowing what is needed on the institutional level.

Coordinating Board Agency

The position of the coordinating board agency between the legislature and institutions of higher education places it in an intermediary role, ideally as a transmission link between the two. When the agency performs the task of consolidating planning, budget, and program data from the various institutions, it can contribute to an orderly and equitable distribution of resources to all institutions, avoiding the earlier pattern of politically powerful institutions benefiting at the expense of smaller institutions having less political power. The position of the agency as an intermediary in bringing equilibrium to the system was well described by Berdahl.

> The quality of the agency's policy recommendations to the state, and certainly its ability to win the institutions' cooperation later in carrying out state-approved policies, are greatly influenced by the nature of its procedural relations with those institutions. Similarly, the degree to which agency recommendations receive state approval and funding will be greatly influenced by the nature of its relations with the organs of state government (1:173).

It is through these procedural relations between the two levels that the coordinating agency has had its greatest challenge. Berdahl concluded, "our field work left us with a distinct impression that few agencies have in fact obtained such a position of equilibrium between higher education and state government, and that none has been able to maintain it for any length of time" (1:187).

Means of communication have sometimes been lacking, and the requirement for the data collection has placed heavy burdens upon the staff and faculties of individual institutions. Such data collection can supplant the intended purpose of an individual on the college staff as bureaucratic requirements supersede those of services to students and faculty. A frequent criticism made about student personnel and institutional research offices has been their tendency to become data collectors for external administrative agencies rather than to provide internal service and direction.

Individual colleges often react negatively when coordinating agencies transmit unsolicited policy directives which might have an adverse effect upon the administration of the institution. This lack of mutual understanding may be the outgrowth of the isolation of the agency from the college, and the agency's inability to pretest its directives in the field. Most states have attempted to correct this problem by establishing advisory committees representative of the colleges being served. Difficulties of communication are not confined to state-college relationships, for the same gaps frequently exist on the local campus. All too often the administration does not effectively communicate information about issues and problems to its own constituencies, thereby creating antagonisms and confusion.

A number of other problems make state-college relationships difficult. In the larger states, the sheer size of the state agency and number of colleges make personal meetings difficult to schedule. The agency staff may also be unenthusiastic about broad participation by individual institutions because of possible dissent and opposition to agency decisions. In such cases there is a desire to maintain informal contacts rather than formal structures for collective advice and involvement. Berdahl found that few coordinating agencies were interested in or maintained any meaningful contacts with trustees, faculty, or students as a part of the communications systems or mechanisms for policy formulation. In general, they were content to work with other state-level agencies having jurisdictions over higher education or with the local administration itself.

The Two-Year College Agency

Some idea of the range of activities of the state agency can be seen in the list of chief functions identified by Wattenbarger, Gager, and Stuckman which the state director for community colleges "should perform."

1. Provide leadership as an articulate state spokesman in promoting the comprehensive junior college program.
2. Provide leadership in developing, defining and coordinating a statewide junior college plan.
3. Clarify the functions and roles of the junior colleges; design criteria for the orderly establishment of new junior colleges.
4. Provide and coordinate statewide junior college research; encourage and coordinate research in the local junior colleges.
5. Advise, recommend, and consult with state officials and legislators concerning the improvement of junior college legislation and finance.
6. Prepare, present, and defend the state junior college budget.
7. Advise and consult with local junior college officials, particularly in the areas of legislation, finance, and budget.
8. Maintain junior college standards and administer state board policies and requirements (13:2–3).

Hurlburt's comprehensive study of state-level planning for community colleges described the growing trend toward state control of the institutions as a consequence, in part, of the failure or inability of the local institutions to solve their own problems (6:8–17).

Most state agencies for community colleges now have professional staffs to work directly with local institutions in such areas as academic affairs, business and finance, vocational and technical education, planning and research, physical facilities, student affairs, evaluation, accreditation and standards, continuing education, and personnel.

The agency can provide leadership through statewide councils composed of institutional participants including presidents, chief academic, student personnel, or business officers, as well as faculty and students. The presidents' council has become an important vehicle for setting goals and planning within the state agency. Such councils can provide effective communication for the system, avoiding the pitfalls of misconceptions or misunderstandings commonly identified with large bureaucratic organizations. The council mechanism, while time-consuming and expensive when great distances are involved, has proven its worth in bringing complementary and unified actions into the system. Addressing himself to this subject, Stuckman concluded:

> Via the council mechanism, equilibrium within the junior college system may be established, the realization of the need for inter-dependent action may be engendered, institutional representatives may participate in statewide policy formulation and reach consensus, and an increased understanding of functioning within the coordinating process may result (10:39–40).

The state central fiscal control agencies represent another possible impingement upon the college, particularly in their pivotal position for operating, capital budgets, authorization of contracts and purchases. Moos and Rourke comment, "nowhere has the cutting edge of this knife (the budgeting, auditing, and purchasing agencies of centralized fiscal control) been felt more keenly than in the area of higher education" (8:54). Their prediction that the move toward centralized fiscal control would increase in the future years certainly has proven correct. Unfortunately, these offices operate on a premise contradictory to that of the local institution. Their role or function is to conserve or preserve tax funds, a task frequently accomplished without any appreciation of potential impact on services at the local level.

On the other hand, it is not uncommon for the local institution to plan programs with the assumption that it is the state's job to find the necessary support for those services. To avoid operating at cross principles, there is a need for constant communication.

Building authorities represent another external source of impingement upon the local institution. Many state authorities operate for all governmental construction projects, making their responsibilities complex indeed. Since authorities are accustomed to hearing about the "critical" need for a given project, whether it be construction of a prison, hospital, or a college, they can become insensitive to even sincere pleas. In a different vein, the local institution can be set back in its facilities planning due to delays that develop at the state level.

Other influences occur as a consequence of the legal ramifications of working with an authority. The local architect must understand specifications, job orders, and other construction requirements of the state. All necessitate a high degree of specialization.

State certification and licensing agencies can provide some of the most complex and restrictive impingements upon local institutions. Special prerequisites for program approval may extend from the qualifications of faculty to square footage per student and prescribed hours of laboratory and classroom instruction. Many of these agencies have jurisdiction over funds or standards through their review powers.

SUMMARY

Influences operating at the state level impinge more directly upon the internal functioning of the two-year college than influences at the national level. An examination of the way such influences function, however, leads to the conclusion that national influences may have greater impact in terms of defining long-range priorities. This is true both because of the greater stability in political processes at the national level and because of the frequent conflicts among state influences relative to immediate as opposed to long-range interests in the allocation of resources. At the same time, inability to resolve conflict in the goal determination process seems to be the rule rather than the exception for state governments.

The kinds of influences exercised by state agencies may be divided into two categories. Directional influences are the consequence of long-range planning, enabling legislation, determination of priorities, and similar processes to shape institutional purposes indirectly. Operational influences are more direct and are the consequence of specific procedures or restraints imposed by legislation, executive order or through agencies exercising controlling powers granted by the legislature.

Among the influences discussed were the legislature, the executive office, coordinating agencies, judicial bodies, and other governmental and nongovernmental organizations. Most of these agencies exercise directional influences primarily, although it is not uncommon for many to exercise operational influences also. Our list of influences has not been all inclusive but it does serve to further identify external forces which shape internal reactions.

REFERENCES

1. BERDAHL, ROBERT O., *Statewide Coordination of Higher Education*. Washington, D. C.: American Council on Education, 1971.

2. BLACKWELL, THOMAS EDWARD, *College Law, A Guide for Administrators*. Washington, D. C.: American Council on Education, 1961.

3. BRUBACHER, JOHN S., *The Courts and Higher Education*. San Francisco: Jossey-Bass Inc., 1971.

4. GLENNY, LYMAN A., *Autonomy of Public Colleges*. New York: McGraw-Hill, 1959.

5. GLENNY, LYMAN A., "State Systems and Plans for Higher Education," in *Emerging Patterns in American Higher Education,* ed. Logan Wilson. Washington, D. C.: American Council on Education, 1965.

6. HURLBURT, ALLAN S., *State Master Plans for Community Colleges.* Washington, D. C.: American Association of Junior Colleges, 1969.

7. MILLER, JAMES L., JR., "Institutional Individualism and State Higher Education Systems," *Compact,* 3:3,27–30 (June 1969).

8. MOOS, MALCOLM and FRANK ROURKE, *The Campus and the State.* Baltimore: Johns Hopkins, 1959.

9. *Report on Higher Education.* Washington, D. C.: USOE, 1971.

10. STUCKMAN, JEFFREY A., *Statewide Coordination of Community Junior Colleges.* Gainesville, Florida: Institute of Higher Education, University of Florida, 1969.

11. *The Capitol and the Campus: State Responsibility for Postsecondary Education.* New York: The Carnegie Foundation for the Advancement of Teaching, 1971.

12. VAUGHAN, GEORGE B., *Some Philosophical and Practical Concepts for Broadening the Base of Higher Education in Virginia.* Topical Paper No. 19. Los Angeles: ERIC Clearinghouse for Junior Colleges, University of California, March 1971.

13. WATTENBARGER, JAMES L., WILLIAM GAGER, and JEFFREY STUCKMAN, *The State Director for Community Junior Colleges.* Gainesville, Florida: Institute of Higher Education, University of Florida, 1969.

14. WATTENBARGER, JAMES L. and MELVYN SAKAGUCHI, *State Level Boards for Community Junior Colleges: Patterns of Control and Coordination.* Gainesville, Fla.: Institute of Higher Education, University of Florida, August, 1971.

three

Local
Influences
and the
Board of Control

A distinguishing characteristic of the community college is its intimate relationship with the community it serves. It is dependent upon the forces at work within the community while at the same time contributing to the process of change. The interdependencies discussed in this chapter are in constant action, not only within the community context but also within the larger universe of the state and nation.

The administrator of a community centered institution must be concerned continually with the impact of the college on those who reside within its service boundaries as well as with its image. Despite the fact that our analysis of state influence supports the conclusion that the percentage of costs borne by local revenues will probably continue to decline, the willingness of the local community to support the institution may well make the difference between an institution which is merely adequate and one which attains some degree of excellence.

The context within which a college is viewed by its supporting community has the likelihood of becoming a self-fulfilling prophecy. If a community has an unfavorable impression of an institution, this idea cannot but affect a faculty's sense of self-worth and attitude toward responsibility. Students, too, are strongly affected by community response to the college. Students who might benefit from its services may elect not to attend. Minority groups in particular are sensitive to the implication that they are attending a second-rate institution.

Every new institution must express its total commitment and purpose through both words and actions as early as possible and on a continuing basis thereafter. A new institution is particularly vulnerable in that it must counter the bias of those who have traditional concepts about the nature and status of higher education, while at the same time reach in a positive way those whose attitudes have not yet been determined. The college that delays establishing certain types of programs during its initial period of development, for whatever reason, runs the risk of creating an image within the community which may make the future of such programs uncertain.

Established institutions must recognize the need for educating their communities before moving in directions that have not been pursued in the past, regardless of how well such directions may be accepted among professional colleagues. An institution cannot become more than its constituency will accept and support. The community college, like no other institution, must simultaneously lead and follow within its community. This is the unique quality of the institution.

WHAT IS THE COMMUNITY?

Whether the college serves a large or small geographic area, an urban or rural setting, its community is made up of individuals, informal groups, formal groups, and coalitions of different groups. In simplest terms, the community is made up of people, but how these people come together and reflect group interest or concern and how they work together through informal or formal organizations will determine the nature of the community. The different levels or stratifications of interest among individuals and groups must be understood in terms of both separate and composite influences if administrative response is to reflect successfully the sociopolitical setting which varies according to group thinking and group action for each community.

Roland L. Warren defines community as, "that combination of social units and systems which perform the major social functions having locality relevance. This is another way of saying that by 'community' we mean that organization of social activities to afford people daily local access to those broad areas of activity which are necessary in day-to-day living" (10:9). Consistent among all communities is effort to provide for man's inner needs of religion, education, recreation, and protection.

Whether the community college is a large multi-institution system serving a great city or a small locally controlled institution, likenesses exist in the need for understanding the community, its groups, its people, their organization, and their institutions.

Even the individual units of a multi-institution district have an identifiable community which guides programming and services. In a study of multi-institution districts, Kintzer, Jensen, and Hansen observed, "The site administrator regards the community in light of students attracted as well as the needs of the adjacent community, whether business or residential" (5:37).

There are a variety of influential groups with which the college works. Various political, civic, ethnic, social, and educational groups exist in all communities but with different degrees of influence and impact. To understand the link between individuals and groups, the work of sociologists and political scientists who have studied the relationship between political power structures of the community and the decision-making process has relevance for the two-year college. College administrators must comprehend the nature and behavioral pattern of political thought and organization within the community if the college is to be an integral part of it.

CONCEPTS OF POWER AND DECISION MAKING

Several studies of community power structure provided insight into the range of procedures through which decisional processes are influenced. Dahl studied New Haven, Connecticut by identifying selected major public issues or policies, examining documents, and interviewing people to identify the most influential policy makers involved. He found a highly pluralistic system in which both leaders and followers were associated with different strata of the community. He also found that politics in New Haven had undergone rapid and dramatic change from oligarchy to pluralism. He observed:

> In the political system of the patrician oligarchy, political resources were marked by a cumulative inequality: when one individual was much better off in almost every other resource—social standing, legitimacy, control over religious and educational institutions, knowledge, office. In the political system of today, inequalities in political resources remain, but they tend to be noncumulative. The political system of New Haven, then, is one of dispersed inequalities (3:85) .

In studying the patterns of influence among subleaders, Dahl found that individuals who might be influential in one sector of public activity were not necessarily the same as those who influenced decisions on other issues. Furthermore, he found that there was a similar difference in the social strata from which leaders came. Coalitions of groups were to prove effective in the exertion of power for policy making. Dahl observed: "Individuals with the same amounts of resources may exert different degrees of influence because they use their resources in different ways" (3:271).

Edward C. Banfield studied the Chicago power structure using methods similar to Dahl's. He found the heads of the Democratic Party's political machine were in virtual monopolistic control of policy making. He found, however, that they elected to test their plans upon groups within the community in order to assess a broad cross-section of opinion before making a final decision. When there was disagreement, a strategy of delay in decision-making was usually followed in order to encourage others to react and to put pressure upon the party itself (1:287).

In contrast to preceding studies conducted in large cities, Kimbrough described two studies of rural counties which exhibited similar characteristics on a more limited scale. In Midway County, an informal competing power structure was found, while the case study of River County revealed the development of a multistructured power system which was becoming a serious threat to a ruling monopolistic power structure. Kimbrough observed:

> Whether the pattern of power is competitive or monopolistic may not ultimately prove to be a major consideration in establishing a theory of power. The one thread which appears to run through analyses of power is that predominant power exists in variations of informal structures. This esoteric, informal nature of power may, in the final analysis, be the common base for a concept of social power which accounts for all of the big decisions and projects at the local school district (4:37).

Presthus has commented on the differences between some of the more recent studies conducted by political scientists and the earlier studies of other sociologists.

> Whereas sociologists have usually found an "elitist" leadership structure, political scientists have often found a "pluralistic" system in which power is shared among several competing groups. Where the former have assumed and found that the economic resources provide the critical basis of community power, the latter has assumed and found that power has many bases, each of which tends to be decisive in a given substantive area (7:8).

While it is probable that most communities will exhibit characteristics of both elitism and pluralism, a number of conclusions seem relevant to two-year colleges. First, it is apparent individuals form coalitions within the community to achieve goals held in common. These coalitions usually form on an ad hoc basis for a given issue and then disband or reorganize.

Second, influential people within the community are not necessarily the elected officials or even the publicly identified policy makers meeting in public view. The college must seek the support of the "invisible" as well as the visible leaders of the community. Often, however, the purpose and mission of the community college is not of great concern or consequence to the invisible elite. They do not have direct involvement with the college and unless it impinges upon their interests, it does not command their attention. Nonetheless, knowledge of their existence and potential in a given issue is of value to the college.

Third, the authority of the office of the president will not necessarily prove powerful in all decision making. The president must know the limitations of his office and the power of external groups and individuals who can be rallied for a specific issue. Fourth, each community has its own unique power structure which must be identified. The board of trustees can be a key to this process.

Fifth, broad-based involvement in the formulation of policies for the community college including faculty, trustees, and even students, can provide potent leverage for influencing top decision makers even when they are not fully identified. Furthermore, the college should not make the mistake of assuming all decisions are made by the power structure. Frequently, the institution can successfully appeal its case to the public, for students, graduates, and other interested citizens can exert pervasive influence upon the decision-making process when given adequate institutional leadership and public confidence.

POLITICAL INTERACTION

A persistent dilemma and opportunity is the interaction of internal constituents with politically powerful individuals and groups. It is naive to assume that higher education is nonpolitical. All of public education has become fair game in the political arena. Many community college districts have highly charged politically oriented elections for trustees. In large urban centers it is not unusual to observe the selection of a college president on political rather than educational grounds.

The college, if it is to be successful, must walk the fine line of securing political support while avoiding political domination. Elected officials form a vital link between the college, the community, and state and national agencies. Frequently, the college will need the assistance of political figures if it is to achieve its objectives. Insensitivity to the concerns of those who work within the political sphere can only result in a lack of cooperation when such consideration may be critical indeed.

Another facet of political affairs which cannot be ignored is the tendency to use group power tactics to achieve political and economic advantages. This trend is clearly apparent with virtually all public service employees. The faculties of community colleges are no exception. The growth of well-disciplined unions which exert pressure upon administrators, trustees, and political office-holders, is an accepted reality in most urban centers.

Educational Agencies

The public image of a two-year college is in part dependent upon the attitudes of those who hold positions of responsibility in other community educational organizations. If the high school counselor does not have a positive impression of the institution, his attitudes will be conveyed to prospective students and to their parents. There are a number of ways in which the college can improve its relationship with local educational agencies and through such improvement enhance its opportunities of functioning effectively within the community.

Opportunities for counselors and teachers to meet with their counterparts in the college often fosters personal relationships which result in cooperation and understanding. Perceiving the achievements of the local high schools can encourage cooperative relationships between various departments. Association with area vocational schools is particularly important for the college. Much doubt or suspicion can be avoided if the college takes the initiative in establishing communications and working for mutual understanding and cooperation.

A primary consideration involves the respect shown by the two-year institution for its educational colleagues. Inevitably, members of the college staff receive questions about the performance of secondary schools whenever the college publicizes its remedial programs. A failure to handle this question carefully can lead public school educators to take advantage of any opportunity to downgrade the programs offered by the community college.

If private institutions of higher education are a part of the community scene, it is imperative that early and positive relationships be established with such institutions. In certain respects, the community college is a threat to the private institution. Most such institutions have long relied upon local commuting students, to some extent, to furnish a part of their income. Obviously, students who commute for financial reasons are likely candidates for the public two-year college. Unless special efforts are made to reassure the private institution that transfers at the junior level will outnumber losses at the freshman level, and unless efforts are made to avoid competing with the private institution, the possibilities for conflict are close.

In addition to public schools and other institutions of higher education, careful attention must also be given to the sensibilities of proprietary institutions. Some have operated within their communities for extended periods achieving positive images and substantial support among the business and industrial community. It is inevitable that the establishment of a two-year college will occasion some loss in revenue to these institutions since the community college normally offers programs providing comparable career preparation at lower costs. While the college cannot abdicate its responsibility for providing career education, it can, through careful assessment of local manpower needs and through limited admission to programs duplicating the offerings of local proprietary institutions, avoid entering into open conflict with these institutions.

Business, Industrial and Professional Organizations

As the college seeks to become more involved in its total community, it becomes involved with organizations related to the occupational structure of the community. Such organizations are important because career programs to be successful must receive support. In addition, the position they take on issues affecting the development of the institution can be significant indeed.

Perhaps no organization is more important than the local chamber of commerce since it includes within its membership a broad spectrum of the occupational life of the community. The college should become a member of the chamber at the earliest possible date. Hopefully, its staff members will be provided with an opportunity to serve on chamber committees. In addition, college information can be provided through the services of the chamber office to chamber members. If the college is successful in conveying to the chamber the sense that its own development contributes to the development of the total community, then the institution has won an important source of community support.

Equally important is the influence of labor organizations. In many communities across the nation, labor organizations have been influential in developing the local thrust for new colleges and for the expansion of services. Most labor organizations are educationally minded. Most of them recognize, too, that the community college has a greater potential for providing services to their members than most other types of institutions of higher education. A liaison between labor organizations and the community college, while natural, is not inevitable. It is important for the college to work actively to secure the support of local labor leaders and to include them on advisory committees and boards. The college that can claim the undivided support of local labor organizations has taken a major step in the direction of securing the kind of community support that will enable continuing growth and effective service.

The most effective way of reaching other community occupational groupings can be through specific career programs offered by the college. A sound legal secretarial program is a natural entrée to the bar association, particularly if the program provides for cooperative experience. Career programs in the health technology area help to secure the support of doctors and dentists. Not only can such groups be a significant factor in mobilizing community sentiment for the college, but not infrequently they can be relied upon to provide substantial support in the way of additional resources through private donations or services.

Public Media

Over a period of time, one of the most influential contributors to the image developed by an institution is the public media. While it is important to have someone within the institution interpreting the institution via the public information program, it is impossible to create a positive image unless such an image is sustained by the day-to-day activities of the institution.

The public information program requires the kind of cohesion and consistency that can only be attained through the direction of a single individual who has primary responsibility for this aspect of the institution's functioning. At the same time, it is important that the president be accessible, particularly in matters of serious community concern. A failure of the chief executive officer to make himself available, to provide information concerning his position on relevant issues will lead to speculation which can be far worse than any information he might have provided.

While favorable attitudes held by representatives of public media toward the institution will not result in their distorting news in favor of the college, such attitudes will result in special efforts to be scrupulously fair to the institution when situations of a negative nature do develop. It is inevitable in the life of any institution that internal actions or even external actions beyond the control of the administration or the board will create the potential for substantial impairment of the public's confidence in the institution. At such times, the way in which the situation is handled by the public media can mitigate much of the potential damage to the public image. It is safe to say that such treatment will be accorded only if the media is assured that the institution is providing full information and is not withholding anything in an attempt to manage the news.

The institution should provide accurate information promptly in any situation where the facts would normally become available to representatives of public media in the normal course of events. Reporters appreciate efforts of the institution to make their job easier and not infrequently demonstrate this appreciation in the way that a story is handled. By the same token, they are by the nature of their position, somewhat skeptical of the information they receive. If for any reason they believe that the institution is withholding information or that deliberate distortion has taken place, they will expend every possible effort to discover the true state of affairs. If the institution is caught in a contradiction, or if the work of reporters is made more difficult by a refusal on the part of an institution's officials to cooperate, the attitudes that this engenders will also be reflected in the way stories are handled.

It is important for the institution to avoid becoming involved in controversies through the public media whenever possible. There is little question controversy creates interest. Consequently, public media, as a matter of policy, normally provide more attention to controversial issues than those where consensus exists. Observing statements in print has a way of hardening attitudes and making conflict resolution more difficult. While the self-restraint required in matters of considerable provocation is often great, the ability to refrain from entering into controversy in the public sector makes it far easier to resolve issues which are a normal part of institutional life.

It is essential that the institution provide information about what it does within some kind of context designed to help present its purpose. Far too many institutions run the risk of misinterpretation because they provide too much information about what they do and not enough information about why it is done. Animosity between the college and other agencies frequently stems from a lack of foresight to explain the reasons for new programs being introduced and their relationship to existing programs within the community.

Advisory Committees and Boards

Relationships between the college and its community constitute a feedback loop through which the college can expect to receive in proportion to what it gives. If the college, through its career programs, through its program of community service, through its continuing education programs, and through the efforts of individual staff members, makes a significant contribution to the ongoing life of the community and to the development of its commerce and services, then it can expect to receive support at a number of distinct levels.

Of central importance in utilizing community support is the local board of trustees. We will discuss the responsibilities of this agency at a subsequent point in the chapter. In states where the method of organization does not provide for a local board of trustees, there is equal or even greater need to provide interchange between the community as an external constituency and the institution as a service organization. A community relations advisory board can play a significant role in the interaction process, even where local boards of trustees do exist.

The activities of the community relations advisory board communicate to members of the community a better understanding of what the college is attempting to achieve. This can be accomplished by presentations of the faculty and staff at periodic meetings, through invitations to programs where outside speakers are brought in for in-service education of staff members, and through a carefully planned program of public information that provides continual information about the college's activities and development. It is important that the flow of information be two-way. Initially, the committee may be helpful in identifying areas where the college may want to concentrate with respect to the development of career programs. As individual career program advisory committees are established the role of the community relations advisory board changes; it then becomes more of a device for explaining the college to the community and for bringing into the orbit of the college people who might have interest in the institution, but who would otherwise have very little understanding of the institution. The college should not hesitate to use advisory board members on an individual or group basis whenever it needs to mobilize community support or learn of community priorities.

Other committees relating to external constituencies include advisory committees of individual programs. Such committees meet once or twice each year after a program has been developed to monitor and evaluate the activities of the program and to interpret the program to its specific constituents. They provide material assistance in the establishment and evaluation of career programs, provide a source for the recruitment of staff members and students, and place graduates.

In addition to the community relations advisory board and the program advisory committees, there may be a variety of *ad hoc* committees dealing with specific needs. Some of these ad hoc committees will become standing advisory committees of the college, others will pass out of existence. Such committees can be particularly valuable for continuing education.

In using advisory committees and boards, it is imperative that their roles be clearly defined and that they be given significant tasks which lead to a sense of accomplishment. An advisory committee which is not utilized is worse than no advisory committee at all in terms of unfulfilled expectations and neglect by a college administration of volunteer service. While the college cannot use all of the advice it receives, it can accept most of it and interpret the remainder in such a way that some use is made of it. Advisory committees and boards are critical elements between the controlling board and the community, if such organizations are used effectively and their membership provides maximum representation.

College Foundations

In the past, it has been relatively unusual for public two-year institutions to practice private fund raising. While there have been some notable exceptions, most community colleges have relied exclusively upon public support or upon the occasional unsolicited private gift. Few have made systematic efforts to include private resources in their plans for development. In the future, however, more colleges can be expected to turn to the college foundation as a legal means of private funding to make it possible for the college to provide a level of service otherwise not feasible.

The college foundation can be organized in most states as a separate corporation under applicable laws. The foundation as a special corporation insures that gifts are used for intended purposes and not diverted by those who direct the affairs of the college, particularly in the case of state boards. The foundation board also gives visibility to the interests of the college in securing private funds. Foundation board members become an important source of support to the college. They also provide advice on how the college can most effectively seek private support and what can be done with private support after it has been obtained.

Endowment funds are sought by private institutions to be used as principal to earn income, with spending restricted to the interest. It does not make sense for most public institutions to seek private support to create such an endowment. Normally, private funds can be used far more effectively as the means by which additional state or federal support can be generated. In addition, a public institution does not have the same requirement for an endowment as does a private institution.

LOCAL BOARD OF TRUSTEES

Arrangements for mediating between internal and external constituencies of an institution have significant implications for the way in which community needs are perceived and the mode of response employed. Two-year colleges, regardless of method of control, establish responsiveness to local needs as an important philosophical commitment. Local priorities and appropriate responses frequently appear quite different to the state capital or state university as opposed to the way they may be perceived by leaders of the local community. Strong local advisory committees can without doubt exert significant influence in calling attention to local needs; but any response by a board of a state or university system is inevitably limited by the scope of its responsibilities, by the need to have uniform policies, by intersystem rivalries for resources, and the need to establish priorities for the system before recognizing those of a local unit.

The local board of control is composed of individuals who know the community best and whose attention is not diverted by the intricacies of attempting to maintain an entire system. It does not follow that a local board will be more responsive to the needs of the local community, or that the existence of a local board will guarantee the development of an institution superior to one of a state or university system. The existence of a local board allows a wider range of responses than is possible for a unit of a system. This can be either an advantage or a disadvantage, depending upon the representativeness of the local board as well as its level of understanding and commitment to the institution it serves (8).

There are three approaches which can aid the local board in becoming more aware of community needs and appropriate responses. The first involves addition of individuals representative of the diverse populations served. Such representation should include major internal and external constituencies. The boards of most public two-year colleges are not in a position to influence their own membership since they are normally appointed or elected by external agencies. Elective and appointive processes are such that they can seldom be depended upon to accomplish the goal of representativeness. This implies the board must seek out ways to ensure consideration of those who are not represented through direct membership, but who can nonetheless exert significant influence.

A second approach is the establishment of local advisory committees to aid the board in understanding the needs of its constituents and the appropriate responses to these needs. Effective advisory committees must have a clearly defined role and established procedures through which their views are communicated directly to the board and reflected in specific reactions. Above all, the committees must feel their work is recognized and they influence the institution's responses.

Finally, a board can become more responsive through a well developed program of orientation to the institution for new trustees as well as periodic reviews of philosophy and commitment for all trustees. Attendance at national or state meetings can help locally oriented trustees gain a sense of perspective on their job as well as the issues that confront the institution. Faculty presentations at board meetings help to promote knowledge about the educational program and instructional techniques. Informal sessions at which philosophical premises are considered in the light of pragmatic realities without the necessity of making decisions can also be an important method for shaping board attitudes.

One comprehensive definition of board responsibilities is contained in a publication of the New York State Regents Advisory Committee on Educational Leadership. Five major responsibilities are suggested:

1. A board of trustees is legally responsible for assuring that the college or university fulfills the distinctive purposes for which it was established.
2. A board of trustees should understand and approve the kind of education offered by the college or university; the board should ascertain that its quality meets the highest standards possible and appropriate to its purposes; and the board should assist in the planning for educational growth.
3. A board of trustees should carefully select, counsel with, and support the president of the college, relying on him for leadership in educational policy planning and assisting him in the exercise of that leadership.
4. A board of trustees should promote understanding and cooperation between society and the college or university, by interpreting the opinions and judgments of each of these to the other, thus fostering quality and effectiveness in the development of the educational program.
5. A board of trustees should oversee the acquisition and investment of funds and the management of facilities for the implementation of the educational program (2:v–vii).

In carrying out its responsibilities, the board must depend upon the president to ensure that adequate information is available for making appropriate decisions. The practice of inviting second echelon administrators to board meetings can make a significant contribution to this process. Obviously the president cannot know in detail the answers to all of the questions which may arise in the course of a given meeting. If second echelon administrators are responsible for submitting and defending agenda items in their respective areas, they can contribute to board understanding on a more intensive level than would be possible for the president unaided. An administrator can benefit from the experience of observing board reactions to recommendations they receive as well as secure satisfaction from the knowledge his priorities have been presented well to the policy-making authority of the college.

Broadening the base upon which recommendations are advanced to the board of trustees leads inevitably to the issue of faculty and student representation. Decisions made by trustees must, of necessity, be a function of the information and recommendations they receive. The major question is to whom the responsibility for specific recommendations should be delegated (6:433). The question is one of how faculty and student viewpoints can best be transmitted to the board. Ziebarth contends that the seating of students on trustee boards has caused as much tension as it has released "because administrators cannot rationalize refusals to respond to student demands by implying . . . the trustees would never approve" (11:214). This is of course the best reason for insisting upon student and faculty representation at all trustee meetings, at least in a nonvoting capacity. Faculty and students are not sufficiently naive to accept the assertions of administrators as evidence of board positions. To establish board and administrative credibility, faculty and students should be present at all deliberations and be permitted to present or defend their points of view.

Yet another problem area is the board's view of administrative structure. Drawing upon their own experiences in business, board members commonly assume the existence of an ordered hierarchy. Faculty members, and increasingly students, do not accept the assumption of subordinate status to administrators. In consequence, boards have sought the assistance of faculty and student organizations to bar administrative dominance. The board's belief that administrators possess the authority to issue and carry out directives despite the rejection of such by students or faculty has direct influence in the unrealistic decisions board members sometimes make.

In addition to suggesting that local boards frequently do a poor job of governing, Tendler and Wilson suggest the three most critical decisions boards are called upon to make involve admissions standards, tuition rates, and instructional programs (9).

This statement can be supported only to the extent decisions in these areas determine accessibility of the institution to the population it is expected to serve. We would suggest that decisions related to structuring relationships for effective functioning as well as those which provide for open communication may be a prerequisite to all other decision making.

In this regard, the existence of written policies and procedures governing board action and relationships among internal constituencies and with the board is extremely vital. Properly utilized, the development and periodic revision of such policies can be a major source of inservice education for the board. When a policy is considered which would authorize student and faculty representation at all formal and informal sessions of the board, the board is required to give serious consideration to a major issue confronting American higher education. In a like manner, developing policies regarding grievances, salary negotiations, student and faculty involvement in the selection of a president, and the creation of channels through which all constituencies can receive just consideration for their concerns is an effective means of focusing board attention on major aspects of institutional functioning.

If the advantages inherent in the review and adoption of policies jointly formulated and supported by students, faculty, and administration are to be achieved for the entire board, it is important that the number of committees be kept to a minimum and that membership on such committees be rotated periodically. Standing committees with fixed memberships and narrowly defined areas of concern limit the opportunity for all board members to profit from the consideration of a given issue, and may create divisions within the board over a period of time when individuals lack equal experience in significant areas. To the extent that time permits, the more issues the board can consider as a whole, the less likely it is to become divided during a crisis.

This leads naturally to the question of openness as opposed to secrecy in board deliberations. Some states have solved this problem by requiring all meetings to be open to the public. It is not uncommon for boards to accomplish much of their business in private meetings. The difficulty with this approach is that it may alienate both internal and external constituencies who are informed of decisions, but are unaware of the considerations leading to the decision. Of course this is the exact opposite of what the board is supposed to accomplish. Inevitably the board is called upon to mediate in areas of great sensitivity, such as higher faculty salaries as opposed to the desire of taxpayers for lower costs; or an uncensored student newspaper contrasted with the concern of the community with the widespread use of four-letter words. The board's decisions in these areas can never satisfy those who are affected. At best, such decisions, if understood, can create a feeling that a just compromise among conflicting interests has been effected. This consequence can only come about when there has been full public discussion of the issue with an opportunity afforded to both sides to present their views. On the balance, public confidence and acceptance, a result of open decision making, outweighs any convenience of conducting business secretly.

In some instances, such as the discussion of personnel or the selection of a site, it may be desirable for boards to conduct discussions in private. Care should be taken, however, to ensure that the exception does not become the rule and to make certain any formal action resulting from private discussions is a matter of public record.

If a board is to function effectively, it must meet with sufficient frequency to provide continuity to its discussions. At the same time, meeting too frequently is an unfair burden on the trustees and invites intervention in administrative matters. The boards of most public two-year institutions meet monthly.

While the right to submit agenda items can be extended to student and faculty representatives and second-echelon administrators, it is important that screening the agenda be done by the president. Items should not be advanced to the board until they have cleared all appropriate organizations. A failure to resolve issues through the use of internal procedures is an open invitation for board involvement in administration, a practice which undermines institutional integrity and effectiveness.

While the president must be in a position to insist issues not be submitted to the board until every defined procedure for obtaining internal consensus has been exhausted, it is equally important that his authority not extend to a veto over item submission. A primary function of the board involves the arbitration of internal disputes which cannot be resolved in any other way. Providing guaranteed access to the board to all college constituencies on issues of major concern prevents the president from using his central position to make decisions in an arbitrary or unilateral fashion without recourse for those affected. It is certainly true that the board can be expected to support the chief executive officer in most disputes. This probability places pressure on faculty and students to compromise in the decision-making process. At the same time, the president is equally aware of the conclusions about his effectiveness that must be drawn by board members if too many unresolved issues are presented for arbitration. This awareness places pressure on the president to ensure an honest attempt on his part to reconcile personal biases with the desires of other staff members.

The mission of an institution is defined by the statutes which authorize its existence as well as by various restraints established by the agencies providing funds. Within these restraints, the board functions to establish specific goals and to define the conditions under which the institution will reach its objectives. Unfortunately, many boards stop at this point and fail to insist that evidence of the effectiveness of the institution in achieving objectives be demonstrated. The concept of accountability is relatively new and procedures for its implementation at the board level have not been clearly defined. We suggest two kinds of evaluative data which every board should require and periodically review.

First of all, the board should require on a regular basis institutional data relative to success in achieving defined missions. Questions related to the attrition rate, numbers of students enrolled in career programs, performance of graduates, and attitudes of those served all contribute to improved board understanding of how well the institution is achieving its objectives. In this regard it is important for the board to establish clearly defined objectives based upon performance criteria, to review and revise these objectives on at least an annual basis, and to agree in advance upon the procedures evaluating achievement. Cost effectiveness must be one significant factor: how much is the institution achieving at what expense in comparison to other institutions performing under similar circumstances.

Secondly, the board has the responsibility of evaluating the effectiveness of the president. Such evaluation should occur not less frequently than once every three years and should include evidence of the reaction of both internal and external constituencies to the quality of presidential leadership. As in the case of assessing institutional effectiveness, there must be previous agreement to what the president is expected to accomplish and upon what criteria his degree of success will be evaluated. Boards are increasingly insisting upon faculty accountability in the learning process. This concept will never be accepted on an operational basis until it can be demonstrated that there is also administrative accountability.

If boards insist upon accountability from administrators and faculty, they must recognize that accountability is a two-way street. As the process of establishing objectives and evaluating outcomes becomes prevalent, it is only natural that board accountability be given to the electorate or the appointing authority, and to internal constituencies. Trustees must understand that unless they create an appropriate level of confidence on the part of students and faculty, the institution will be unable to achieve the level of interaction essential to productivity and quality of performance. The periodic review by staff of board functioning can be helpful in identifying areas which may require more attention or additional communication.

It is clear that boards represent the critical intermediary between internal and external constituencies. In the next chapter we will suggest that role conflict among trustees, administrators, faculty, and students is a major source of the unrest characterizing many institutions during the past several years. It is unrealistic to expect that such conflicts can be resolved by one-sided concessions on the part of students and faculty. The need for redefinition of role has as many implications for trustees as for other constituencies. As various restraints in the form of legislation, sources of funding, and coordinating bodies limit the range of board alternatives, boards will find themselves less frequently in the position of being able to achieve objectives without the voluntary cooperation of all involved. Securing such cooperation will be more time consuming and more demanding than the arbitrary decisions which frequently served as the basis for institutional direction in the past. At the same time, the possibility exists for an institution to attain a level of performance hitherto impossible under the old authoritarian model.

SUMMARY

In this chapter we have considered the importance of relationships between the two-year college and its immediate environment. No other American institution of higher education is so inextricably bound to the local community for its sense of direction and priorities. At the same time, the unique degree of interaction affords the college an opportunity to be a significant force in shaping the community.

Contemporary analysis of community power structures has tended to focus on the question of elitism versus pluralism. In point of fact, it would seem that both forces are at work to varying degrees in each community. An understanding of how things get done is indispensable to effective interaction with an environment. Since action is induced by the political process through a complex interaction of individuals and groups, the college must develop procedures for relating effectively to those group: and individuals who contribute to issue determination.

In addition to commenting upon the nature of the community and its political processes, we discussed a number of specific organizations with which the institution must interact, including educational agencies, business, industrial, and professional groups, and the public media. It was suggested that advisory committees and boards can serve the purpose of interpreting the concerns and capabilities of community organizations to the college and vice versa.

Finally, we identified the governing board as the critical agent between external influences and internal constituencies. While a local board does not guarantee an institution that is more responsive to local concerns, it does create this possibility. Systems which lack local boards of control need to develop arrangements to ensure that the local community does not become alienated from the institution created to serve it.

With our discussion of the local board of control, we conclude our analysis of external influences as they determine the context within which internal processes of governance must evolve. The remainder of this book concentrates upon forms of governance which can respond effectively to the forces and trends previously identified.

REFERENCES

1. BANFIELD, EDWARD C., *Political Influence*. New York: Free Press, 1961.

2. *College and University Trustees and Trusteeship,* Recommendations and Report of a Survey. New York: The New York State Regents Committee on Educational Leadership, 1966.

3. DAHL, ROBERT A., *Who Governs?* New Haven: Yale University Press, 1961.

4. KIMBROUGH, RALPH B., *Political Power and Educational Decision-Making*. Chicago: Rand McNally, 1964.

5. KINTZER, FREDERICK C., ARTHUR M. JENSEN, and JOHN S. HANSEN, *The Multi-Institution Junior College District*. Washington, D. C.: American Association of Junior Colleges, 1969.

6. NEWTON, RICHARD F., "The Trustees: A Look at Some Bureaucratic Models," *School and Society,* 97 (November 1969), 433–34.

7. PRESTHUS, ROBERT, *Men at the Top*. New York: Oxford University Press, 1964.

8. SYKES, ABEL B., JR., "Junior College Boards of Trustees," *Junior College Research Review*, 4:10 (June 1970).

9. TENDLER, MITCHELL and RICHARD E. WILSON, *Community College Trustees: Responsibilities and Opportunities*. Washington, D. C.: American Association of Junior Colleges, 1970.

10. WARREN, ROLAND L., *The Community in America*. Chicago: Rand McNally, 1963.

11. ZIEBARTH, E. WILLIAM, "Trustees in the Academic Revolution," in *Perspectives on Campus Tensions*, ed. David C. Nichols. Washington, D. C.: American Council on Education, 1970.

part II

THE THEORY

four

The Nature
of
Human
Interaction

Administration is the science of managing human behavior. The administrator accomplishes his objectives through the effort of others. If he fails to comprehend the importance of role perception, interpersonal dynamics and motivational forces, then he will either fail to achieve his objectives, or he will achieve them with limited success at a greater cost than might otherwise be necessary.

An examination of the quality of human relationships in our colleges today would be sufficient cause for concern. We are experiencing a lack of institutional equilibrium whereby the energy of those involved seems to be expended more in internal conflict than on the objectives for which the organization exists.

On many campuses student activism, sometimes taking destructive form, provides evidence of inadequate communication and of the extreme frustration felt by those whose grievances, legitimate or otherwise, do not seem to receive a fair degree of recognition. The advent of collective bargaining legislation has encouraged the development of adversary relationships where faculty and administration seek to promote their own concerns, not infrequently at the expense of the institution. Tax issues fail, as citizens, angered by events they do not fully comprehend, demonstrate their lack of confidence in the trustees and the college staff. Trustees cling to outdated notions concerning the degree of authority they should exercise over students and faculty. On every side we find instances which illustrate poor judgment, lack of good faith, inadequate communication, hostility, and tension (27:123–25).

For the purpose of our analysis, it will be helpful if we refer to student militancy, faculty activism, administrative obstinacy, trustee insensitivity, and taxpayer revolt as observed behavior. These are obviously examples of undesirable behavior which interfere with the defined objectives of two-year colleges. While it is not our intention to imply such behavior is the rule and while there are many examples of constructive and effective behavior within our institutions, we do assert there is far more undesirable behavior at present than was true a few years ago. To say things are not as bad as they could be is not the same as saying there is no room for improvement. We are experiencing more than our share of difficulties and not all of these difficulties are the inevitable consequences of circumstances beyond our control.

Here we will propose a model conceived to capitalize upon the most positive and constructive aspects of human interaction. First, however, it is necessary to analyze those dimensions of current role definition for students, faculty and administration which seem to be at the root of many of our problems. An understanding of the basic causes of intrainstitutional conflict can lead to a restructuring of relationships within the organization toward a solution that will restore the equilibrium so vital to continued growth and public confidence in our two-year colleges. We do not seek the millennium in which all differences between individuals and institutions are resolved. Indeed, Argyris suggests a certain degree of incongruence may be healthy. "It is our hypothesis that the incongruence between the individual and the organization can provide the basis for a continued challenge which, as it is fulfilled, will tend to help man enhance his own growth and to develop organizations that will tend to be viable and effective" (1:7).

The important thing to recognize, however, is that we must understand the nature of the incongruence and be in a position to move in the direction of resolving it. Public confidence is not so much destroyed by the problems which develop within our institutions of higher education as it is by the evidence that those in responsible positions do not understand the nature of the problems and have not planned for their orderly resolution.

INTERACTION OF INSTITUTION AND INDIVIDUAL

A major concept within Getzel's theory of administration is that observed behavior is a result of interaction between the personality of the individual and the quality of the institutional environment. See Figure 4.1 (14:150–65). It is Getzel's contention that the needs of the social system give rise to institutions which incorporate certain roles and expectations. The institutions, in turn, interact with individuals whose personalities and needs dispositions give rise to certain observed behavior. This behavior is the product of interaction between the role assigned by the institution and the degree of congruence between that role and the individual's personal needs disposition.

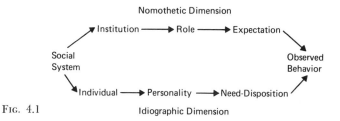

Fig. 4.1

Some kind of balance or equilibrium between the needs of the social system which supports the institution and the needs of the individuals within the institution is required. Therefore let us now analyze the extent to which the personality and needs of students, faculty, administrators and trustees have been affected by societal change. First, we will examine some of the motivational aspects of behavior and then analyze the role dimension of students, faculty and administrators.

Some Motivational Aspects of Behavior

Maslow developed a theory of human motivation based on clinical experience in which he describes a hierarchy of basic needs classified as psychological needs, safety needs, love needs, self-esteem needs, and at the highest level, self-actualization needs (21). The physiological needs include food, rest, shelter, and exercise while safety needs involve protection against danger, threat, or deprivation. As one moves up the hierarchy of needs, it soon becomes apparent that a higher degree of human motivation is involved. We share physiological needs for food and air with all living things but as we ascend the hierarchy, according to Maslow's theory, only man has self-actualization needs. Maslow also theorized that needs which are satisfied no longer act as motivators of behavior; rather, man moves to a higher level of unsatisfied need to motivate his subsequent actions. Maslow points out that satisfaction of the self-esteem need leads to feelings of self-confidence, worth, strength, capability, and adequacy of being useful and necessary in the world. Thwarting of such needs produces feelings of inferiority, inadequacy, and frustration (21:91). Maslow describes self-actualization as man's need to become more and more what he is capable of becoming.

Successful achievement of higher needs can come only after satisfaction of the physiological, safety, love, and esteem needs, and requires appropriate positive environmental conditions as well. It should be recognized that all needs are interdependent and overlapping, and that higher needs emerge before all the lower needs are completely satisfied. Higher needs then require an opportunity for an individual to develop to his capacity including freedom to think, act, investigate, and to develop.

The satisfaction of needs is influenced by intervening variables which make up the distinct and unique personality and life-style of each individual. These variables include life experiences, cognitive factors, the individual's affective style, his psychophysical makeup, group memberships, and levels of aspiration.

After translation of basic needs by the intervening variables, individuals establish personal goals, such as choice of occupation, commitment to a family group, membership in compatible groups, economic security, and freedom from physical deprivation.

Figure 4.2 illustrates how needs, as defined by Maslow, are translated into goal-seeking behavior.

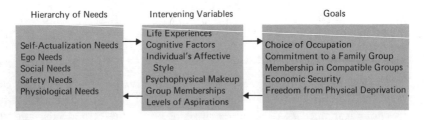

Hierarchy of Needs	Intervening Variables	Goals
Self-Actualization Needs Ego Needs Social Needs Safety Needs Physiological Needs	Life Experiences Cognitive Factors Individual's Affective Style Psychophysical Makeup Group Memberships Levels of Aspirations	Choice of Occupation Commitment to a Family Group Membership in Compatible Groups Economic Security Freedom from Physical Deprivation

FIG. 4.2 NEEDS, INTERVENING VARIABLES, AND GOALS

McGregor uses the hierarchy of human needs postulated by Maslow to serve as the basis for a theory of human behavior as it relates to the achievement of organizational objectives (22). In a comparable discussion of the characteristics of individuals within organizations, Argyris writes of the importance of competence, self-awareness, self-esteem and confirmation to what he defines as self within the organization (1:24–

28). Both Argyris and McGregor emphasize the importance of incorporating an understanding of the role of motivational factors in governing human behavior within the organization. Argyris speaks of psychological success and psychological growth as the highest of human needs. This concept is similar to McGregor's highest need which is the need for self-fulfillment or realizing one's full potential. Both McGregor and Argyris emphasize that conditions of modern society, combined with problems of role definition, may operate to inhibit opportunities for the fulfillment of higher level needs.

Men who are deprived of the opportunity to satisfy both low level and high level needs will exhibit behavioral consequences which are likely to be undesirable for the organization. Assembly line workers have perhaps the least opportunity to satisfy higher level needs in their work situation. Cases of intentional sabotage have been observed among such workers who feel bored and confined by the narrow limits of their job environment. Among the union activities of faculty members in many educational systems, we can observe similar dissatisfaction with the restraints imposed on faculty by administrators, trustees, and the community. We can conclude from these and other observations of human behavior that unless an organization provides for the satisfaction of the entire range of needs in its role definitions, there will be undesirable consequences in terms of observed behavior.

What we frequently fail to recognize is the difficulty of meeting human needs in organizations exhibiting nontraditional characteristics. Toffler, in his book, *Future Shock,* defines some of the conditions which apply to human life at this point in our evolution. He writes of the concept of transciences, "the new feeling of temporariness in everyday lives" (30:42). This feeling of impermanence must characterize the educator, who is among the most mobile of all professionals, as well as the two-year college student who spends less of his time associated with a single educational setting than any other student at any stage in the educational process. Our relationships with people, organizations, places and things are subject to transcience, for as Toffler also points out, it is necessary to "turn over our conceptions of reality, our mental images of the world, at shorter and shorter intervals" (30:161). We know the search for identity is characteristic of late adolescence. This search has always been a difficult one; most institutions of higher education recognize in their statements of philosophy some responsibility for promoting this self-development. But if we are to believe Toffler, the search for identity increasingly becomes the pursuit of a moving objective accelerating at an undefined rate. Under such circumstances it is difficult to understand how traditional solutions dependent upon eternal verities have relevance for our current generation of students or faculty.

It is essential for us to understand that it is not only the students who are seeking a sense of identity and relevance but also the faculty. It is not inaccurate to say that the attractiveness of a nontraditional approach to education in two-year colleges has drawn to them many young people who are still trying to find out who they are. Indeed, older and more experienced members of the faculty are also searching. We must thus recognize that both students and faculty are groping for self-understanding. Klapp puts it this way:

> My view, briefly, is that a collective identity search is symptomatic of the fact that some modern social systems deprive people of psychological "payoffs," the lack of which, expressed by terms such as alienation, meaninglessness, identity problem, motivates a mass groping for activities and symbols with which to restore or find new identity. People grope because they do not really know what is wrong, especially when there is physical prosperity *yet* a sense of being cheated (17:vii).

Klapp points out further that the search for self-identity is occurring *"outside the organizational and institutional channels,"* primarily because of a breakdown of feedback through discursive and nondiscursive symbols. Given the serious disturbance of the symbolic balance and the loss of non-discursive symbolism, many individuals are attempting to achieve a socially confirmed self-concept in unorthodox ways (17:ix).

Theory of Adaptation

McGregor suggests two views of human behavior, each resting upon a different set of assumptions. Theory X, the traditional view, requires that human beings adapt themselves to the organization. Theory Y encourages, at least in part, the adaptation of the organization to a clearer view of human needs. Theory X views human nature as essentially unchanging and suggests, at least implicitly, that certain behavior patterns are characteristics of interaction within an organization. We may summarize these assumptions as follows:

1. The individual works primarily to satisfy his material needs.
2. The individual needs to be told what to do and how to do it.
3. There needs to be close supervision to ensure that instructions are carried out.
4. Evaluation is the responsibility of the supervisor who uses the offering or withholding of rewards to promote efficiency.
5. The individual will perform at the minimum level at which he can get by and will seek to reduce the minimum level required wherever possible; thus there is constant tension between administration which is production-oriented and the individual who seeks to protect himself from the demands imposed (22:33–43).

It is obvious that theory X assumptions about human behavior lead to role definitions essentially oriented toward lower level needs. We know most lower physiological level needs are reasonably well satisfied in our technological society. If the premise that satisfied needs are not motivators of behavior is accepted, it becomes evident that role definitions based on theory X assumptions have only limited influence in motivating behavior. In seeking to fulfill higher needs, role incumbents will seek to redefine the characteristics of their positions. In turn this process will lead inevitably to conflict among those involved in attempting to perpetuate existing definitions and those who feel the need for redefinition.

In contrast to theory X, theory Y capitalizes upon the information we have concerning human needs as motivators of behavior. Theory Y assumptions may be summarized to include the following:

1. The individual works to achieve a sense of self-worth and fulfillment, as well as to satisfy material requirements. Where material requirements are reasonably satisfied, they become secondary considerations as a motivation for behavior.
2. To achieve satisfaction of nonmaterial needs, the individual must be involved in the definition of what is to be done and how it is to be done.
3. The individual needs to be self-directing. Once an agreement has been reached on a specific objective, responsibility for achieving that objective passes to the individual who has agreed to the assignment.
4. Evaluation is the responsibility of the individual who establishes performance targets and methods of assessing the degree to which these targets are achieved.
5. The individual will seek to do the best job possible under the circumstances and can be expected to establish his own standards for productivity and quality. The relationship between the administration and the individual is creative and cooperative with both concerned about achieving maximum effectiveness within the context of healthy human relationships (22:45–53).

The acceptance of theory Y assumptions accommodates the need for role redefinition and encourages individual freedom and flexibility which must characterize human relationships if we are to cope successfully with the stresses of accelerating change. Traditionally we have placed our major emphasis upon ferreting out the occasional malingerer who does not seem inclined to observe minimal standards. In the process of attempting to carry out this task we have been forced to define roles in terms of minimum standards. Since human behavior is conditioned by expectations, not surprisingly, minimum standards have become maximum goals.

As we will see in subsequent discussion, a fundamental dilemma faced by higher education is, first, the differences between role demands and role performance; and second, rapidly changing perceptions of roles.

Until recent years, college students were expected to be quiescent and adolescent. Any suggestion that they participate in a mature adult way in policy formulation and college governance was virtually unthinkable. We now know that student participation in the affairs of the institution is a reality we can no longer avoid (19:87–97).

In the past, the faculty had reasonably well delineated responsibilities within a context that was changing very slowly. Faculty were generally expected to be nonpolitical and essentially insulated from the larger community. Now their role demands are much more diffuse, for they include the whole range of human interaction as well as responsibilities for teaching and counseling students. The situation is complicated further in that individual perceptions of role may vary widely.

The impact of value change and society's expectations of higher education have also been felt by college administrators and trustees. The dilemmas induced by organizational rigidity in the face of a rapidly shifting value system become a major source of frustration as individuals seek self-fulfillment (5).

Even the most casual review of the faculties of our colleges would provide evidence that we have not been very successful in weeding out the incompetent. We would also discover much dissatisfaction among the competent who do not satisfy their higher level needs through the observance of minimum standards but who are not motivated to use their full resources in the existing climate. We must stop concentrating our efforts on the incompetent few who do not seem to be benefiting from our attention, and focus our attention instead upon the qualified majority and challenge them to achieve for the sake of self-fulfillment.

At a later point, we will suggest organizational concepts designed to promote an environment attuned to the satisfaction of higher level needs. We will also be concerned with how role participants function within such an environment. Let us first turn our attention to defining with some clarity the role expectations and conflicts among the internal constituents of the college community.

ROLE ANALYSIS

Student Role

What are the concepts which govern interaction insofar as the student is concerned? In the past the student has been viewed as a client who receives services. The assumption was made that the institution defines the nature of the services and the conditions under which they are to be received. In the future, this does not appear to be a safe assumption for in the words of Thresher, "College, to change the metaphor, is a crutch not a stretcher." In other words, as Thresher points out, the student "must learn to see the college as an incidental aid and supplement to his own effort, not as the source from which all enlightenments stream down" (29:36).

There have been numerous studies of students to determine their role expectations. One of the most recent illustrates clearly the incongruence between students' role expectations and the role demands placed upon them in the educational setting.

Teenagers are not needed enough.

Adults don't listen to them.

They mature early physically but are in economic bondage.

Young people think they are wasting time by going through a twelve-year school system.

Some insisted, a very small number, that students completely take over the administration of their college.

Students have higher expectations of their courses and teachers than do parents and school administrators and school board members.

The more able the young person the more severe his criticism and protest.

There is too much adversary relationship between youth and adults (25).

Alvin Toffler critically states, "the student-consumer is forced to fight to make the education industry responsive to his demand for diversity" (30:241). That students will fight in two-year colleges seems evident from the scope of organized student protest as described by Gaddy (13). Leading the list of issues promoting activism was the category of student-administration conflicts, including services and grievances.

Of course, not all protests are organized. Two year-colleges have long been notorious for their high percentage of drop-outs. The drop-out can be viewed as a protester, albeit a silent one. Cohen and Brawer's comprehensive study found little to suggest that major differences of an easily identifiable sort exist between those who persist and those who do not (8). Chickering asserts those who drop out may do so because of the need for an improved environment within which to grow and change (7).

The administration is concerned above all else with the creation of an environment within which growth and change can occur. If we examine the writings of Cross, we must conclude a major function of the two-year college lies in serving what may generally be defined as nontraditional students (10). Such students do not score well on tests designed to predict success in traditional curricula. They are more oriented toward practical rather than intellectual pursuits. They often come from lower socioeconomic groups with different sociocultural value systems, and frequently their aspirations are high in relation to the backgrounds from which they come. Perhaps more significant is Cross' finding that two-year college students score lower on measures of autonomy and nonauthoritarianism and are less likely to be venturesome and flexible in their thinking than their four-year counterparts. Knoell's study, dealing with the potential of the community college for serving disadvantaged students, also raises serious questions about the effectiveness of the institutional environment (18).

There is little evidence to suggest serious consideration has been given to structuring the role dimension for students in the two-year college upon the basis of their observed characteristics (20). Most responses to human interaction embody some attempt to maintain an authoritarian structure in which emphasis is placed upon controlling behavior rather than guiding development. Such a relationship is in the tradition of *in loco parentis* and rests upon certain assumptions concerning student values and attitudes which the writers believe to be highly questionable.

The major criticism leveled at students is that they are apathetic. Evidence to support this claim includes lack of interest in student government elections, poor involvement in student activities, and widespread indifference to participation on committees involved in the development of college policies. We should not delude ourselves by assuming such behavior warrants the assumption that two-year college students are indifferent toward student life and administrative relationships.

An additional dimension regarding student apathy should be considered here. Students' roles in higher education have been subjected to extensive criticism by students themselves (25).

The essential question relative to students in the community college is whether they actually have thought through and understand a viable role for themselves within the institutional context. Keeping in mind that these students come from "noncollege" families, by and large, it becomes evident that their lack of collegiate experience inhibits adequate role definition. This, coupled with institutional rigidities, may well constitute the major contribution to lack of interest and apathy among students.

If we examine the nature of student governments, we usually find them buried within the organizational framework with little authority and less prestige. We may discover the committees on which a college advertises voting membership of students are heavily weighted in the direction of administrative and faculty membership; furthermore, such committees probably report their recommendations to institutional bodies on which students have no representation. Under such circumstances, many students lose faith in the established procedures for involvement in governance processes, then boycott such procedures as a mark of their contempt. Similarly student activities frequently are designed around institutional considerations and public expectations rather than developing from the actual needs of students.

Kenneston has described three categories of students in an analysis of dissent. He identifies the "excluded," the "tenuously in," and the "solidly in" (15). Within each of these groups one will find at least four distinct types of individuals. The dissident is one who clearly rejects some or all the conventions of his immediate environment or society in general. The indifferent constitutes the majority of students who are willing to accept new ideas, for they have not yet committed themselves irrevocably to the general modes and ideals of society. The disaffected are those having marginal status, generalized social anxieties, and disillusionment. The last group are the resentful who have been excluded from the mainstream and have nothing to lose through changes in the system (2:381).

Among the excluded are those who are also described by Knoell (18). Such students are predominantly those who come from minority group backgrounds and who would not have been in college at all until the recent democratization of higher education. The tenuously in probably constitute the majority of those found on two-year college campuses and include the vocationally oriented, upwardly mobile, first-generation college students who are actively seeking integration with the system as it now exists. The solidly in are made up of the sons and daughters of the affluent who are, themselves, college graduates and who are generally regarded as operating within the power structures of their respective communities. This last group is under represented but not absent from two-year college campuses.

Interestingly, the most likely source of activism is the solidly ins, while the excluded are the second most likely source. Kenneston warns, however, that the potential discontents of the more vocationally oriented students may lead, in the future, to a growing polarization, particularly as these students see their values threatened by demands from both the militant minorities and the affluent activists (13:59). Two-year colleges may alienate and polarize their own nontraditional student bodies to the extent they attempt to imitate practices of the selective four-year institutions. If environment is based upon an analysis of needs and numbers, greater attention will have to be given to minority group needs and to needs of the large silent majority for whom the two-year college represents the pathway to an American dream which has not yet lost its luster.

If we accept the broadened concept of the student using the college as a resource for self-development and higher need fulfillment, certain fundamental considerations emerge which hold implications for the structuring of relationships and responsibilities. First we must assume students will choose not to involve themselves in activities they regard as peripheral to their needs. In many, perhaps in most, areas of institutional decision making, a majority of students will regard decisions as irrelevant to their goals. At the same time, they can be expected to pursue issues they view as important with great vigor, for the lesson of dissent has not been lost upon them. In consequence of this lesson, they will often pursue their goals outside established channels. Obstinacy or hostility on the part of faculty or administration invites confrontation and acceleration of tensions (6). Passivity invites excesses and abuse. The challenge is to find a middle ground for conceptualizing student role.

It will be helpful in viewing interaction to define those areas of greatest student concern. These can be divided into a number of categories. The first, and perhaps the most important, is the quality of services. Within a broad range of tolerance, instruction, counseling, and food service are examples of student services capable of mobilizing student opinion and motivating involvement in the decision-making process. A second classification of concerns extends to those who provide services. A decision to retain a staff member whose services are regarded by students as unsatisfactory or a decision to terminate the services of a popular staff member may generate substantial concern.

Next we may consider the range of issues related to student rights and freedom from unnecessary regulation. Increasingly students have given evidence that their behavior will not be prescribed in areas unrelated to the academic process (28). Organizations such as the National Student Association have created an awareness that like faculty, students too are entitled to academic freedom. Documents such as the Joint Statement on Rights and Freedoms of Students have outlined ideas in areas such as speakers, college newspapers, and disciplinary procedures which have not infrequently been in direct contradiction to prevailing institutional practice. Courts have held, in a number of instances, that withholding college funds cannot be used as a means of denying students the rights they are entitled to as citizens under the constitution. Reducing the voting age to eighteen may have an impact on the effectiveness of the college student as a consumer and a client far beyond anything that has yet occurred (12).

Because student concerns about most issues seldom surface in the absence of strongly provocative circumstances combined with serious errors in judgment, many institutions continue to overlook the importance of redefining both the students' role within the institution and the procedures through which such a role can be effectively exercised. The lack of procedures and methods for relating student concerns to the policy-making process within the institution represents a dangerous situation.

To say the student is a client is not to say his opinions are unimportant. He may lack the professional knowledge and the experience of the faculty and the administration but what he lacks in those areas is more than compensated for by his numbers and his centrality to the entire process of education. He can tell where it hurts, so he is capable of cooperating in the process of improvement. Any assumption that the student is an inferior person, subject to the wisdom and authority of his betters in the persons of the faculty and the administration, will stand only so long as it is not tested. The student must and will be viewed as a full partner in the process of education.

Faculty Role

Faculty role is difficult to analyze because of the complications introduced by a number of developments which have occurred within the past three to five years. The advent of collective bargaining, accompanied by the rapid growth of faculty organizations with welfare objectives similar to those identified by unions, has created substantial internal controversy as well as a growing number of institutional crises. The faculty as union member does not in many instances represent a radical departure from past practice. Perhaps the predominant role definition for faculty members in many of our institutions has been as union member without the benefits of union membership. By that we imply he has been subjected to constraints typical of a bureaucratic situation in which no union existed, including the definition of the nature of his job, the amount of work to be accomplished, the evaluation of his performance, and the determination of remuneration to be authorized by administration.

In a variety of ways the situation is changing. Collective bargaining legislation has accorded faculty the right to negotiate with administrators and trustees about salaries, fringe benefits and working conditions. Issues involving working conditions have created the stage for a new level of confrontation. Employers have sought to alter the definition of working conditions so as to remove many of the areas of decision making which have, in the past, been determined by joint faculty-administrative participation, and more recently with student involvement. Faculty organizations have sought to broaden dimensions to provide welfare organizations with a virtual veto over all aspects of institutional policy formulation. If faculty organizations such as those sponsored by the National Education Association and the American Federation of Teachers are successful in current efforts, the eventual result could be the establishment of a parallel administrative structure to which faculty would owe their first allegiance. How student interests might fare in such an arrangement is open to conjecture.

Perhaps the root of the problem of role definition of faculty rests with the nature of the practice of education. Millett indicates that the profession of scholarship is socialized (23). One aspect of this condition is the absence of faculty control over remuneration. There is also the problem of the lack of a code of ethics for the educational profession combined with an acknowledged reluctance to be self-policing. The consequence has been the establishment of institutional arrangements whereby faculty has been evaluated by administrators. Administrators have also assumed the responsibility for determining, often with little participation from faculty, such questions as the allocation of institutional resources, standards for retention and promotion, criteria for recognition, and similar matters not directly related to the educational program.

It is a well-known fact that administrative values do not always coincide with faculty values. Furthermore, while dominance of administrators in the decision-making process during the past few years may be more implied than real, faculty members tend to feel most administrators have and utilize far more power than they actually do.

The study by Dykes indicated that there was a marked discrepancy between the faculty's ideal role and its concept of its actual role. Dykes points out that:

> Comments from the respondents suggested that the discrepancy is primarily attributable to two related convictions: that the faculty's actual involvement in decision making is for the most part focused on rather insignificant matters; and that the faculty should have a larger, more active, and more influential role in the decision-making processes. According to respondents, the truth of their first conviction renders impossible the attainment of the second. Many expressed frustration and exasperation with extensive involvement in what seemed to them relatively unimportant matters (11:11).

Both these contribute to faculty frustrations and to faculty resentment. Just as students have viewed with suspicion machinery for their involvement in policy formulation established by a paternalistic faculty and administration, so too have faculty demonstrated little faith in administratively conceived schemes for their participation. In more than a few instances, the passage of collective bargaining legislation has been accompanied by a movement to discard all existing procedures for college governance and to substitute the adversary relationships of the collective bargaining unit.

It would be wrong to imply a consensus exists among faculty concerning the direction their involvement in the governance process should take. Corwin differentiates between bureaucratic employee expectations and professional employee expectations (9). Among other characteristics the former tend to stress loyalty to the institution and to superiors, task orientation, uniformity of client problems, and rules stated as universals and specifics. The latter, by comparison, are concerned more with loyalty to professional associations and clients, client orientation, uniqueness of clients' problems and rules stated as alternative and diffuse. For our purposes, we may assume most two-year colleges will include faculty members representing both these points of view. Perhaps one of the most difficult situations with respect to inducing change involves the established institution with its core of bureaucratically oriented older faculty members confronted by a growing number of professionally oriented younger faculty.

In two-year colleges the professional organization to which a faculty member's loyalties may be drawn is more likely to be a welfare group than a scholarly organization. In consequence, some of Corwin's assumptions may prove false, since a tendency of welfare organizations is to substitute one bureaucracy for another. Indeed those who have had some experience with institutions subsequent to the organization of collective bargaining units report a distinct reduction in flexibility and a hardening of institutional arteries of communication. The result may decrease the possibilities of change in promoting a recognition of higher needs even more than those associated with security and peer group recognition of the past.

Perhaps the major implication of the foregoing is the recognition that redefinition is now in process; moreover, it will probably accelerate in the immediate future. While such redefinition may reduce incongruencies between institutional expectations and faculty needs, such reductions may be accomplished at the expense of flexibility and responsiveness to the needs of a nontraditional student body. In passing it may also be observed that a socialized profession is not particularly sensitive to the attitudes of those who provide resources for their remuneration. In the past such insensitivity has been much in evidence, even though faculty have been insulated by only a single bureaucracy as represented by administrative structures. The establishment of a secondary bureaucracy in the form of a parallel faculty organization can only increase insensitivity and consequently the potential for conflict in the matter of institutional resources.

Because of the previously mentioned conflict among faculty between loyalty to institutions and loyalty to professional organizations, it is easy for administrators to misread the direction and intensity of current efforts toward role redefinition. It is not uncommon for people to hear what they wish to hear and to ignore or rationalize input which does not confirm their biases. Despite differences of opinion as to the desirability of faculty welfare organizations as a substitute for prevailing governance practices, the weight of faculty opinion in most two-year institutions is clearly in this direction. Perhaps this is true because faculty have tried existing procedures and have not been satisfied with the rate of change. Perhaps it represents distrust of any procedure which has been unilaterally established and which presumably could be unilaterally changed by an external authority. Under any circumstances the pressures are there; little time remains for the exploration of viable alternatives to the collective bargaining unit. Many institutions have already passed over the divide. While the writers are in no way opposed to labor unions as one way of resolving differences, we should not accept this pattern as representative of the most promising and creative relationship between professionals in institutions of higher education. Nevertheless, we would be less than realistic if we did not admit that this is the probable direction of the future.

Faculty preoccupation with welfare activities has not prevented the development of lively controversies in other areas. The advent of behavioral objectives and the systems approach to learning has deeply divided faculty opinion among those who advocate traditional practices and those who wish to pursue actively the new methodology. Faculty members have, in some instances, been subjected to pressures by administrators committed to the concept of innovation and who have controlled the system of rewards to encourage new techniques. In the absence of compulsion, the use of multiple approaches to teaching has frequently resulted in a creative and dynamic environment. Student involvement and reaction have sometimes provided the necessary thrust to encourage traditionally oriented faculty to experiment with new approaches, while at the same time curbing excesses not infrequently perpetrated in the name of innovation.

The public demand for accountability has added another dimension of conflict. Administrators are hard pressed to respond to the growing requirements passed down from legislatures to state agencies to institutions to demonstrate measurable outputs upon which dollar allocations can be justified. Faculty find such concerns less important in their day-to-day activities, frequently giving only minimal response and support to the endeavor.

Faculty are also divided over the role students should play in the decision-making process. In many institutions faculty have enjoyed only limited responsibilities in this process, so they cannot be expected to be overly enthusiastic about any further dilution of their influence. A first prerequisite to faculty acceptance of students as partners in the process of education involves appropriate recognition of the faculty as professional practitioners by administration and by the larger community. Until the faculty member feels secure in his professional status with respect to areas such as evaluation, promotion, salary increases and role definition, he is unlikely to extend to students more than the token participation he has long perceived as his lot.

Faculty age and rank are important factors contributing to the process of role redefinition (30). Toffler has indicated that older people react more strongly to further accelerations of change while the impatience of the young may be in proportion to their perception of a given time period as it differs from the perception of an older person who has had a longer time span with which to make comparisons (30:38). Older faculty members are less likely to transfer their allegiance to an external organization. They are also generally in a position to control the process of change with respect to the development of new programs and personnel decisions. This problem may be particularly acute in some two-year colleges where the majority of all faculty members currently teaching have been employed within the last ten years.

From this review it is apparent many issues and conditions have created ferment among the ranks of our faculty. The mists created by catalytic reactions obscure the forms in process of reshaping. There are definite readings which can be taken, however, and they yield evidence of direction, if not of final form. Boyan has suggested a number of these have implications for the governance process (4). In the future we may expect increased levels of preparation and expertise among our professional staffs combined with a growing disenchantment with authoritarian and paternalistic administration. There will be a tendency for faculty to assume greater responsibility for decision making and to turn increasingly to professional organizations for the machinery to implement such involvement. Professional organizations with their promise of security will encourage greater faculty militancy. Increasing concern is likely to be evidenced with the allocation of institutional resources. This process carries with it the potential for professional role conflicts in such areas as standardization, centralization of authority and specialization.

Role of Administrators

Administrators are the focal point for developing pressures in the role redefinition process. The student and faculty thrust toward greater involvement in processes formerly dominated administratively has resulted in fears about status and power on the part of many administrators who correctly perceive their traditional prerogatives eroding. Not only must administrators contend with fears of losing power but also they must face continuing pressures from trustees and the general public to behave in traditional patterns. This leads to a serious dilemma.

If administrators cling to the modes of behavior that coincide with public stereotypes, they run the risk of further antagonizing faculty and students, thus provoking confrontations which culminate in public censure and lack of confidence. On the other hand, administrators who tend to relate creatively to the new forces at work within the institution are likely to be labeled as liberals and severely castigated, if incidents arise over issues unrelated to the internal affairs of the institution and consequently beyond the control of the administrators. Demonstrations against the war in Vietnam or national policy were illustrations of this dilemma. If administrators seek to gain public confidence by preventing demonstrations, they alienate students and faculty and may, in the process, escalate the violence of the confrontation. If they support the causes espoused by the demonstrators, they become the targets of outraged citizens who feel such issues are clearly beyond the scope of student concern.

Perhaps more dangerous than either of these extremes is an attempt to occupy a compromise position. Administrators must recognize there is no possibility at present for a middle ground between those who maintain a traditional view of the administrator's role and those who seek the reconstruction of relationships among the internal constituencies of the college. Any attempt to compromise is likely to alienate both the public and internal constituencies. The ultimate solution to this dilemma must await general acceptance of a new concept of the role of an administrator in an institution of higher education.

Clark Kerr has identified a series of concerns central to an understanding of the administrative role in the 70s. Among these concerns he includes fiscal problems, faculty relations, control of the institution, student relations, new directions for programs, and aims and purposes (16:141). Fiscal problems have become one of the dominant issues of the current era, perhaps the source of greatest concern to administrators. Enrollment growth has leveled off and begun to decline for many private institutions. While students continue to pour into community college systems, public support has not kept pace with enrollment pressures or with the effects of economic inflation. Consequently, institutional development has been hampered; in some instances services have been reduced while in others the continued stability of the institution has been placed in serious jeopardy.

Faculty actions have added to the fiscal crisis. It has not been uncommon, in the past, for data on institutional resources to be withheld from faculty groups or to be deliberately misrepresented. As a result, faculty groups frequently take the position the source of funds is of no concern to them. On this basis they have sought simultaneously to decrease workloads while increasing salaries. Reductions in credit hour loads combined with limitations imposed on class size have increased costs faster than salary increments. Consequently, administrators have, with some justification, interpreted faculty concern with their own welfare as being to the detriment of the welfare of their clients or the institution. Such attitudes have been reinforced by instances of faculty resistance to change, faculty movement toward unionization, and other actions having the implication of lessened confidence in administrative competence and fairness. Confrontation and adversary relationships between faculty and administrators is the rule rather than the exception in many of our two-year colleges.

The issue of institutional control has not simply been one of balancing the demands of faculty and students for greater involvement in the processes of institutional governance against the need to reserve some authority for administrators. Pressures from external sources including political bodies and public opinion have impaired the ability of the college to preserve academic freedom. Public two-year colleges are, by their nature, particularly susceptible to community pressures. The growing number of court cases as well as censorship reports in the AAUP Bulletin give evidence of pressure infringing upon the rights of students and faculty.

Student relations are another source of institutional concern even though they may rank well down the list for administrators. Administrators are sympathetic with student pressures oriented toward increasing student involvement in the academic sphere, yet at the same time they are likely to resist student involvement in areas of administrative concern including observance of moral standards. The transient nature of the student body has been used both as a rationalization for preventing greater student involvement and as a device for limiting student influence. It has not been uncommon for decisions to be postponed in the hope graduation or attrition might remove those promoting changes viewed as undesirable.

Administrators tend to have different priorities for the use of institutional resources than either faculty or students. Faculty members tend to accord top priority to areas involving faculty welfare. Students tend to emphasize the importance of instruction and student services. Administrators are concerned with the image and perpetuation of the institution as well as the development of new programs or services directed toward long-range objectives. The difference in values extends also to the objectives of the institution including philosophical considerations. Administrators tend to be very knowledgeable about and highly committed to the philosophical values guiding the two-year college movement. Faculty are less aware of and, generally speaking, less committed to these philosophical considerations, particularly when they come into conflict with traditional concepts in areas such as services to the disadvantaged, selectivity in the admissions process, and the focus of instructional objectives. Not surprisingly, students are likely to be the most resistent to emphasis upon long-range goals at the expense of present requirements.

The obvious is often overlooked. The responsibility of the administrator for the management of the total educational enterprise of the institution as well as all its resources frequently seems unnoticed by faculty, students, trustees and even the general public. The tasks of planning, organizing, directing, evaluating and redirecting must be performed. Sadly, we need not look long or far to see the unfortunate consequence to institutions where internal or external demands and pressures resulted in costly absence of management planning or management evaluation.

A final source of administrative tension involves the development of multicampus networks in many large cities and even total state systems directed by a central state agency. Under such circumstances, the question of centralization versus decentralization becomes a key issue. Unfortunately, it is never possible for the central unit to provide sufficient self-determination to system components, since one effect of providing increased autonomy is to create a desire for even greater autonomy. While there may be less tension related to this issue among highly centralized systems where the idea of self-governance has never been articulated, such systems encounter other disadvantages including problems of communication and coordination, general lack of flexibility, and inability to respond to the demands of the local community. Administrators in multicampus or state controlled systems must contend with the impact of more complex constraints and relationships in addition to adapting to most of the other forces previously defined. Administrators confronted by the variety of issues and crises generated by role conflict have reacted in a number of ways, depending upon personality and perception of the dynamics of human interaction. One approach to understanding the administrative role involves the categorization of administrative behavior on the basis of response to the individuals with whom they work.

Blake and Mouton have devised an approach for this purpose (3). Termed the Managerial Grid, the system involves two intersecting axes with the horizontal axis representing concern for institutional objectives and the vertical axis concern for people. Each axis is divided on the basis of a 9 point scale with the higher numbers representing an increasing degree of concern. A 9,1 administrator, for example, is one with maximum concern for objectives and minimum concern for people. A 1,1 administrator, by contrast, has minimum concern for both objectives and people. While eighty-one different combinations are theoretically possible, Blake and Mouton have confined their efforts to the definition of five ideal type positions. An examination of each of these five categories can help to explain the variety of administrative roles which currently can be observed within our two-year colleges. See Figure 4.3 (3:9–11).

The 9,1 administrator subscribes to the theory X view of human behavior. Because he places a high priority on the achievement of institutional objectives, he is likely to be highly resistant to role redefinition. He operates on the basis of his authority and he expects obedience from his subordinates. He is likely to place emphasis upon procedures for organiz-

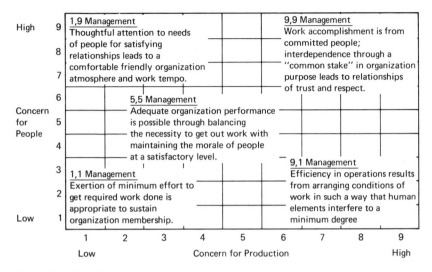

FIG. 4.3   THE MANAGERIAL GRID

ing work and to be little concerned with such considerations as conflict, creativity, or commitment except as these may relate to goal achievement. His relationships with others will be impersonal and he will drive himself and others (3:48).

Administrators with a 9,1 orientation are most likely to survive in small institutions and in institutions isolated from the mainstream of the changes previously described. The basic position lacks the flexibility necessary to adjust to the process of role redefinition other than through confrontation techniques. Despite the high degree of emphasis placed upon goal attainment, the 9,1 administrator is limited in his effectiveness because his concept of human behavior relies upon relatively low level needs to motivate the achievement of subordinates. In contemporary administrative practice, the 9,1 administrator is an anachronism and can survive only as long as there is no challenge to the assumptions upon which his behavior is based.

The 1,9 administrator is concerned with keeping people happy. Whenever decisions must be made, values involving human relationships, friendliness and harmony will take precedence over the objectives of the institution. People are encouraged to do sufficient work to avoid causing problems but there is no sustained effort to improve the quality or quantity of output (3:79–80).

Relationships between administrators and faculty in the 1,9 environment will be pleasant, because expectations of faculty members are low and there is a great deal of individual freedom combined with very little accountability. The students are the real losers in the 1,9 situation since their best interests are seldom represented in the decision-making process. The 1,9 administrator appeals to social needs such as peer acceptance and friendship. Morale research has demonstrated there is no consistent correlation between employee satisfaction and productivity. Understanding the mode of operation of the 1,9 administrator is the key to understanding the lack of relationship between satisfaction and productivity. Because the 1,9 administrator does not appeal to higher needs, the staff member is not motivated to achieve near the maximum level.

The 1,1 administrator is really a drop-out. Overwhelmed by the forces which surround him, he wants simply to be left alone. He is likely to be an expert at rationalizing failure in order to insure the blame is placed elsewhere. His criticism is not goal directed but rather intended to protect himself. The 1,1 administrator is essentially a message carrier who seeks minimum involvement in the human relationships that are a part of goal achievement.

The 1,1 administrators have been defeated by their environment. They hope to survive until retirement but have no real expectation or desire to influence organizational purpose. Such administrators are sometimes sought out by trustees in a conflict situation as a means of minimizing confrontations between contending factions. Unfortunately, such administrators also minimize direction and achievement and may continue in their positions by creating only small problems.

The 5,5 administrator is a manipulator. Having correctly identified the forces with which he must contend, he seeks accommodation through balancing the demands for goal achievement with the requirements for maintaining cordial relationships among the staff. The 5,5 administrator is likely to place considerable reliance upon informal procedures for making decisions and informal procedures for communicating the results of decisions. Under such circumstances, the informal system becomes a method of testing decisions. If the decisions seem to function satisfactorily, they will be formalized as written policies. Much of the energy of those involved in the 5,5 environment must be directed toward maintaining the dual systems in operation (3:135–36).

The 5,5 administrator may be an individual of great personal integrity. In such cases, his manipulation is aimed, not at promoting any selfish interests, but rather in the direction of what he perceives as the best interests of the institution. The 5,5 administrator is the great compromiser. He recognizes the challenges but attempts to resolve matters in terms of accepting some kind of a balance between the needs of people and the objectives of the institution. He does not seek to combine these forces, rather he uses the incongruencies creatively to maximize institutional achievement. Unfortunately, the appeal of motivational forces continues to be at a level no higher than the social needs level for the 1,9 administrator. Again, the student may be the loser in the 5,5 environment because he is not in a position to defend his interests to the same extent that other parties in the compromise are.

The 9,9 administrator has as his basic framework the theory Y concept of human behavior. While elements of theory Y are also present in other marginal styles the 9,9 administrator places greater emphasis upon the higher needs of people to be involved and committed to productive work. Goal setting is a cooperative process involving all of those who will be affected by the decisions reached. The 9,9 administrator is convinced that as individuals are involved in the process of goal setting, they will be committed to the achievement of these goals, and in turn, will find self-fulfillment through goal achievement. Strong emphasis is also placed upon the importance of conflict confrontation as an aspect of interdependent relationships (3:180).

It is probable that the 5,5 administrator will be found in greater abundance among the ranks of administrators in two-year colleges today than any of the other types mentioned. Next in order of frequency would probably be 9,1 administrators and 1,9 administrators which we might expect to find in almost equal numbers. The 1,1 administrator would be found less frequently. It is difficult to predict the number of 9,9 administrators since there is little evidence that the concepts of human behavior, which must of necessity underlie the 9,9 approach to administration, are well understood. Hopefully, one effect of this volume will be to encourage more administrators to move in the direction of 9,9 philosophy.

SUMMARY

We are now in a position to define the nature of our problem. We know a college, to function effectively, requires a certain degree of congruence between the needs of those who function within its setting and the requirements imposed upon them by the role expectations built into the institutional structure. It is apparent that role expectations, because they are institutionalized, will change more slowly than the society which shapes the personalities and need dispositions of those who fill the roles. We have reached a critical point in our colleges where role expectations have become so obsolete in terms of our faculty and student needs that a state of rebellion exists directed against the institution.

The effect of this revolt has been to polarize those who are attacking and those who are defending the status quo. Administrators and trustees who are, by and large, satisfied with existing role definitions, especially since these tend to create an imbalance of power in favor of administrators and trustees, are fighting to preserve the conditions which have provided them with a measure of security in the past. Faculty and students have lost faith in the ability of the institution to change from within, using established governance procedures. Consequently, they have turned to outside agencies or have established separate procedures. This process has been interpreted by trustees and administrators as lack of loyalty.

In consequence, the battle is on. The nature of warfare is such that it is difficult to confine relationships to an impersonal level. The dust of the conflict and resultant emotions have obscured the real causes and alternative solutions. The time has come when we must persuade ourselves that the real culprit is not an irresponsible student, a disloyal faculty member, an authoritarian administrator, or a meddling trustee. We must begin to understand that the basis of our problem is an outmoded view of human behavior which has led us to define roles in such a way as to exclude students and faculty from the satisfaction of their higher-level needs.

Like administrators and trustees, students and faculty have needs for self-esteem, self-respect, autonomy, achievement, and competence. They also have needs for status, recognition, appreciation and the respect of their colleagues. Above all, they have needs for self-fulfillment. Until we change our concept of human behavior as it relates to the procedures we use in establishing goals, evaluating performance, and providing rewards, we can expect to continue to experience distress in the form of unsatisfactory behavior. Student activism, faculty militancy, attrition rates, and a host of other factors can be attributed, in large part, to this failure to revise our role expectations in accordance with vastly altered societal conditions.

An examination of some of the characteristics of the roles currently defined for students, faculty, and administrators, in comparison with the changes necessary to bring them into congruence with personality and need dispositions of role incumbents reveals the extent of the disparity. Having identified the problem and analyzed the need for change, the question now to be considered is how such change can be effected. It is axiomatic that stating a hypothesis with verification and obtaining acceptance of that hypothesis can be two quite different matters, particularly when vested interests are concerned and a crisis exists. In the next chapter we will consider the organizational dimension of the institution as it relates to the resolution of this problem.

REFERENCES

1. ARGYRIS, CHRIS, *Integrating the Individual and the Organization.* New York: John Wiley, 1964.

2. BARNETT, H. G., *Innovation: The Basis of Cultural Change.* New York: McGraw-Hill, 1953.

3. BLAKE, ROBERT ROGERS and JANE S. MOUTON, *The Managerial Grid: Key Orientations for Achieving Production Through People.* Houston, Texas: Gulf Publishing Co., 1964.

4. BOYAN, NORMAN J., "The Emergent Role of the Teacher in the Authority Structure of the School," in *Organizations and Human Behavior: Focus on Schools,* eds. Carver and Sergio Vanni. New York: McGraw-Hill, 1969.

5. BRAWER, FLORENCE B., *Personality Characteristics of College and University Faculty: Implications for the Community College.* Washington, D. C.: American Association of Junior Colleges, 1968.

6. *Campus Tensions: Analysis and Recommendations.* Report of the Special Committee on Campus Tensions. Washington, D. C.: American Council on Education, 1970.

7. CHICKERING, ARTHUR W., "The Best Colleges Have the Least Effect," *Saturday Review,* January 16, 1971, pp. 48–50, 54.

8. COHEN, ARTHUR M. and FLORENCE B. BRAWER, *Student Characteristics: Personality and Drop-Out Propensity.* Washington, D. C.: American Association of Junior Colleges, 1970.

9. CORWIN, RONALD, "Professional Persons in Public Organizations," *Educational Administration Quarterly,* 1:1–22 (1965).

10. CROSS, K. PATRICIA, *The Junior College Student—A Research Description.* Princeton, N. J.: Educational Testing Service, 1968.

11. DYKES, ARCHIE R., *Faculty Participation in Academic Decision Making.* Washington, D. C.: American Council on Education, 1968.

12. FISCHER, THOMAS C., *Due Process in the Student Institutional Relationship.* Washington, D. C.: American Association of State Colleges and Universities, 1970.

13. GADDY, DALE, *The Scope of Organized Student Protest in Junior Colleges.* Washington, D. C.: American Association of Junior Colleges, 1970.

14. GETZEL, JACOB W., "Administration as a Social Process," in *Administrative Theory in Education,* ed. Andrew W. Halpin. Chicago: Mid-West Administration Center, 1958.

15. KENNESTON, KENNETH, "What's Bugging the Students?" in *Perspectives on Campus Tensions,* ed. David C. Nichols. Washington, D. C.: American Council on Education, 1970.

16. KERR, CLARK, "Presidential Discontent," in *Perspectives on Campus Tensions,* ed. David C. Nichols. Washington, D. C.: American Council on Education, 1970.

17. KLAPP, ORRIN E., *Collective Search for Identity.* New York: Holt, Rinehart & Winston, 1969.

18. KNOELL, DOROTHY M., *People Who Need College.* Washington, D. C.: American Association of Junior Colleges, 1970.

19. LLOYD-JONES, SUSAN S., "Student Interests in Value Change and Power Conflict," in *Value Change and Power Conflict in Higher Education,* eds. W. John Minter and Patricia O. Snyder. Boulder, Colo.: Western Interstate Commission for Higher Education, 1969.

20. LOMBARDI, JOHN, *The President's Reaction to Black Student Activism,* Topical Paper No. 16. Los Angeles: ERIC Clearinghouse for Junior Colleges, University of California, January 1971.

21. MASLOW, A. H., *Motivation and Personality.* New York: Harper & Row, 1954.

22. MCGREGOR, DOUGLAS, *The Human Side of Enterprise.* New York: McGraw-Hill, 1960.

23. MILLETT, JOHN D., *The Academic Community: An Essay on Organization.* New York: McGraw-Hill, 1962.

24. RICHARDSON, RICHARD C., JR., "Restructuring the Human Dimensions of Our Colleges," *Junior College Journal,* 41:20–24 (February 1971).

25. SABINE, GORDON, *When You Listen, This Is What You Can Hear. . . .* Iowa City, Iowa: The American College Testing Program, 1971.

26. SEYMOUR, MARTIN LIPSET, "The Politics of Academia," in *Perspectives on Campus Tensions,* ed. David C. Nichols. Washington, D. C.: American Council on Education, 1970.

27. STERN, GEORGE G., "Campus Environments and Student Unrest," in *Current Issues in Higher Education,* ed. G. Kerry Smith. San Francisco: Jossey-Bass, 1969.

28. The Beliefs and Attitudes of Male College Seniors, Freshmen and Alumni. A Study by Roper Research Associates, Inc., prepared for Standard Oil Company (New Jersey), May 1969.

29. THRESHER, P. ALDEN, *College Admissions and the Public Interest.* New York: College Entrance Examination Board, 1966.

30. TOFFLER, ALVIN, *Future Shock.* New York: Random House, 1970.

five

Theory

and

Structure

of Organization

Behavior resulting from role conflict is closely related to the structure of institutions and their administrative leadership. Much undesirable behavior can be attributed directly to the demands imposed upon faculty and students by organizational precepts (7:7–25).

Most attempts to analyze social organization have utilized some form of the bureaucratic model advanced by Weber (9). Merton's description serves as well as any to summarize the essential aspects of this type of organization.

> A formal, rationally organized social structure involves clearly defined patterns of activity in which, ideally, every series of actions is functionally related to the purposes of the organization. In such an organization, there is integrated a series of offices, of hierarchized statuses, in which inhere a number of obligations and privileges closely defined by limited and specific rules. Each of these offices contains an area of imputed competence and responsibility. Authority, the power of control which derives from an acknowledged status, inheres in the office and not in the person who performs the official rule. Official action ordinarily occurs within the framework of pre-existing rules of the organization (13:195).

Several points should be noted. Actions are related to the purposes of the organization, purposes which are precisely defined and whose success is subject to quantitative evaluation. Offices are arranged in a hierarchical order, the functions of each office being carefully circumscribed by established rules and procedures; authority rests with the office and not with the person.

A careful analysis of institutions of higher education reveals that their basic structure rests, first of all, upon organizational theory as defined by the concept of the bureaucratic organization; and secondly, upon scientific management which, in essence, is a refinement of the theory of bureaucratic organizations. Argyris has summarized the principles of scientific management, paraphrased and made applicable to the educational environment:

1. Work tends to be specialized with the scope of responsibilities for each employee kept as narrow and uncomplicated as possible.
2. Responsibility for establishing objectives and determining how they shall be reached is placed primarily in the hands of administration.
3. Responsibility for determining the scope of an employee's activities, his place of work, and for issuing directives governing the work to be performed is in the hands of administration.
4. The responsibility for evaluating performance and for distributing rewards and penalties rests with administration.
5. The responsibility for employment and dismissal rests with administration (2).

The pyramidal structure, typical of the bureaucratic model, is designed to insure that the greatest influence over people, information and procedures is exercised by those who operate at the top of the structure (1:39). This concentration of authority and decision making in the hands of the few has created a gap between psychological needs and opportunities for meeting them which grows wider as one descends the chain of command. The lack of congruency between organizational demands and individual needs to which we alluded in the preceding chapter has as its consequences frustration, failure, and conflict for employees and for students also. Argyris summarizes this point:

> The formal organization and the administrative control system typically used in complex formal organizations may be viewed as part of a grand strategy to organize human effort to achieve specific objectives, and this strategy is based on such principles of administration as specialization of work, chain of command, unity of direction and span of control. The strategy creates a complex of organizational demands that tend to require individuals to experience dependency and submissiveness and to utilize few of their relatively peripheral abilities (1:58).

Argyris goes on to say that the frustration of employees results in adaptive types of behavior which may include: absenteeism, turnover, trade unions, increasing emphasis on material factors, decreasing emphasis on human factors (1:92). Two of the major criticisms that have been leveled at faculty members in recent years is their tendency to turn to professional organizations which are in reality thinly disguised trade unions; and that faculty members are more concerned with their own material well-being than with the satisfactory performance of their professional responsibilities. If the two-year college is viewed as a bureaucratic organization, then it is apparent that faculty members must occupy the lower levels within this structure. It is equally apparent that at such levels they will have only limited opportunities to satisfy psychological needs. Consequently, they will be motivated to resort to adaptive behavior that will reduce the incongruency between the demands that are imposed upon them by the organization and the environment which they perceive as essential to their well-being.

Of course, it follows logically that if the two-year college is in fact a pyramidal structure, built along the lines of the traditional model, then students must occupy an even lower level within the organization than that occupied by faculty members. This was amply demonstrated by a study of faculty attitudes toward student participation in decision making (14). Faculty responding to the questionnaire (1) agreed that students should participate in nonacademic policy development; (2) felt that students should participate in evaluating teachers, the results being available to the teacher only; (3) rejected student participation in affairs of the governing board; (4) indicated student ideas should be obtained; and (5) tended to be conventional in their thinking about teaching-learning issues in general.

In the light of halting acceptance or outright rejection by the faculty of expansion of the student role in governance, might we not anticipate students' adaptive behavior to be even more violent or apathetic than the faculty's? We find this to be the case in many institutions. Generally speaking, as one analyzes the level of satisfaction reported by role incumbents within the two-year college, the reactions of the trustees and administration will be most positive. The reactions of the faculty members will be less positive and the reactions of students will be most critical.

The conclusions stated above must be regarded as relative rather than absolute. It is obvious that special conditions may intervene to alter the degree of dissatisfaction experienced by faculty members in comparison with students. For example, Simon notes:

> . . . the objectives of the customer are very closely . . . related to the objectives of the organization, the objectives of the entrepreneur are closely related to the survival of the organization; while the objectives of the employee are directly related to neither of these, but are brought into the organization's scheme by the existence of his area of acceptance (18:18) .

We may consider the customer to be the student, the entrepreneur the administrator, and the employee the faculty. Using this analogy, we can conclude that as long as the services rendered are satisfactory and as long as the organization gives evidence of being able to perpetuate itself, certain basic requirements of the administrator and of the student are fulfilled. However, satisfaction for faculty members is more directly related to the conditions under which services are provided than is true for either the administrator or the student. Consequently, unless faculty discontent affects the quality of student services or unless there is a deliberate attempt by dissatisfied faculty members to influence students unfavorably, it is possible for the degree of satisfaction for students to be higher than that of faculty. However, it is probable that even under optimum conditions, students will have less opportunity to achieve their psychological needs within the organizational structure than administrators or trustees.

THE CONCEPT OF ORGANIZATION

Simon has defined a formal organization as a plan for the division of work and the allocation of authority. The organization also gives to each member of the group his status and role in relation to the other members, but it specifies the content of his work and his decisional function only in very general terms. Argyris indicates that certain basic organizational processes must exist and be functioning in a mutually interdependent manner for an organization to exist. Among these processes he includes work flow, reward and penalty, authority, perpetuation, identification, communication, and status (1:131). Bennis talks of organizations of the future as "adaptive, rapidly changing temporary systems organized around problems to be" (3:45).

From these sources it can be concluded that decisional processes are essential to any understanding of the nature of the organization. Simon has defined the kinds of decisions that organizations make for individuals as function-defining the scope and nature of duties, allocation of authority, and establishing such other limits to choice as may be necessary to accomplish coordination. Simon shows further the three steps of the decision-making process as:

1. The identification of alternative strategies.
2. The determination of the probable consequences of each strategy.
3. A comparative evaluation of the desirability of each set of consequences (18:8–9) .

Authority

Before proceeding further with an analysis of the decision-making process as it functions in the college setting, it will be necessary to identify and define certain terms. First, let us consider the concept of authority. The classical definition of authority insofar as management literature is concerned, has been supplied by Barnard.

> Authority is another name for the willingness and capacity of individuals to submit to the necessities of cooperative systems. Authority arises from the technological and social limitations of comparative systems on the one hand and of individuals on the other. Hence the status of authority in a society is a measure both of individuals and of the technological and social conditions of society (4:184).

Several aspects of this definition deserve particular attention. In the first place, Barnard recognized authority as being based upon the extent to which individuals would voluntarily relinquish their own decisional autonomy in the interests of promoting common objectives. It is also apparent that Barnard conceived of authority as a relative and not an absolute quality. His emphasis upon the social conditions of society implies that as such conditions change, so too, will the nature and effectiveness of authority.

Two different types of authority are discussed by Barnard. The first type, authority of position, is related to the assumption within the bureaucratic model that in each office rests a level of authority necessary to carry out the responsibilities of that office. Logical questions are how the authority came to repose in the office initially and how we can be certain it is still there. The second type Barnard discusses is authority of leadership (4:173). Such authority is based upon the naturally recognized competence of an individual rather than upon the position he may hold within the organization. Ideally, of course, the two types of leadership would be exhibited by the same individual and where this is the case, the effect is to broaden the zone of indifference for the individual. Barnard uses this term, "zone of indifference," to imply that each individual has a range of directives that he will obey without question.

Duryea refers to the same concept with the phrase "zone of acceptance" (8:32). Both authors imply that the authority within an organization rests upon the assent of those governed. Authority thus lies in a specific office, both as a result of upward delegation from those governed by the office, and as a consequence of downward delegation by those legally responsible for overseeing the organization's activities.

We can now examine the dimensions and limitations of the downward delegation of authority. There are three primary reasons why an individual might be guided by the directives of a specific office. First of all, he might be mindful of the sanctions which could be exercised by that office in the form of rewards or penalties. This, of course, is why the emphasis in scientific management is upon retaining control of the rewards and penalties system since it tends to enhance administrative authority. However, we must consider the special case in the college setting where a faculty organization may become involved in collective bargaining to determine the nature of rewards in the form of salaries and fringe benefits. Such a faculty organization will certainly insist, as one of its first prerogatives, upon being able to define and control the circumstances under which an employee may be dismissed. Further, under the broad rubric of working conditions, the faculty organization will seek insofar as possible to limit administrative control over professional responsibilities such as number of students, length of the working day, and number of class hours. It seems apparent that the downward delegation of authority, based upon control of rewards and penalties, has serious limitations and might well disappear in most organizations in the near future (17:1).

Second, an individual might be inclined to follow the directives of a higher office due to his recognition of the natural competence of the holder of that office. With respect to this aspect of authority, it would be desirable if we could assume most faculty members hold most administrators in such high regard that there would be a natural tendency on their part to be guided by the administrative directives. If we examine the attitudes of faculty members, we must conclude that there exists no such general regard. Further, despite some noteworthy exceptions, the assumption of superior competence does not seem sufficient to assure continuing acceptance of the exercise of authority by administrators. This leaves, as our final reason for the acceptance of authority, the recognition that the decision that has been made is in the best interest of the institution and of the individual. Returning briefly to Barnard, we find that "a person can and will accept a communication as authoritative only when four conditions simultaneously obtain: (a) he can and does understand the communication; (b) at the time of his decision he believes that it is not inconsistent with the purpose of the organization; (c) at the time of his decision he believes it to be compatible with his personal interests as a whole, and (d) he is able mentally and physically to comply with it" (4:165). In other words, the decision must lie within the individual's zone of acceptance.

To this point we have talked of the zone of acceptance as if it were fixed for each individual. Obviously, this is not the case. The zone of acceptance will vary depending upon the extent to which an individual is involved in making the decisions he is expected to carry out. Individuals become a part of organizations to achieve ends they perceive to be held in common. If they have been misled with respect to organizational purposes or if organizational purposes shift to such an extent that values are no longer held in common, the individual refuses to cooperate either overtly or covertly or terminates his relationship with the organization.

Homans speaks of it from a different perspective: "If men have not found a society satisfying, they will not find its beliefs satisfying either" (10:458).

The crucial nature of the decision-making process becomes immediately apparent as we analyze the nature of authority. Our problem is to make certain that the values of the individual are consistent with the purposes of the organization. Since organizational purposes will shift in accordance with societal demands, some way must be found of modifying the values and hence the zone of acceptance of the individuals who constitute a part of the organization. The procedure through which this can be accomplished is the decision-making process. A failure to develop it to the extent that all subgroups within the institution use it effectively will result in disparities among individuals in their ability to adapt to change and consequent dysfunctions within the institution itself. Again, referring to Homans, we find that "a decrease in the frequency of interaction between the members of a group and in the number of activities they participate in together entails a decline in the extent to which norms are common and clear" (10:362).

In connection with the need to maintain values and norms in common, it is interesting to examine colleges that have been established for a period of time and which have experienced continuing growth. In such institutions it is not uncommon to find that the faculty is divided into two groups, with those having the longest tenure being the most out of touch with the needs of the institution as it seeks to adapt to new circumstances. As long as decision-making processes are such that they can be controlled by older members of the faculty (and this is frequently the case), the frustration and resentment of new members of the faculty—who may have been recruited in the hope of inducing change—can promote a substantial degree of conflict within the institution.

We must consider that in the decision-making process no one individual or group exercises absolute authority. Further, the attempt to act as if such authority does exist has not infrequently been the cause of conflict between groups and sometimes among members of the same group. If we conclude that authority can serve as the single basis for making a decision only in instances where it goes unchallenged, then we must define an alternative for those instances where significant differences of opinion render authority ineffective. Simon thinks that influence, based on a potential resort to authority, may play a role; but it should be obvious that if a difference of opinion exists immune to resolution by authority alone, it is unlikely that it can be resolved by influence either.

In concluding our discussion of authority, several points need to be emphasized. The first of these is that when an authority relationship exists, individuals have delegated their decision-making autonomy in certain areas to another individual or to an office. Defined in this way, authority is in reality delegated upward, downward, and laterally.

Authority and influence can be effective in the decision-making process only when the matters to be decided fall within the zone of acceptance of those to be affected by them. This fact creates the requirements for two characteristics of the decision-making process. First, the decision-making process must provide for sufficient involvement to insure that values and norms continue to be held in common by all or most of those who are members. Second, where substantive differences of opinion develop, some alternative to the use of authority must be provided by institutional procedures.

Communication and Coordination

Central to the decision-making process is the existence of recognized lines of communication. To a large extent, an organizational chart defines such prescribed lines of communication. Simon defines the media of formal communication as oral communication, memoranda and letters, paper flow, records, reports, and manuals (18:157–59). Effective involvement in the decision-making process depends upon accurate information. It is obvious that administrators can control the flow of formal media to a substantial degree and through such control exercise a major degree of influence on the decision-making process. It is equally apparent, however, that they will be unable to control the informal flow; consequently, decisions will be made by nonadministrators on the basis of whatever information is available. The consequences of this to institutional tranquility are obvious indeed. We may also note that in many institutions administrators deliberately use the technique of oral communication, the least effective of the media, to attempt to limit the number who may participate in the decision-making process and the degree of influence they can exercise.

Blau and Scott summarize the findings of research in the field of communications and perceptively define an institutional dilemma (6). The free flow of information contributes to problem solving; however, status differentiations which develop as a part of the organizational process impede the free flow of communication and hence affect the decision-making process as it applies to problem solving. The use of such titles as Dean, Division Chairman, Professor, and Instructor contributes to the development of communication barriers. When differential salaries and fringe benefits, as well as unequal access to parking places and secretarial assistance are added to the titles, the ingredients are present to promote the concept and consequences of the bureaucratic structure, insuring that the upward flow of communications will be severely modified.

The type of structure which promotes the free flow of communication and effective involvement in the decision-making process impairs the ability of an organization to achieve coordination, because clarity of function is sacrificed in order to avoid status differentiations. Coordination involves the procedures through which an organization insures that interrelated activities will be carried out at times and places that will be convenient and accessible to those who are involved. The better an institution coordinates its activities, the less likely it is to be able to solve problems effectively, since coordination requires emphasis upon specialization and restriction of the flow of communication to avoid contradictory directives.

Elsewhere, one of the authors has suggested that the solution to the dilemma involves the redefinition of institutional objectives in such a way that problem solving is given a higher priority than coordination. It would appear from the study of most contemporary institutions that their structures and priorities are better suited to coordination than solving problems (15:19).

While communication and coordination are both essential to the decision-making process, the relative importance of communications linked to problem solving as opposed to those concerned with coordination must be emphasized. Previously in this chapter, we noted authority could provide a basis for decisions only when it is not challenged. Normally, in the coordinating areas, such as class scheduling, periods for final examination and registration, decisions are rarely, if ever, challenged and the primary task is one of communicating information. In controversial areas such as salary settlements, grievance procedures and dismissals, decisions are likely to be challenged, creating a requirement for problem solving as an alternative to the use of authority.

Given the relative importance of problem solving as opposed to coordinating communications, we would expect institutions to give at least as much attention to the former as to the latter. This is very obviously not the case. Where communication problems develop, these are invariably in the problem-solving areas and not in the coordinating areas. We also find that the effort to restrict or block the free flow of communication is greatest in problem-solving areas. There is far more use of secrecy, oral communication, and other techniques aimed at sharing with a select few information required for decision making in such areas (16). This can be interpreted as further evidence of the bureaucratic nature of most colleges today. It also provides insight into the reasons for institutions encountering difficulty in obtaining overall involvement even when they profess to want it. It may also help to explain why there is substantial disparity between the norms of the leadership of many of our institutions and the norms held by faculty and by students.

Establishing Goals and Evaluating Effectiveness

Every institution must have a procedure through which objectives are established, plans for achieving these objectives designed, and procedures developed to evaluate institutional effectiveness as well as the relative contribution of the persons involved. As a concomitant, a system of rewards and sanctions may also be defined in order to influence cooperative endeavor. The manner in which the decision-making process functions can increase or reduce the incongruities between the needs of those involved and the requirements of the process itself. McGregor describes two polar approaches based upon assumptions made by the administrative leadership. These assumptions, which have already been examined in Chapter 4, can lead, in the case of theory X assumptions, to administration by direction and control; or, in the case of theory Y assumptions, administration by integration and self-control. It is worth examining the two approaches in greater detail because of the implications they hold for the ultimate effectiveness of the decision-making process.

First we need to distinguish between two aspects of the decision-making process. The first involves the decisions made concerning the organization's structure, with respect to the division of responsibilities and the relation of positions to the objectives of the institution. The second aspect focuses on the establishment of broad institutional objectives dependent on the general purposes of the organization and how these purposes can most effectively be carried out. We will begin by examining the consequences of the two theoretical assumptions in terms of four aspects of structure.

GENERAL REQUIREMENTS OF THE POSITION. Under the concept of administration by direction and control, each job within the organization is defined by a formal position description developed by a superior based upon his knowledge of organizational requirements. Relatively little attention is given to the growth potential of the subordinate who may fill the position or to the subordinate's feelings concerning what he would like to have the job encompass. The decision-making process is highly centralized and involves primarily downward communication.

In contrast, using concepts of administration by integration and self-control, job descriptions and their implications as well as relative priorities are developed through mutual discussion with full two-way communication. The objective is to enhance growth possibilities and opportunities for satisfaction of the subordinate's higher-level needs by making him responsible for analyzing organizational requirements in terms of his future position and his relative competencies.

It should be noted that theory Y assumptions do not eliminate planning for specialization. Such planning, however, emphasizes broader involvement with the role of the superior primarily that of catalyst and reactor. Equal attention is given to the requirements of the organization and to the higher level needs of the individual.

SHORT RANGE OBJECTIVES. Operating by direction and control, the superior establishes a series of objectives which are usually based upon his estimate of the requirements of the organization. These objectives are communicated to the subordinate along with the implication that they constitute a minimum standard for satisfactory performance.

When the emphasis is upon integration and self-control, the subordinate is encouraged to take responsibility for planning his own intermediate objectives. The assumption behind this approach is that genuine commitment by the subordinate will only occur when objectives have been internalized, a process which rarely occurs when objectives are imposed.

Intermediate objectives are discussed with the superior who has an opportunity to react to them in terms of his perspective on institutional needs and his beliefs about the capabilities of his subordinate. The objective of this type of involvement in the decision-making process is to reach agreement on intermediate goals in such a way as to secure commitment to their attainment. The subordinate is encouraged to establish his own standards rather than being asked to adhere to unilaterally established minimum criteria.

IMPLEMENTATION. The conventional approach involves monitoring the performance of the subordinate through such techniques as required reports, conferences and observations. Behavior which seems to be effective is encouraged through a system of rewards while penalties, ranging from criticism to threats of imposed sanctions, may be used when performance does not appear to be meeting standards of the superior. Close supervision will be used to prevent mistakes whenever possible by substituting the knowledge of the superior for that of the subordinate. The goal is control of the subordinate's behavior to promote the best interests of the organization.

In the contrasting approach, the subordinate is provided with as much freedom as possible. Premature evaluations of the effectiveness of the subordinate's performance are avoided. The emphasis is upon the growth and development of the subordinate. Consequently, the principle of supportive relationships is used to avoid threatening the subordinate and to encourage the greatest creativity and effort. Periodic consultations with the superior provide for a free exchange of information without imposing unnecessary restraints. Advice is given upon request. Mistakes which do not have major consequences are permitted as a part of the learning process for the subordinate. The goal is to achieve integration between the needs of the individual and the objectives of the organization through promoting increased competence and acceptance of responsibility.

APPRAISAL. The superior obtains measurements of the extent to which the goals previously established have been met. New goals are established by the superior based upon the same criteria used in establishing initial goals. If the subordinate has reached the goals established, he has done nothing more than come up to the expectations of his superior. Even exceeding objectives brings limited satisfaction, for the goals were determined by a decisional process external to the subordinate. Failure to reach goals lowers self-esteem and is normally accompanied by threats of the imposition of sanctions.

Repeated failures destroy the effectiveness of the subordinate to such an extent that he may have to be replaced. Repeated successes are followed by economic rewards and forms of social recognition such as promotions. Even in the case of success, however, satisfaction received is limited since it is based primarily upon lower-level needs. The individual performs in an arena shaped by someone else and is evaluated under a set of rules established without his involvement. He either has the ability for success initially, or he fails since the possibilities for self-growth are extremely limited.

Under the opposite assumptions, the subordinate was responsible in the goal-setting stage for establishing his own criteria for evaluation. These were established through consultations with the superior, but they were chosen by the subordinate along with the methods for the collection of information. Under such circumstances, the individual evaluates himself. In effect, the individual is competing against his own standards. He will experience some successes and some failures but they will be his successes and his failures. Further, he will be motivated to seek out ways in which he can reduce failures and these, in turn, will be reflected in the self-improvement objectives which he establishes for the next intermediate period. The self-evaluation, along with the information on which it is based, is discussed fully with the superior who has an opportunity in an essentially nonthreatening atmosphere to react to the self-appraisal by concurring or dissenting and giving his reasons. The process of goal setting and appraisal leading to the establishment of new goals becomes a part of the behavior pattern of the subordinate.

Failure is conditional both because it involves self-established goals and because it is balanced against positive achievement. Neither success nor failure are guaranteed by the abilities of an individual when he accepts a position. Both are a reflection of his personal development as well as his ability to satisfy his own needs within the context of institutional requirements.

Decision Making and Institutional Goals

Most administrators can readily see the advantages to the individual of the theory Y approach to decisions involving the establishment of position objectives. They may also be able to generalize these concepts to perceive how the establishment of institutional objectives through wide involvement of those responsible for implementing them can improve commitment and enhance institutional effectiveness. Two major objections normally arise, however, both based upon a somewhat erroneous interpretation of the limits of authority and a concern about the quality of decisions reached when values, differing from those who occupy top positions of leadership, are permitted to exercise strong influence upon the decision-making process.

The first and most obvious objection arises in the case of the individual who is judged to be incompetent to perform his responsibilities. If such an individual is permitted to define his own goals and to evaluate himself, conventional wisdom would hold that there is nothing to prevent the full effect of the Peter Principle, with the consequence that soon the organization will be staffed exclusively by incompetents.

The writers believe it is essential for two-year college administrators to reappraise their thinking with respect to this conclusion. Presumably the best judgment of superiors is used in filling subordinate positions. Unless the superiors themselves are incompetent, we must expect that in most instances they will select capable subordinates. Why then should our administrative practices be oriented exclusively toward the small percentage of subordinates who would be unsuccessful? The answer, of course, is that they should not be. The only way that we can weed out incompetence through the use of decisional techniques involving direction and control requires the establishment of minimum standards. It is well recognized that minimum standards soon become maximum objectives with the consequence that achievement and self-growth by the more capable are discouraged. It would be far better if we concentrated upon encouraging the capable to achieve to the limits of their abilities rather than trying to insure that everyone reaches some lower standard.

The use by administration of integration and self-control does not preclude the identification and removal of incompetence, but it does extend substantially the period required for its accomplishment. Under theory Y conditions, we assume that an individual is capable of performing satisfactorily in his position and when given an appropriate environment will meet the challenges of integrating organizational requirements and personal needs. Because of this belief, we do not search carefully for the first signs of incompetence and then use this evidence to undermine the confidence of a position incumbent; rather, we provide a suitable time period together with all possible assistance to encourage the individual to meet the challenges of integrating organizational requirements and personal needs. The decision that the individual is not suited for a particular position should be reached by mutual agreement, since an individual can come to see his deficiencies as well as his strengths and can relate these to the needs of the organization. This process, on the whole, even if it leads ultimately to a decision to terminate the individual's association with the organization, will be far less destructive to him and ultimately to the organization, because the termination procedure is implemented only after the individual has been given a full and fair opportunity under optimum circumstances to develop his capabilities.

The second objection to maximum involvement in the decision-making process concerns perceived threats to organizational objectives when points of view of faculty and administrators are widely divergent. If faculty are involved in setting admission standards, their desire to teach well-qualified students may motivate them to establish highly selective admission practices, or their academic preferences may result in less emphasis upon viable career programs. While it is true that there is a risk associated with true involvement of those holding widely divergent points of view, our past concentration on this risk has blinded us to the advantages which, on the whole, far outweigh the risks. We use the term "true involvement" to distinguish a process whereby the participants agree to be bound by the results as opposed to a situation where such involvement is considered advisory. It is the position of the writers that advisory involvement is not oriented toward taking advantage of the opportunity so much as it is toward minimizing the risks while giving the external appearance of involvement.

To identify the major advantage that is a concomitant of true involvement, we must consider the consequences of two approaches. When administration by direction and control is used, objectives are determined at the top of the organization and communicated downward to those who are to implement them. Controls are established to insure compliance. Such controls must, of necessity, represent minimum standards, in that they are keyed to the lowest common denominator. In the case of open-door admissions, we may succeed in getting students into the institution physically, but once there, they may face an unsympathetic faculty with little or no commitment to such necessities as remedial instruction and individualized learning techniques. Such consequences are reflected by the term "revolving door," suggested by some critics as a more apt description of open-door practices of some two-year colleges.

In the case of technical programs, top administrators reach a decision that such courses will be implemented. The absence of faculty commitment may be reflected by the teachers' refusal to structure general education courses around the requirements of career students or by attitudes ascribing lower status to faculty members who teach in these programs.

In an institution committed to administration by integration and self-control, a determination with respect to admissions or to the relative priority of technical programs would be made only after all who would be affected had been fully involved in the decision-making process. Faculty members would have the opportunity to expose their biases relative to low-achieving students and nontraditional programs. Administration could rebut using evidence from the community. The risk of selective admission practices or fewer career programs would more than be balanced by the advantages of securing the highest degree of faculty commitment to those students admitted and to those programs initiated. In addition, the process of participating in the battleground of ideas requires examination of one's values. Only through such self-examination can attitudes regarding norms be changed.

Institutions must rely upon changing the values of those who serve them to maintain relevancy. No one can direct that staff members be genuinely concerned about the needs of nontraditional students. Either the concern is there or it must be developed within the institutional environment. A failure to fully utilize the decisional process with maximum involvement implies that the institution must rely exclusively on its recruiting procedures to ensure the desired attitudes. It should be noted that so-called inservice programs which are frequently required as a means of influencing attitudes are ineffective in the absence of active participation of faculty in the decision-making process. In fact, such programs may do more harm than good in that they bring to the surface latent concerns and, in some instances, encourage hostility.

Even if the recruiting process is successful (and this is highly unlikely), there still remains the problem of societal changes which require adaptation and growth by staff members who have been with the institution for extended periods of time. Such growth requires the type of environment that can be created only through the acceptance of the risks that are a part of true involvement in the decision-making process.

Decision Making and Specialization

It is appropriate, at this point, to comment upon the role of specialization in organizations. The trend in educational institutions, as in other forms of complex enterprises, has been in the direction of increased specialization. The function of specialization within the organization is clearly recognized. Simon indicates that it is necessary to subdivide the decision-making process to insure that decisions requiring special knowledge are made by individuals with such knowledge (18:10). The impact of scientific management has been to subdivide responsibilities into smaller and smaller packages under the general thesis that such specialization promotes efficiency. While this may be true, the process is also marked by decreasing interest in larger objectives since the contribution of the individual constitutes a diminished part of the total effort required to achieve them.

Specialization is essential since the growth of knowledge has precluded the ability of any one individual to comprehend the total scope of information required to make an effective decision. At the same time, it can have detrimental effects on staff attitudes, interests, and commitments. Under the influence of the concepts of scientific management, our colleges have tended to emphasize degrees of specialization that may go beyond the optimum level for integrating the needs of the individual with the requirements of the organization. It is not uncommon for institutions to seek out staff members whose depth of preparation in a subject matter field is greater than that required for the responsibilities. Subject matter expertise may be equated with pedagogical ability. In consequence, the orientation of the instructional program in many institutions meets the needs of only a minority of the students.

Student personnel services constitute another area of specialization that has created mixed benefits. Counselors have been encouraged to assume sole responsibility for certain student needs previously met through the efforts of all faculty members. The concept has been enthusiastically endorsed by many highly specialized members of the faculty with the consequence that the institution as a whole has lost sight of its commitment to the total development of the student. Frequently, there may be little coordination or communication between counselors and faculty members, each of whom is busy performing his own particular specialty. The fragmentation of educational services has resulted in student dissatisfaction and at national meetings of faculty and professional counselors it has been suggested repeatedly that the student must be put back together again (in terms of the specialties of the particular group discussing the matter).

As in the case of other concepts, inherited, for the most part uncritically, from the advocates of scientific management, we must reexamine the scope and function of specialization. We most certainly can reduce the level of specialization in many areas; and in others, teams of diverse specialists can be structured to ensure coordinated effort and promote the feeling of satisfaction that comes from being a part of the total process. In addition to a critical examination of the kinds and levels of specialization necessary, we must also examine the assignments and distribution of specialists within the organization to determine how the resources they represent can be utilized most effectively.

Decision Making and Accountability

We have previously suggested authority can serve as a basis for decisions only in situations which do not involve substantial differences of opinion. When differences do exist, the decision-making process has been identified as the procedure through which a consensus may be reached. Implicit in this analysis is the assumption that consensus will represent a compromise which will incorporate the least objectionable aspects of the positions of those who are involved. We are not proposing a utopian arrangement which will have as its consequence a higher degree of satisfaction for the participants (with respect to a particular decision) than can be obtained under traditional practices. To the contrary, we assume decisions in controversial areas will create as much dissatisfaction under either arrangement; but such dissatisfaction can be distributed more uniformly among administrators, faculty, and students rather than being distributed hierarchically as in the case of the traditional pyramidal organization with the lowest levels experiencing the greatest degree of dissatisfaction.

This is an important point. Compromises seldom satisfy anyone yet they can redress imbalances which resulted in the past from administrative domination of the decisional process. It is equally important to note that while the amount of satisfaction available as a consequence of a particular decision remains relatively constant and is essentially redistributed among those affected, the level of satisfaction for a series of decisions resulting from full involvement is greater than the sum of the consequences of individual decisions. This is due to access to the satisfaction of higher-level needs for those who participate in the decision-making process. In other words, genuine involvement produces identifiable results capable of providing satisfaction separate from the effects of the decisions themselves. The individual who participates feels a stronger sense of identification with the institution, an improved sense of status, and the feeling of accomplishment which follows successful problem solving.

In the absence of authority relationships supported by a system of administratively controlled rewards and penalties, how can we be sure participants in the decision-making process will behave responsibly? The answer to this question may be found in the concept of accountability. Essentially, accountability is nothing more than the recognition of the interdependent relationships of the component parts of a system (12:231–35). Unless there exists a commitment to the destruction of the system, the behavior of individuals who constitute specific constituencies, such as students, faculty, administrators, will be guided by their wish to influence other constituencies by the most effective means. We may note in passing that an attempt to destroy the system normally arises only when the system is perceived as being immune to change by other types of influence.

If we accept the thesis that the interdependencies operating within a system can cause one group of individuals to permit their behavior to be guided by another in order to induce a desired response, we can see how a system can operate in the absence of authority. If the decision-making process is perceived as equitable to the interests of those involved, the consensus decision will emerge as a series of commitments on the part of one group in return for desired concessions by the other. Both parties will be bound by the decision, for they violate the agreement only at the risk of losing an agreed upon objective. Thus there are two kinds of pressures operating to maintain accountability; the threat of undesirable reactions from the other party to the agreement, and peer-group influence to prevent the individual from jeopardizing concessions won by the group.

In place of the hierarchical system held together by authority presumably delegated downward from some inexhaustable source, we postulate a dynamic and flexible pattern of interdependent relationships based upon accountability arising from agreements reached among the participants within the system and between the system, and the social context out of which it was created and by which it must be sustained. For accountability to function effectively, an extremely high level of accurate communication must exist. An inability to predict the consequences of specific decisions either in terms of the adaptive behavior by other constituencies or in terms of the responses of the societal context can be serious indeed.

It is our thesis that it is this interdependency which provides the necessary regulatory effect on the relationships within the organization in order to maintain a state of balance. Bettelheim speaks of dependency in which one individual must rely upon another in order to meet his needs (5:69). Thus we say that a parent exercises power over a child because that child is dependent upon the parent. The strength of this dependency relationship transcends the strength of an authority relationship dependent upon the exercise of sanctions. Fear of the loss of a parent's love is a more powerful motivator than any threat of physical abuse or withdrawal of material benefits.

A recognition that the constituents of a college are mutually interdependent is an acceptance of the fact that they must rely upon one another to satisfy basic requirements. The administrator is dependent upon both the faculty member and the student for the perpetuation of the institution. The student is dependent upon the administration for planning and for securing the necessary resources to ensure that he has an opportunity to learn. The faculty member is similarly dependent upon the administration for procuring and allocating resources, as well as providing the framework in which a faculty member can practice. At the same time, the faculty member is dependent upon the student, both to establish the need for his services, and to provide certain kinds of emotional gratification. Because each constituent group is dependent upon other constituent groups for their well-being, each group exercises power over the others. It is this relationship of interdependency which creates the limitations necessary to ensure proper internal functioning. In a mature organization where the nature of interdependency is well recognized and procedures established for the recognition and maintenance of necessary limits, there should be little need for an appeal to external agencies for the resolution of disputes.

ADMINISTRATIVE LEADERSHIP IN THE MATURE INSTITUTION

We have previously indicated that the institutional context or the nature of relationships between individuals and functions give rise to adaptive behavior on the part of role incumbents which can be, and frequently is, detrimental to the achievement of institutional objectives. We have discussed the nature of authority as a means of controlling behavior and have suggested that it is the most effective in areas where consensus exists, and the least effective in situations involving differences of opinion or conflict. Since the concerns of contemporary administrators must center upon conflict resolution to a considerable degree, we have postulated the concept of interdependency as an alternative to authority for the control of institutional relationships in the decision-making process.

We know that the state of dependency involves a condition where power is exercised over an affiliated individual. From this knowledge, we can define interdependency as the simultaneous existence of power relationships flowing in both directions between two or more individuals or groups of individuals with related interests. In the complex institution, each individual or group of individuals exercises power in those functions upon which others are dependent. In turn, their own behavior is subject to controls in areas where they, themselves, are dependent. A failure to recognize the nature of interdependent relationships can lead to inappropriate role definition with resultant ineffective behavior, conflict, and frustration. Our task must now be to examine the characteristics of organizations within which the greatest advantage can be gained from this knowledge.

Likert defines the characteristics of four different management systems based on comparative analysis (11:14). The systems are ranged along a continuum from extremely authoritative to participative, depending upon the behavioral considerations that govern the relationships within each system. The systems, arranged in order, are termed exploitive authoritative, benevolent authoritative, consultative, and participative group. The first two systems rely primarily upon theory X assumptions about human behavior, while the last two rely to varying degrees upon theory Y assumptions. Likert has succinctly summarized the behavioral differences generated within each of the four systems (see Figure 5.1). For our purposes, a brief review of the two polar systems will provide insight relative to differences in functioning (11:197–211).

System 1—Exploitive Authoritative

The motivational forces used are related to economic security with some attention to status. The individual derives little satisfaction from the achievement of institutional objectives and the sense of responsibility for such objectives diminishes as one moves downward in the organization. The direction of communication is primarily downward. Upward communication is distorted. There is little understanding between superiors and subordinates. The interaction-influence process is designed to maximize the position of superiors, although the objective may not be achieved to the degree desired due to inherent limitations in the assumptions made about motivational forces. Subordinates perceive their position as powerless to effect change. The decision-making process involves little influence from subordinates due both to the inadequacy of upward communication and the downward direction of the interaction-influence process. Decisions may be made at higher levels than where the greatest expertise exists. Decision-making is not used to influence values or to encourage motivation. Goals are established at the highest levels and impressed upon the remainder of the organization. In consequence, it is normal for a highly developed, informal organization to exist, which frequently works in opposition to the formal organization. Performance characteristics include mediocre productivity, excessive absence and turnover, and difficulty in enforcing quality standards.

System 4—Participative Group

Full use is made of economic, ego, and self-fulfillment motives through group involvement in setting goals, improving methods, and appraising success. Satisfaction is relatively high throughout the organization based upon identification with the progress of the group and the growth of the individual. Communication moves upward, downward, and laterally, with little distortion and few errors. Superiors and subordinates have accurate perceptions of the characteristics and needs of each other. There is a substantial degree of interaction and influence exercised by all levels within the organization. Subordinates feel that they exercise considerable influence over organizational direction and objectives. Decision making occurs throughout the organization and includes the use of overlapping groups to ensure that decisions are made with the involvement of all who have something to contribute, as well as taking place at the point within the organization where the greatest degree of expert opinion may be brought to bear. Decision making encourages team work and cooperation. Goals are established through group participation and are largely internalized by all participants within the organization. The informal and formal organization tend to be one and the same, since the adaptive orientation of the organization tends to change structure in the direction of the needs of both individuals and the organization. Productivity is high, turnover and absenteeism is low. Group members provide substantial control over the quality of their own efforts through the group interactive process.

It is immediately apparent that we can relate leadership behavior as previously discussed under administrative role in Chapter 4 to organizational characteristics. The 9,1 administrator with his emphasis upon productivity and lack of concern about people would tend to adopt System 1 techniques. The 1,9 administrator would be less harsh in his use of authority because of his primary concern for people, and hence would tend to develop a System 2, or benevolent authoritative approach. It is interesting to note that despite a similarity in characteristics, the concern for people will be reflected in generally higher productivity for the System 2 approach. While the techniques do not work more effectively, there is less active hostility and resistance generated.

A System 3, or consultative approach, would probably be chosen by the 5,5 administrator. In essence, System 3 is a transitional model attempting to compromise the conflicting assumptions of the two polar positions. Finally, System 4—Participative Group, relates to the 9,9 administrator and does have the potential of achieving the highest level of productivity of the four systems.

In order to fully understand the use of interdependent relationships in a System 4 approach to improve productivity and the quality of institutional environment for the individual, it will be necessary to examine several other factors. Likert speaks of three types of variables within the institutional environment: causal variables, intervening variables, and end-result variables.

"Causal variables are independent variables which determine the course of developments within an organization and the results achieved by an organization. These causal variables include only the independent variables which can be altered or changed by the organization and its management" (11:29). Examples of causal variables include the principle of supportive relationships, group decision making in a multiple, overlapping group structure, high performance goals, high pressure

PROFILE OF ORGANIZATIONAL CHARACTERISTICS

		SYSTEM 1	SYSTEM 2	SYSTEM 3	SYSTEM 4
Leadership	1) How much confidence is shown in subordinates?	None	Condescending	Substantial	Complete
	2) How free do they feel to talk to superiors about job?	Not at all	Not very	Rather free	Fully free
	3) Are subordinates' ideas sought and used, if worthy?	Seldom	Sometimes	Usually	Always
Motivation	4) Is predominant use made of 1) fear, 2) threats, 3) punishment, 4) rewards, 5) involvement?	1, 2, 3 occasionally 4	4, some 3	4, some 3 and 5	5,4, based on group set goals
	5) Where is responsibility felt for achieving org. goals?	Mostly at top	Top and middle	Fairly general	At all levels
Communication	6) What is the direc. of info. flow?	Downward	Mostly downward	Down and up	Down, up, & sideways
	7) How is downward comm. accepted?	With suspicion	Poss. with suspicion	With caution	With open mind
	8) How accurate is upward comm.?	Often wrong	Censored for boss	Limited accuracy	Accurate
	9) How well do superiors know problems faced by subordinates?	Know little	Some knowledge	Quite well	Very well
Interaction	10) What is character of interaction?	Little, always with fear and distrust	Little, usually with some condescension	Mod., often fair amt. confidence and trust	Extensive, high degree confid. & trust
	11) How much cooperative teamwork is present?	None	Relatively little	Moderate amount	Very substantial amt. throughout organ.

		System 1	System 2	System 3	System 4
Making Decisions	12) At what level are decisions formally made?	Mostly at top	Policy at top. Some delegation	Broad policy at top, more delegation	Throughout but well integrated
	13) What is the origin of technical and professional knowledge used in decision making?	Top management	Upper and middle	To certain extent throughout	To a great extent throughout
	14) Are subordinates involved in decisions related to their work?	Not at all	Occasionally cons.	Generally consulted	Fully involved
	15) What does decision making process contribute to motivation?	Nothing, often weakens it	Relatively little	Some contribution	Substantial
Setting Goals	16) How are org. goals established?	Orders issued	Orders. Some comm. inv.	Aft. disc. by orders	Group action (except crisis)
	17) How much covert resistance to goals is present?	Strong resistance	Moderate resistance	Some resistance at times	Little or none
Feedback Control	18) How concentrated are review and control functions?	Highly at top	Relatively high at top	Moderate delegation to lower levels	Quite widely shared
	19) Is there an informal organization resisting the formal one?	Yes	Usually	Sometimes	No - same goals as formal
	20) What are cost, productivity, and other control data used for?	Policing, punishment	Reward and punishment	Reward, some self-guidance	Self-guidance, problem solving

FIG. 5.1 PROFILE OF ORGANIZATIONAL CHARACTERISTICS

Source: From *The Human Organization* by Rensis Likert. Copyright © 1967 by McGraw-Hill, Inc. Used by permission of McGraw-Hill Book Company.

through imposing tight work standards, personnel limitations, and tight budgets. Causal variables may be considered the characteristics of the institutional environment established through administrative behavior. Obviously, supportive relationships and group decision making contribute to a System 4 setting, while high pressure and the external imposition of high standards relate to a System 1 approach. Note too, that the causal variables are the only ones that lend themselves to direct influence by administrators.

Intervening variables "reflect the internal state and health of the organization, . . . the loyalties, attitudes, motivations, performance goals, and perceptions of all members and their collective capacity for effective interaction, communication, and decision making" (11:29). Examples of intervening variables for a System 1 approach would include compliance based on fear, unfavorable attitudes, little confidence and trust, poor communications, low levels of influence, low levels of cooperative motivation, and low peer performance goals. For a System 4 approach, comparable intervening variables would be favorable attitudes towards superiors, high confidence and trust, high reciprocal influence, excellent upward, downward, and lateral communication, and high peer performance goals.

"End-result variables are the dependent variables which reflect the achievement of the organization, such as its productivity, costs" (11:29). Examples of end-result variables for System 1 include high absence and turnover, high productivity over the short run, and low productivity over the long run. System 4 produces low absence and turnover and high productivity. It is important to note that the time factor assumes great significance in evaluating the effectiveness of one management system over another. Likert emphasizes that an organization must take into consideration its human assets (11:115). This would seem to be particularly important for educational institutions. While an organization, like a piece of machinery, may be forced to yield very high returns over a short time span by subjecting it to unwise pressures, the excessive wear that results will inevitably bring about an attrition which will compromise the long-range goals. The problem in organizational dynamics is to define that point at which the institution can sustain its highest effort, while at the same time renew itself as may be necessary.

It must be emphasized that a shift in management styles cannot be expected to produce immediate consequences in terms of end-result variables. Such variables as productivity are dependent, not only upon the style of administration that is used, but also upon the period of time during which the style has been employed and the extent to which it has had the opportunity to influence intervening variables. This may explain why administrators who attempt to change their approach to problem solving feel frustrated when their efforts seem to yield no immediate discernible results. It would appear that most educational administrators have greatly underestimated the time that may be required to effect fundamental organizational change due to a failure to take into consideration the influence of intervening variables.

For example, the pressures of contemporary practice may lead an administrator to conclude that the effectiveness of his institution will be improved if an attempt is made to secure greater faculty involvement in decision making. Accordingly, procedures are structured to secure such involvement. Inevitably, the action encounters resistance from the faculty whose attitudes (intervening variables) have been conditioned by long exposure to a contradictory set of administrative actions (causal variables). If, in the case of a System 1 setting, the faculty acquiesce to the wishes of the administrator and do involve themselves, or give the appearance of involvement, administration and faculty are likely to be mutually suspicious of the motivation behind the other's new approach. When immediate results are not forthcoming, attempts to promote greater involvement may be given up, since group participation is time-consuming and requires the learning of new behavior.

Because of intervening variables which can be affected only indirectly, administrators must be prepared to wait as long as three years to see any significant change in end-result variables, and wait as long as ten years to see a maximization of such results. During the interim, there will be many temptations to achieve short-range goals through System 1 techniques at the expense of any progress that may have been made in the direction of long-range objectives. Administrators must be prepared not only to wait long periods to see major consequences of changes in administrative behavior, but they must also be aware of the need to learn new modes of behavior which will be significantly different from those which they have experienced or practiced.

On one point Likert is particularly clear. "The management system of an organization must have compatible component parts if it is to function effectively" (11:123). The implication is that you cannot substitute certain types of behavior which are characteristic of a System 4 approach in a System 2 setting and expect to achieve satisfactory results. The approach to administration must, first of all, be based upon assumptions about human behavior which are translated into administrative behavior that is internally consistent. System 4 behavior is learned behavior and it can be learned effectively, but such learning must occur as a part of a total systems movement. A System 4 dean, under a System 1 president would have little chance to function effectively. In fact, we may say that it is essential for any change in the direction of System 4 concepts to come from the top levels within the institution. A failure to secure a commitment at the presidential level is almost certain to culminate in internal conflict and a resultant inability to alter intervening variables in the direction of necessary change.

It is probable that there is no such thing as a System 1 or a System 4 college. Most two-year institutions would probably be grouped somewhere in between with a majority of them falling somewhat below the median; in other words, somewhere between benevolent authoritative and consultative. It is the writers' thesis that theory X assumptions predominate at present and that it is these assumptions, combined with the administrative systems they produce, that have resulted in the intense role conflict that is evident in our institutions. As a corollary, we must conclude that there is a need to move toward a System 4 approach with greater reliance upon theory Y assumptions. Such a movement, because of its emphasis upon participation in goal setting, combined with a reliance upon higher-level needs as motivational forces, could provide the means through which faculty and students become involved in redefining their own roles with full recognition of the interdependency and, hence, accountability that must be characteristic of their new definitions.

Likert demonstrates that improved labor-management relationships occur in industrial organizations where effective problem solving replaces irreconcilable conflict through a shift in management style toward the System 4 approach (11:44). He also speaks of long-range improvements in productivity, labor relationships, costs and earnings. He cautions, however, that System 4 behavior is much more complex and requires greater skill on the part of those who use it.

The multicampus or multicollege environment is obviously a special type of complex organization. In such an institution, consideration must be given to geographic as well as functional specialization. To this point, the argument has been primarily one of centralization versus decentralization. A review of current solutions to the question of institutional autonomy makes it readily apparent that this issue remains unresolved. One solution to the problems of multicampus decision making is to organize simultaneously along functional and geographic lines, thus providing two separate channels of communication; one for coordination, and one for decision making. Two or more separate channels lead inevitably to the requirement for more than one superior. Such an approach is not feasible under the assumptions governing Systems 1 through 3; however, it is entirely consistent with System 4. We need only be sure that in decisions involving personnel, one superior is designated to take the initiative. The decision, it must be noted, will still reflect a consensus (11:162). The use of alternate channels need not be limited to multicampus situations, although, obviously, it may be more essential to that type of setting.

AN EMERGING MODEL FOR THE TWO-YEAR COLLEGE

We have examined at length two polar models of organization, along with two transitional models. We have also identified the assumptions about human behavior upon which each rests, and the logical consequences of implementing these models in the educational setting. Our purpose has been to suggest the lack of suitability of the bureaucratic model and its consequences for communication, problem solving, role conflict, and other facets of organizational life. We can now proceed to suggest an alternative model. Before doing so, however, let us summarize the characteristics of the bureaucratic model which seem inappropriate for the tasks facing two-year colleges in the final decades of the 20th Century. Figure 5.2 is a graphic representation of the traditional model. External influences are interpreted through the administrative structure which defines priorities, allocates resources, issues directives governing faculty and student performance, and controls the resultant process through the measurement of intervening or end-result variables. The basis for controlling behavior is an authority relationship created by the downward delegation of powers vested in the governing body by a legitimizing agency.

Communication is predominantly downward with most written directives concerned with achieving coordination. The structure resists change introduced from the bottom because of the poor quality of upward communication and status differentials which depreciate the value of recommendations originating at low levels within the hierarchy. The organization is passively resistant to the introduction of change from the top because of the attitudes of faculty members and students towards administrators. The opportunities for gratification of higher-level needs are concentrated near the top of the organization. The resultant frustration of faculty and students dissatisfied with their assigned roles creates frequent conflicts that impair the ability of the institution to achieve its objectives.

Objectives are established at the top of the organization with various methods, including inservice training used to secure acceptance of these objectives at lower levels. Differences of opinion, if recognized, are usually resolved along lines of authority. An informal organization is present and may frequently be engaged in attempting to defeat the objectives of the formal organization. Specialization is predominantly along functional lines with inadequate provision for overcoming the communication and status problems that may result.

Leadership is predominantly authoritarian, although it may be disguised through use of committees which give the appearance of participation without endangering administrative control over the decision-

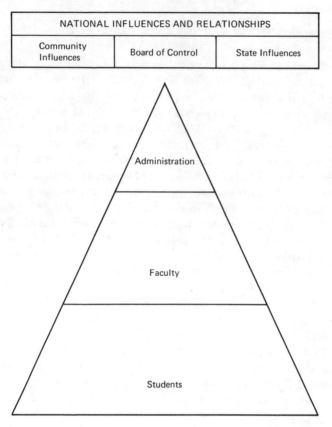

NATIONAL INFLUENCES AND RELATIONSHIPS		
Community Influences	Board of Control	State Influences

Administration

Faculty

Students

FIG. 5.2   TRADITIONAL BUREAUCRATIC MODEL OF AN ORGANIZATION

making process. Objectives concerning human behavior relate to the enforcement of standards and the weeding out of the incompetent. There is little real opportunity for individual growth, nor is this process considered as one of the primary objectives of the institution.

In contrast, let us now examine Figure 5.3 which represents an attempt to portray graphically the participational model. In this model there are the same three major internal constituencies and the same external influences. Rather than being mediated exclusively through the administrative structure, external influences may impinge upon the internal environment through faculty and students as well. Such an assumption seems to have two important assets. First, it implies that information required for decision making is not the exclusive property of any single group. Second, it appears to correspond more closely to what we know about the transmission of information under the influence of modern media.

Within the institution, administration, faculty, and students are not

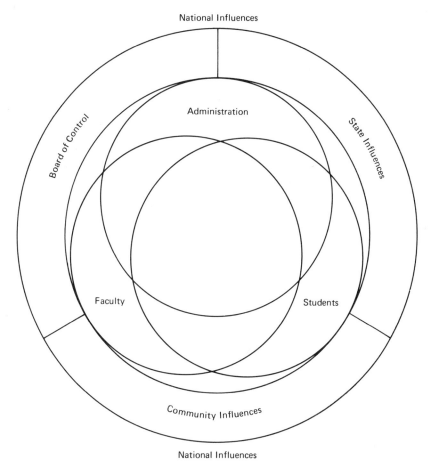

FIG. 5.3   PARTICIPATIONAL MODEL OF AN ORGANIZATION

arranged in a hierarchical order, but rather occupy individual spheres of responsibility and influence. The overlapping nature of the circles is intended to convey the impression of interdependency which replaces authority as the mode of control for institutional behavior. The definition of priorities, allocation of resources, and the determination of roles is accomplished through group participation. In addition to the measurement of intervening and end-result variables, procedures exist for examining and altering, when necessary, the causal variables.

Communication occurs in all directions, depending upon the nature of the task. The focus is upon problem solving, although the requirements of coordination are not overlooked. The nature of the overlap implies that in some instances problem solving may occur between administrators and faculty, or faculty and students, or administrators and students. In other instances where the decisions to be made involve matters that are central to the interests of the entire community, communication procedures exist to ensure that all three groups are centrally involved in the decision-making process.

The organizational structure is pliable and changes frequently to coincide with new requirements or conditions. Consequently, there is substantial congruency between the formal and informal organization, with both working to promote the objectives of the institution. Objectives are developed jointly, with the result that there is substantial commitment to their achievement by all members within the organization, and corresponding satisfaction when they are achieved. Thus, access to the satisfaction of higher-level needs is not exclusively the province of administrators but is shared with faculty and students. The degree of role conflict is also reduced since, in effect, role incumbents have a major voice in determining their own responsibilities. Those areas of the circle which do not involve overlap imply that when the actions of one group of role incumbents do not impinge upon the interests of another, the group should be free to pursue its own course of action without unnecessary interference.

The concept of mutual accountability prevents decision making of a unilateral or arbitrary manner when the interests of more than a single group are involved. Decision making is a shared responsibility with all of those affected by a decision represented in the decisional processes. Involvement in decision making, in turn, provides the mechanism through which values and attitudes are changed to keep them consistent with organizational purposes.

Specialization may be either functional or geographic, with attention given to the need to maintain effective relationships between specialties through involvement in decisional processes. Relationships are cooperative rather than adversary; positive attitudes exist toward institutional purposes.

Leadership is multiple and the use of committees represents a real commitment to the solution of differences of opinion through compromise rather than by decree. Administrators, through leadership behavior, seek to encourage both high performance goals and the satisfaction of higher-level human needs. Care is taken to ensure that communication is maintained at a sufficiently high level so that those who need to be involved in the decision-making process have the information required for maximum contribution. Individual growth is integrated with institutional goals and constitutes a central purpose for institutional existence.

SUMMARY

We have discussed two models of college administration which can lead to radically different end results. In the remaining chapters, we shall relate the concepts defined in this section to administrative practices and procedures. We do not propose to dwell excessively upon what is, except as this is necessary to define what ought to be. Our focus is upon a new direction which must be explored if we are to continue and expand the impact of the two-year college on societal problems. Our goal is to suggest an approach through which internal conflicts can be resolved to the end that our resources may be devoted to the attainment of institutional goals.

REFERENCES

1. ARGYRIS, CHRIS, *Executive Leadership.* New York: Archon Books, 1967.

2. ARGYRIS, CHRIS, *Integrating the Individual and the Organization.* New York: John Wiley, 1964.

3. BENNIS, WARREN V., "Post-Bureaucratic Leadership," *Trans-Action* (July/August 1969).

4. BARNARD, CHESTER I., *The Functions of the Executive.* Cambridge: Harvard University Press, 1968.

5. BETTELHEIM, BRUNO, *The Children of the Dream.* New York: Macmillan, 1969.

6. BLAU, PETER M. and W. RICHARD SCOTT, *Formal Organizations.* San Francisco: Chandler, 1962.

7. BRIDGES, EDWIN M., "Administrative Man: Origin or Pawn in Decision Making?" *Educational Administration Quarterly,* 6:7–25 (Winter 1970).

8. DURYEA, E. D., "The Theory and Practice of Administration," in *Administrators in Higher Education,* ed. Gerald P. Burns. New York: Harper & Row, 1962.

9. EISENSTADT, S. N. (ed.), *Max Weber on Charisma and Institution Building.* Chicago: University of Chicago Press, 1968.

10. HOMANS, GEORGE C., *The Human Group.* New York: Harcourt Brace Jovanovich, 1950.

11. LIKERT, RENSIS, *The Human Organization: Its Management and Value.* New York: McGraw-Hill, 1967.

12. LOPEZ, FELIX M., "Accountability in Education," *Phi Delta Kappan,* 52:231–235 (December 1970).

13. MERTON, ROBERT K., *Social Theory and Social Structure.* New York: Free Press, 1963.

14. MILTON, OHMER, *Survey of Faculty Views on Student Participation in Decision Making*. Washington, D. C.: USOE, Bureau of Research, Project No. 7–D–037, May 1968.

15. RICHARDSON, RICHARD C., JR., "Needed New Directions in Administration," *Junior College Journal* (March 1970).

16. ROTTER, JULIAN B., "Generalized Expectancies for Interpersonal Trust," *American Psychologist*, 26:443–452 (May 1971).

17. SCULLY, MALCOLM G. and WILLIAM A. SIEVERT, "Collective Bargaining Gains Converts Among Teachers: 3 National Organizations Vie to Represent Faculties," *The Chronicle of Higher Education*, 5:1 (May 10, 1971).

18. SIMON, HERBERT A., *Administrative Behavior: A Study of Decision Making Processes in Administrative Organization* (2nd ed.). New York: Macmillan, 1965.

part III

THE
ORGANIZATION

six

Administrative

Organization:

Chief

Executive Officer

When we speak of the structure of administration in this chapter, we distinguish a part of the institution from the whole. The bureaucratic model previously discussed makes the assumption that everyone in the institution can be fitted into some position within the administrative structure. The implications of this assumption, basically divergent from our own, are evident in the problems of authority and status which consequently appear.

Administrative structure is the most visible aspect of an organization. This is true for a number of reasons. First, the administrative building represents the first contact for most outsiders with the total institution. Second, administration is a coordinating and an implementing activity; as a result, administration becomes a focus through which both internal and external constituencies interact. Third, it is standard practice to attempt to convey the responsibilities of a specific office through a distinctive title. For this reason, an institution will have only one Director of Financial Aid although it may have twenty instructors of English. Both the distinctive title and position in the organizational chart will probably convey that the former is more important than the latter, although this distinction may not be reflected in a salary differential.

The highly organized nature of the administrative structure has contributed to the centralization of power in the hands of administrators. Faculty members, if organized at all, are likely to have a much less tightly defined structure, and the officers within this structure exercise their functions as a secondary aspect of their primary role, the providing of professional services. The same statement can be made for students. While they too have a structure of sorts, it is not well suited to administrative activity. At best, it provides a forum through which their concerns may be formulated and conveyed to other constituent groups.

Because of the differences of organizational characteristics, we will discuss faculty and student structure in Chapter 9 as an aspect of the governance process. But while it is true that faculty structure occurs primarily as a part of the process of governance, faculty members have correctly perceived the power that can be wielded when they are sensitive to the hierarchical control of resources. Consequently, when faculty members organize for collective bargaining, they are likely to devise a structure which parallels the administrative structure in form. There will be an attempt to provide released time to officeholders in the organization, and the active officeholders will seek increasingly to influence and participate in the administration of the institution. The objective of this activity is to provide faculty with greater authority by interposing a secondary bureaucracy (that of the faculty organization) between the faculty members and the primary bureaucracy represented by the administrative structure.

The participative model of governance, which strives to avoid this kind of "aberrant" bureaucratic outgrowth, affects more strongly the overall governance structure of the institutions than it does the administrative structure alone. There are, in the final analysis, certain standards of efficiency demanded by administrative operation which can be achieved most effectively through the use of traditional bureaucratic techniques or organization. Therefore, the administrative structure, part of the participative model, when viewed by itself from the vantage point of the organizational chart, will appear similar to the administrative structure of the traditional model.

Within the structure of administration, it is important that the principles previously identified in Chapter 5 govern relationships among role incumbents. If effective interaction, substantial involvement in decision making, the use of supportive relationships, and management by objectives are not characteristic of relationships within the administrative structure, then we can be assured by our knowledge of the requirement for consistency within a system that such principles will not appear in relationships between the administrative structure and the faculty or students.

We may say, then, that in the institution of higher education there exists a unique constellation of factors which does not correspond to most other types of organization. We have three distinct internal constituencies each with its own structure but interrelated both through functional requirements and through a governance structure. While students may be regarded to some extent as clients, or consumers, they also have a relationship different from that characteristic of other social institutions. They are not patients, nor are they inmates. Neither do they consume a product. While faculty members are employees, they are also practitioners of a profession which demands by its nature a relationship to the organization different from that required in the typical business or production enterprise.

The failure of the primary groups involved in college governance (trustees, administrators, faculty, and students) to recognize these differences, while attempting to utilize similarities, has led them to draw certain conclusions about the relationships of faculty and students to the administrative structure which are no longer valid. While we will use the traditional organizational chart as the device for examining the structure of administration, we wish to emphasize our premise that faculty and students, usually certified parts of the structure, are *not* included in the structure as we conceive it. In reference to the circular model previously described, we are dealing exclusively with the sphere of influence labeled administration (7:176–80).

ORGANIZATIONAL GRAPHICS

The organizational chart is the most common representation of the structure of our institutions of higher education. Such charts are useful because they provide a portrayal of the positions and functions within an institution as well as the relationship that each position has to others. Organizational charts assist staff members in defining their relationships to the institution as a whole and to one another. At the same time, it is important to understand the limitations of such charts as true indicators of the relationships within a complex organization.

Organizational charts define relationships between positions. In the past, it has been assumed that they also designated status and authority. We have seen from the analysis presented in Chapter 5 that it is no longer safe to make assumptions about authority and status on the basis of the traditional bureaucratic structure. Organized groups of faculty or students may succeed in interposing a secondary bureaucracy between themselves and the primary bureaucracy through use of power politics or collective bargaining techniques. In extreme circumstances, they may through violence succeed temporarily in turning the pyramid upside down. While some may argue that the second example does not truly reflect a loss of status or authority since civil authority exists and can be used to restore the original arrangement, the writers would contend that no institutional administration has survived such a confrontation without incurring losses of personnel from among its ranks.

The organizational chart illustrates the prescribed channels through which the formal media of communication theoretically flow. Presumably, control of the organizational structure implies control over the communication channels. At the same time, it is well known that informal procedures of communication develop and, under certain conditions, act to subvert the prescribed channels. Unless the official channels serve the purposes of all role incumbents satisfactorily, they may easily fall into disuse or, worse, be subject to calculated distortion (13:8).

The strength of the organizational chart as a representation of administrative structure lies in its ability to convey a concept of the ways in which the institution has chosen to specialize in order to accomplish its objectives. The best organizational structure is one which is responsive to the needs of those who belong to the institution while at the same time promoting the objectives for which the institution exists. Such a structure presumes knowledge of motivational factors related to the satisfaction of role incumbents as well as the careful identification of institutional objectives and planning to relate such objectives to human capabilities.

It is safe to say that few organizational structures actually reflect the conditions identified above. In the first place, one of the most common criticisms leveled at educators is their failure to define objectives clearly. The current emphasis on accountability reflects, in part, a serious effort to force more considered planning with respect to objectives. As previously noted in Chapter 4, most existing organizations pay little heed to the needs of those who are perceived as occupying the lower levels of the hierarchy.

The truth of the matter is that the structures of many established institutions represent not so much the consequences of considered planning as the results of haphazard growth. Positions are added in shortsighted response to problem areas and to the personalities and competencies already integrated into the structure. The organizational chart of an established college not uncommonly reflects the random addition of positions with unusual and sometimes confusing lines of communications in clouded, overlapping areas of responsibility. In new institutions, the structure is likely to reflect similar problems combined with the lack of experienced personnel who keep the machinery operating.

A major weakness of the organizational chart and the structure it reflects is the two-dimensional nature of the representation. An organizational chart conveys only horizontal and lateral relationships. It cannot convey the quality of depth which is characteristic of relationships involving people. Neither can it demonstrate the changes that occur over time. If an organizational chart met all of the conditions previously enumerated and at the same time represented a perfect reproduction of the actual structure, it would be completely accurate only for a brief moment. Almost immediately, the dynamic quality of organizational life would act to change the structure. The chart would become increasingly irrelevant to the reality of organizational life over an extended period of time.

While it is true that all organizational charts are at best distorted representations of institutional interaction, they are nonetheless useful in the study of administrative structure. A comparison of the organizational chart for a structure based upon bureaucratic premises with one influenced by the concepts of participational structure reveals significant differences in such areas as the number of hierarchical levels, span of control, and arrangements for specialization.

COMPARISON OF BUREAUCRATIC AND
PARTICIPATIONAL MODELS

Figure 6.1 represents one method of implementing specialization for a bureaucratic model which has previously been suggested as the most common organizational pattern among two-year colleges. The structure emphasizes unity of command. Each individual reports to only one other individual within the chain of command. The organization is relatively inflexible since specialization is carefully controlled in both the horizontal and vertical dimensions to avoid overlap wherever possible. Emphasis upon limiting the span of control, as well as upon unity of command, has resulted in six somewhat distinct levels within the organization. While level three is shown in the figure as a staff function and theoretically should not increase the height of the organization, in many organizations this level would represent a line function. In others, the insertion of an executive vice-president could further increase vertical stratification.

The primary focus of this type of organization stresses coordination, since the various hierarchical levels impede communication and consequently limit effectiveness in solving problems related to the initiation of change. Within such an organization, one assumes that faculty and

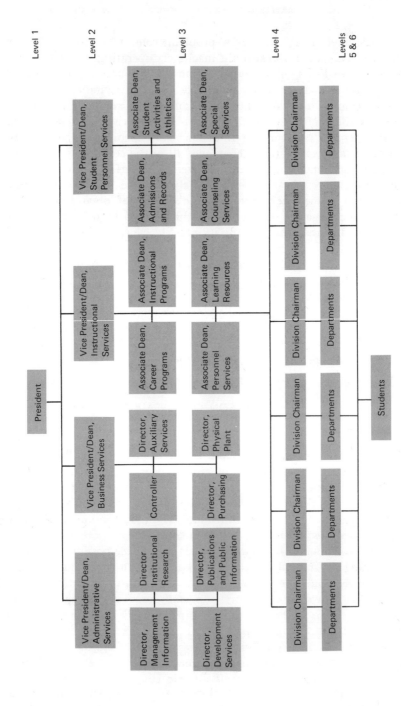

FIG. 6.1 SPECIALIZATION WITHIN THE ADMINISTRATIVE STRUCTURE: A BUREAUCRATIC MODEL

students have their respective positions at the lower levels of the hierarchy. In this regard, we would argue that while Stroup may be right concerning bureaucratic pervasiveness in higher education, we cannot agree that his model is the most desirable alternative. It will be our purpose in the pages which follow to suggest a different approach—the participational model (12:41).

Figure 6.2 provides one arrangement for distributing administrative responsibilities for a participational model. Three levels of responsibilities are defined with four areas of specialization at the second level. The participational model is dynamic and flexible. Each area of specialization is interdependent with all other areas, both vertically and horizontally. Specialization may repeat itself at each level with a somewhat different emphasis since overlapping responsibilities are considered natural and desirable. The multiple channels of communication combined with an attempt to keep hierarchical levels to a minimum encourage two-way communication and problem solving in the organization.

Administrative structure recognizes the existence of faculty and student constituencies which, while related to the structure, are not regarded as a part of it in any hierarchical sense. This type of organization does not manage change through control over the decision-making process, as suggested by Roueche, Baker, and Brownell (8:25–26). Neither is accountability considered primarily or exclusively an administrative responsibility. The principle of unity of command is deliberately violated to improve communication and to encourage a unified approach to institutional objectives by all constituencies.

It has been demonstrated previously that two-dimensional graphics cannot adequately portray the complexity of relationships within an organization. This statement is certainly true with respect to this representation of the participational model. Student Personnel Services has the same need for interaction with Business Services as does Instructional Services. The lines of communication and interaction shown are not intended to convey the implication that these are the only relationships that exist. In reality, each area of specialization must interact and communicate effectively both laterally and between levels with every other area of specialization. It is also important that such interaction and influence flow in both directions since according to our theory, one level or area of specialization within the organization will be able to exercise influence over other levels or areas only to the extent that there exists a willingness to have its own behavior influenced in turn.

There are no irrefutable arguments that can be presented for four second-level areas as opposed to three or five. In part, the size of an institution as well as its objectives may determine these features of the organization. By the same token, it can be argued that functions assigned

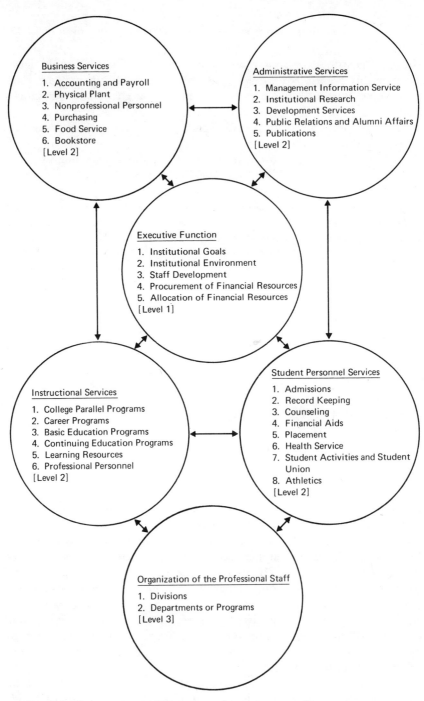

Business Services

1. Accounting and Payroll
2. Physical Plant
3. Nonprofessional Personnel
4. Purchasing
5. Food Service
6. Bookstore
[Level 2]

Administrative Services

1. Management Information Service
2. Institutional Research
3. Development Services
4. Public Relations and Alumni Affairs
5. Publications
[Level 2]

Executive Function

1. Institutional Goals
2. Institutional Environment
3. Staff Development
4. Procurement of Financial Resources
5. Allocation of Financial Resources
[Level 1]

Instructional Services

1. College Parallel Programs
2. Career Programs
3. Basic Education Programs
4. Continuing Education Programs
5. Learning Resources
6. Professional Personnel
[Level 2]

Student Personnel Services

1. Admissions
2. Record Keeping
3. Counseling
4. Financial Aids
5. Placement
6. Health Service
7. Student Activities and Student Union
8. Athletics
[Level 2]

Organization of the Professional Staff

1. Divisions
2. Departments or Programs
[Level 3]

FIG. 6.2   SPECIALIZATION WITHIN THE ADMINISTRATIVE STRUCTURE:
A PARTICIPATIVE MODEL

to one area of specialization could just as easily be transferred to another. Again, each institution must make its own decisions in these matters based upon an examination of priorities and personnel. The arrangement suggested does provide a comprehensive outline of administrative responsibilities while at the same time demonstrating one logical organization of these responsibilities.

MULTI-INSTITUTION DISTRICTS

There is an unmistakable trend for urban districts to develop more than a single campus. A number of states have chosen to establish two-year colleges as units of a single state system. Even some suburban or rural colleges have added a second campus in preference to developing residence halls when confronted with long distances or geographic barriers. The development of such systems has important implications for our discussion.

Regardless of the degree of decentralization, there are significant differences between a free standing institution and one that is a part of a system. There is little possibility that the degree of autonomy afforded can ever approach the level that is desired by the constituents of a campus. Even in districts that have sought to provide maximum autonomy to campus units by calling them colleges and by providing the chief executive with the title of president, there is still a constant tension accompanied by the ever-present realization that the needs and priorities of the system take priority over the aspirations of the individual units.

Kintzer and his colleagues have discussed in some detail different systems for organizing multi-institutional districts (4). Without becoming involved in the merits of these systems, several points relevant to our analysis can be made. The concepts we will suggest apply to a system whether that system includes a single college or twenty. Their applicability to a unit of a multi-institutional system is dependent upon inter-relationships between the central administration and units of the system. It would probably not be feasible to develop a participational model for a campus if the system was highly bureaucratic. Since systems depend upon internal consistency for cohesiveness and integrity, all units of a system must have similar forms of interaction at least at points where interfaces occur. Any unit that differs significantly from the norm will create tensions. The impact of these tensions insofar as changing central administration is concerned will depend upon the number of units within the system, their relative size, and the ability of the system as a whole to tolerate diversity and to accommodate change.

A multi-institutional district, like any organization, is more than the sum of the interactions which occur among the individual units and between the units and the central office. In talking about structure, we tend to focus upon relationships between administrators in the central office and those on the individual campuses. While we recognize that the administrators on the various campuses will interact with each other and with central administration, there is far less recognition of the implications of interactions between faculty and student groups among the various campuses and the tendency for such groups to organize themselves in order to exert direct influence on central administration in addition to the indirect influence they exert through their respective campus administrators.

We may say that all of the problems that can be attributed to the bureaucratic structure as an organizational form for the individual college are raised to the nth power in a multi-institutional district with n representing the number of campuses. If the multi-institutional district is to remain responsive to the needs of each locality it serves, the concepts of the participative model assume increased importance. There must be multiple channels through which two-way communication occurs. Competition between units must take place within a cooperative and mutually sustaining frame of reference. Bureaucratic authority must be replaced by the principles of shared authority, and governance patterns must be focused upon the creative resolution of problems and not upon unnecessary coordination.

The highly publicized Newman Report carried the following statement which is closely related to our concern: "The junior college scenario is thus one of transformation of community institutions into amorphous, bland, increasingly large, increasingly state-dominated, two year institutions which serve a number of interests other than that of their own students" (6:74). It is in the nature of all large bureaucratic organizations to become increasingly remote from the needs of their constituencies while at the same time remaining remarkably impervious to change. If the multi-institutional district is to escape this fate, alternatives which go beyond the centralization-decentralization issue will need to be carefully explored. In this process, the participational model has much to recommend it as a starting point.

We have discussed the general nature of the structure of administration and compared two polar approaches to the definition of such structure. We have also suggested that the need for a participational model may be even greater in the multi-institutional district than for a single college. Let us now consider the responsibilities of the chief executive officer.

THE EXECUTIVE FUNCTION

The functions of the chief executive officer have been identified by Simon as raising money, balancing the budget, participating in the establishment of institutional goals, working with faculty to create an environment that encourages learning, and recruiting, and maintaining a high quality of faculty. Simon also draws a parallel between the responsibilities of the college president and the top executives in other types of concerns, giving particularly strong attention to the concept of accountability (10:68–78).

The president's function has had many interpretations, most of which are obsolete. As sometimes sentimental portrayals of what a chief executive officer's life has been in the past, they have value. As a guide for future behavior, they leave much to be desired (11, 9).

If we accept the premise that there is a need for role redefinition, it becomes immediately apparent that the president of the future will need to possess a far greater expertise in managerial competencies and at the same time exercise such competencies in a manner that will make his position far less central to institutional functioning than has been true. Galbraith makes the point that leaders in industry have become far less visible and far less central to many institutional operations than was the case with their predecessors (2:106). Educational institutions, particularly large public ones, in which the bulk of our faculty and students are located, are caught up in a growth process which must parallel in many respects the experience of industry. Presidents will become less visible, less central to the functioning of their institutions; however, this will not necessarily lead to a zero-sum process whereby the chief executive will lose authority and influence equal to that gained by others within the institution. Rather, the president may need to exercise his influence in different causes and in more complex ways.

A central responsibility of the president which relates to everything else he undertakes is the establishment of an institutional environment conducive to learning. The president does not establish such an environment through the force of his own personality so much as he makes possible its development through the ways in which he works with his staff officers and other constituencies of the institution. A president who sets an example by insisting upon clear communication in all directions and who refuses to countenance the use of arbitrary sanctions to enforce administrative preeminence is making a significant contribution to developing one type of institutional environment (1:11).

Equally important is the manner in which he opens access to participation for all who will be affected in establishing goals and formulating policies. To stimulate effective participation, the president must support a policy of open access to information about the institution. He must insist that the roles of administrators be clearly defined and interpreted to all who are affected by their actions. The institution must have a decision-making process which is highly visible, operated without secrecy and susceptible to interaction and influence by all segments of the college community. The stance taken by the chief executive officer on such issues will establish prevailing practice for the entire institution. The credibility of the procedures established by the president for resolving conflict will govern the extent to which they are used by faculty and students. If the president resorts to the use of power or displays arbitrary judgment in his relationships with the faculty, he can expect that the faculty will behave similarly in their relationship with students and administration.

There is the view that the new president of a previously established institution may provoke changes in the institution to move toward greater accountability merely by encouraging a conservative faculty to take advantage of a less authoritarian atmosphere. Failing success through this method, he may use the lever of expressed student concern on the fulcrum of his own leadership to promote student participation in the decision-making process (1:29).

The president is no longer the supreme arbiter or the power figure in institutional politics. He is a mediator who has a major responsibility, the reconciliation of opposing interests while at the same time preserving institutional goals and directions. Not only must he be able to provide a credible structure through which conflict can be resolved on acceptable terms, but he must also be prepared to recognize when appeal must be made to an external constituency because the problem cannot be resolved internally. It is important that the president avoid advocacy of a particular position. As a mediator, it is his responsibility to seek consensus rather than lock himself into an adversary role. This is not to say that a president should avoid taking positions or that he simply floats on the currents of institutional opinion. It is rather to say that the president must be able to see the advantages and disadvantages of both sides of a position and that he gives clear recognition to the legitimacy of opposing points of view.

The recommended role of a president in the collective bargaining process is illuminating in this respect. Most authorities advise the president to remain strictly aloof from this process, delegating responsibility for administrative participation to a staff officer. There are two very good reasons for this recommendation. First, the president, who may be the person to whom a final appeal for judgment is directed, must not have been previously involved in the bargaining in a way that would void his role as arbitrator. Equally important, however, is a second reason. When the collective bargaining process has been completed, there must be someone within the institution with sufficient moral capital to bring adversaries back into cooperative working relationships and to heal the wounds inflicted during the adversary process. The president who has been aware of the problems but not closely identified with either of the protagonists occupies such a position.

Even in the absence of collective bargaining the chief executive must recognize the dangers inherent in placing the weight of his office prematurely on one side of an issue. There are very few differences of opinion that develop within a college where institutional objectives are so critically involved that there is no room for compromise. Of course, it is essential that the president recognize such issues but it is equally important that there be firm recognition of his own fallibility. Arrangements must exist to appeal an issue beyond the office of the president when such an issue cannot be appropriately resolved within the institution. In this regard, it is pertinent to make reference to a statement advanced a number of years ago by John Millett (5:241). It was his thesis, and it is ours, that a president can no more operate without student and faculty support than he can operate without board support.

If the president properly recognizes those issues where resolution requires appeal to an external source of reference, it will be no longer necessary to consider him infallible in his judgments. After providing for appropriate review of decisions that create intense institutional antipathies, it becomes possible for students and faculty to have confidence in the processes established by a president without agreeing that he should have the final word on all issues. It is apparent that when appeals are made to an external reference group such as the board, we can expect that under normal circumstances the president's view will prevail. By the same token, if a board is required to deal with too many routine controversies, they must inevitably come to question the effectiveness of their chief executive. In essence, the appeal process becomes the legitimizing machinery through which pressures are brought to bear on all internal constituencies to encourage them to solve their own problems through a mutual give-and-take rather than through power tactics.

The president who can successfully implement the mediating role is in a strong position to reconcile the opposing interests which are inevitably generated by the process of specialization. One of the weaknesses of specialists is that they experience great difficulty in seeing the needs of their area of expertise in relation to the needs of the total institution. The president as generalist must take the broad view and, in addition, must hold in perspective both short- and long-range objectives. Again, the extent to which constituencies are involved in the process of establishing both short- and long-range goals will have a significant impact upon the president's success when working in such areas as resource allocation, without creating unnecessary hostility in the process.

The establishment of goals is a particularly challenging aspect of the president's role. Not infrequently, a president may be selected because he has strong ideas which are consistent with those held by the board of trustees. Many presidents inevitably come to grief in attempting to implement these ideas, for they fail to understand the interdependencies involved in the goal-setting process. Hughes has pointed out:

> The organizational system bears little relationship in fact to the conventional organization chart, which may not represent realistically the way to the achievement of the accompanying goals. This is because organizational units are interactive; that is, people in them interact with each other in ways that are not defined and described by formal "boxes" and lines of authority. Research shows that far more time is spent in lateral than in vertical relationships. In other words, we get our work done not so much through the management principles of authority, responsibility, and accountability, as through negotiations with people in our same level (3:92–93).

If the president wishes to influence a faculty, he must in turn be prepared to be influenced by them. His top priority should be sufficiently different from the faculty's to allow each to support the other in hopes of reciprocation. There are instances, however, when differences are too great and compromise becomes the only answer. While compromises by their very nature create dissatisfaction, it is important for the president to recognize the dangers to the achievement of future goals if the dissatisfaction is not felt rather evenly by all who are involved. A president who cannot compromise effectively is unlikely to endure very long in today's campus conditions. More important, he will not effect lasting change.

The president must be accessible to the various constituencies he serves on a more or less equal basis. This is far more complex than it may seem. The announcement of an open-door policy does not necessarily guarantee accessibility. The president needs to plan his schedule and his activities so that he is in contact with a variety of students and faculty under conditions less formal than an office visit. While it is desirable that he be accessible, care must be exercised to ensure that such accessibility does not undermine staff functioning by short-circuiting the decision-making process. The president is the most visible element in the governance of the institution, and his positive influence in informal situations can do much to promote the appropriate learning environment, while at the same time providing him with important informational inputs that are different from those prescribed in the organizational chart.

Many writers have specified the multitude of tasks which may be carried out by the president. Studies have been done showing the allocation of a chief executive's time spent in such areas as budgeting, fund raising, building construction, and public relations. Such job descriptions and studies have very limited usefulness for the practicing administrator. The emphasis upon particular areas and the amount of time devoted to each are bound to vary with the size of the institution, its direction at a given point in time, the personality and competencies of the president and of other members of his staff, the presence or absence of crises and a host of factors which combine to make each position different in important respects from all other positions. The one thing that the president cannot afford to forget is that he is providing leadership to an organization that involves shifting and complex patterns of human relationships. He must pay attention, simultaneously, to structures and processes, and he must be capable of blending the two so as to encourage successive adaptations to an ever evolving series of challenges. He is not in the business of providing answers, but rather responsible for providing credible leadership in seeking answers, conscious always that the answers will turn out to be parts of new questions.

While the chief executive officer no longer exercises the authority to make final decisions in matters involving substantial differences of opinion, his central position in the communication network contributes to the significant influence of the office in conflict resolution. The role of the chief executive is also central to relationships with external constituencies. To a considerable degree, the effectiveness of the president in his relationships with the board of trustees is both a measure and a consequence of his impact upon other external constituencies. The president cannot escape the close identification of his office with the successes and failures experienced by the institution as a whole.

In the eyes of the local community, the accessibility of the chief executive officer and his interest in community affairs establishes the tone for the entire institution. His comments upon an issue will be regarded by external constituencies as the official position of the institution. This places a major responsibility upon the executive officer to reconcile through his decisions and his statements the emerging norms of a new generation with the prevailing norms of the establishment. The continuing effectiveness of any institution requires that it operate or at least be perceived as operating within the narrow boundaries between established and developing value patterns. While the range of responses that will receive the acceptance of both internal and external constituencies is broader in some areas than others, the limits always exist and a failure by the chief executive to observe them invariably diminishes his moral capital with one group or the other.

Leadership obviously involves departure from accepted norms when the importance of an issue justifies the conflict involved. It is important in the exercise of leadership that the president refrain from taking positions which consistently diminish his credibility with a single constituency, for a failure to maintain a reputation for impartiality is the first step in the loss of confidence, a process which if consummated destroys the ability of the president to continue to function effectively. If, for example, the chief executive lends his support to the faculty in discussions involving salary increases, he may suffer some loss of moral capital with taxpayers. The situation can be balanced by equal insistence upon maintaining productivity and upon accountability.

It should be apparent that the chief executive officer cannot afford to indulge himself in private biases. His view must weigh the concerns of special interest groups in terms of the well-being of the institution as a totality. If he is consistently fair in dealing with both internal and external constituencies, and if his judgment proves sound in predicting the consequences of actions that he recommends, he will retain the respect of all the groups with which he must contend and with that respect the ability to effect compromises which not only resolve conflict but, in addition, offer qualitative responses to the challenges of mission implementation.

The board of trustees represents a microcosm of the publics to which the institution must be interpreted and with which effective interaction must occur. Substantial board reaction against a specific recommendation should alert the president to the probability that similar reactions can be expected from the community. The temptation to assume a favorable vote from the board resolves the issue should be rejectd in favor of careful analysis of the segments of the community that will be affected, as well as ways in which the issue can be interpreted to avoid permanent alienation. In some instances, chief executive officers would be well advised to avoid implementing a plan which has the potential for serious disruption of relationships with external constituencies even if board support can be obtained. The board looks to the president for guidance in foreseeing the probable consequences of specific courses of action in terms of the attitudes of community groups. The board does not have to be misled very often before losing confidence in the president's judgment in this area. Since trustees are seldom representative of the individuals their institutions serve, the overly conservative board may simply be a board that is relying exclusively on its own judgment of probable community reaction because of a lack of confidence in the judgment of the chief executive.

The degree of difficulty experienced by the chief executive officer in influencing a particular constituency will bear a direct relationship to the geographic and political distance between that constituency and the institution. It is this fact that makes it more difficult for institutions operated as parts of state systems or as campuses of a state university to influence and respond to local constituencies. By the same token it is easier for them to influence state and national forces since the organization and magnitude of such systems makes them more visible and accessible at these levels. For this reason it is important for state and university systems to give special attention to procedures for interacting with the local community. In a like manner, institutions operating under the aegis of local control must devise effective coalitions with suitable leadership in order for their views to receive significant consideration at state and national levels.

It is important in terminating our discussion of the chief executive officer to emphasize his role with respect to evaluation and accountability. In its broadest sense, accountability involves nothing more than the assurance that objectives previously defined are being achieved at a satisfactory level within the range of resources available. "Within the range of resources available" implies that these objectives are achieved with participation of all who are linked to them (not in spite of the participation of some, as is often the case). Thus, the dimension of accountability flows in many directions; administrators are accountable to faculty and vice versa. And the president must insist upon evaluation of everything that is done since accountability as a concept is meaningless in the absence of evaluative information.

SUMMARY

Administration organization is highly specialized in order to perform a variety of complex functions with a maximum degree of efficiency. It is highly visible because the prescribed lines of communication within an institution are defined by administrative organization. In the past we have made certain assumptions concerning the inclusiveness and authority dimensions of the administrative organization which no longer seem viable. The assumption that students and faculty are a part of the administrative organization does not seem consistent with the realities of emerging institutional relationships. This is particularly true when we consider the low level positions traditionally assigned to students and faculty by the organizational chart. Faculty and students have successfully challenged the assumptions concerning administrative authority in a number of significant areas. It is well recognized that they have long ignored prescribed channels of communication when it was perceived as being in their interests to do so.

When we postulate the participational model as a logical successor to the bureaucratic model, it is important to recognize that this alternative changes relationships for faculty and students far more than it does for administrators. Within the administrative structure, the bureaucratic model of organization continues to be viable because it is efficient. At the same time, certain modifications must be made with respect to the assumptions that govern administrative functioning to articulate the structure of administration with internal constituencies. Assumptions concerning the authority exercised by the administrative structure, the concepts of span of control and unity of command must all be reexamined and altered if the bureaucratic structure is to remain functional in a participational setting.

The chief executive officer has the responsibility for controlling the interface which occurs between internal and external constituencies. In implementing this role he must recognize the existence of overlapping areas where prevailing and emerging norms can be reconciled. While leadership may involve departure from the range of decisions that may be within the zone of acceptance for a particular constituency, the chief executive may retain the confidence of necessary groups through limiting the frequency of such decisions and through ensuring that over time the interests of one constituency are balanced against the interests of others.

While the board of trustees represents a microcosm of the community served, interpreting a course of action in such a way that it receives majority endorsement of the board is not the same as reconciling the concerns of community groups reflected by board reactions. The ability of the chief executive to read community attitudes and to avoid compromising board credibility through too frequent controversial recommendations will be a critical determinant in the willingness of board members to initiate new programs. Finally, the effectiveness of the executive officer depends upon his ability to distribute dissatisfaction evenly to the end that all constituencies, both internal and external, retain confidence in his impartiality and judgment.

REFERENCES

1. COHEN, ARTHUR M. and JOHN E. ROUECHE, *Institutional Administrator or Educational Leader? The Junior College President.* Washington, D. C.: American Association of Junior Colleges, 1969.

2. GALBRAITH, JOHN K., *The New Industrial State.* Boston: Houghton Mifflin, 1967.

3. HUGHES, CHARLES L., *Goal Setting: Key to Individual and Organizational Effectiveness.* New York: American Management Association, 1965.

4. KINTZER, FREDERICK C., ARTHUR M. JENSEN, and JOHN S. HANSEN, *The Multi-Institutional Junior College District.* Washington, D.C.: American Association of Junior Colleges, 1969.

5. MILLETT, JOHN D., *The Academic Community.* New York: McGraw-Hill, Inc., 1960.

6. *Report on Higher Education.* Washington, D. C.: USOE, 1971.

7. ROMINE, STEPHEN, "Alternatives to Politicalizing Higher Education," *Educational Record,* 52:176–180 (Spring 1971).

8. ROUECHE, JOHN A., GEORGE BAKER, and RICHARD BROWNELL, *Accountability and the Community College.* Washington, D. C.: American Association of Junior Colleges, 1971.

9. SAMMARTINO, PETER, *The President of a Small College.* Rutherford, N. J.: Fairleigh Dickinson College Press, 1954.

10. SIMON, HERBERT A., "The Job of a College President," *Educational Record,* 48:68–78 (Winter 1967).

11. STOKE, HAROLD W., *The American College President.* New York: Harper & Row, 1959.

12. STROUP, HERBERT, *Bureaucracy in Higher Education.* New York: Free Press, 1966.

13. THOMPSON, JAMES D., *Organizations in Action.* New York: McGraw-Hill, 1967.

seven

Administrative Specialization: Administrative and Business Services

An administrative organization is designed to assist the chief executive in carrying out the responsibilities of the managerial function. An important characteristic of the organization is specialization, the purpose of which is to increase the proficiency of an individual by limiting the scope of his responsibilities and taking advantage of repetitive experience. The relationship of the administrative organization to the president is both qualitatively and quantitatively different from that of the faculty or student organizations. An individual who spends most of his time carrying out administrative functions will have as his primary reference group others who are similarly involved. As a consequence, patterns of relationships for administrators will be quite different from those whose primary responsibility is providing a professional service.

We have already pointed out the hierarchical nature of the administrative organization and the implications this has for the power that can be exercised by administrators. The structural difference between those concerned primarily with administration in comparison with those who furnish professional services also helps to account for the feelings of ambivalence and insecurity frequently observed among individuals holding transitional positions such as division chairmen. It is also important to recognize the stress experienced by administrators when an organization is moving in the direction of a participational model.

As long as the entire organization, including students and faculty, is viewed as a bureaucratic structure, then all role incumbents are subject to the same set of rules. When the institution adopts the shared-authority concept, administrators must continue to abide by some of the rules of bureaucracy because of the nature of their work. At the same time, they are expected to act as if bureaucratic expectations of authority and status no longer apply to their relationships with students and faculty (5:141).

It requires a great deal of learning and experience to understand why the administrative structure both can and should be operated along bureaucratic lines, while the institution as a whole can be better served by the tenets of a participational model. It is only after the participational model has functioned for a period of time that administrators can perceive the advantages which result from this method of operation. It is more difficult to function as an administrator within a participational model, but the levels of achievement and the opportunities for organizational change possible through the interaction process will more than compensate for the additional effort required. Although bureaucratic principles to some extent continue to govern the administrative structure, transition to a participational model requires different administrative behavior, particularly in the decision-making process, the observance of status differentials, and the use of communication media.

One of the most significant and essential departures from conventional practice is the concept of multiple channels for reporting and problem solving. In the traditional approach, each person reports to one and only one other individual. Thus, the second-echelon administrator assigned responsibility for instructional services is the individual to whom all staff members having instructional responsibilities report. Such a practice convinces faculty members that instruction is the principal purpose of a college and that those concerned with instruction are somehow more important than those concerned with other functions. In the participational model division chairmen report concurrently to all second-echelon (level two) administrators and are accountable to each for certain responsibilities. This helps to convey the idea that all staff members are responsible for the total process of human development and consequently must be prepared at appropriate times to learn, to teach, or to perform administrative functions. While the percentage of time spent in each of these activities will vary for different staff members, the interdependent nature of institutional requirements must be recognized and encouraged by the structure of administration.

The idea that the principle of unity of command should be violated when there is good reason to do so is not original with the authors. More than ten years ago, Simon analyzed the weaknesses of the assumptions upon which the principle is based (7:22). More recently, Likert has suggested the importance of such a step, warning it could be effectively implemented only within the participatory model, since lack of unity of command is inconsistent with other assumptions of the authoritarian model (4:158).

In practice, when an individual is asked to report to more than one colleague, it is advisable that position relationships be as carefully clarified as possible, that a procedure to resolve jurisdictional disputes be established, and that one office be designated to take the initiative in personnel matters.

Administrative specialization in the horizontal plane can be divided into two general classifications. The first involves activities related primarily to maintenance and servicing of the organization with relatively little impact on faculty and students in the absence of system failure. The second involves activities carried out directly through faculty and students and consequently having an immediate and significant impact on these two groups. Administrative and business services which will be discussed in this chapter normally fall into the first classification. To describe them as less central to faculty and student concerns than other aspects of the administrative organization is not to imply any attenuation of their potential for contributing to the success or failure of the institutional mission.

ADMINISTRATIVE SERVICES

Vice President/Dean, Administrative Services, Level 2

The area of administrative services is the last to emerge as a distinct entity in the pattern of growth for most institutions. It is not uncommon to find development services and public information managed by an assistant to the president. Management information services may be incorporated within the business office while institutional research may be supervised by student personnel services. The responsibility for publications is frequently given to a number of separate offices. At the same time, there are some good arguments that can be advanced for giving these services a stronger identity, more unified leadership, and less opportunity to be dominated by areas of specialization when they should serve the entire institution. (See Figure 7.1)

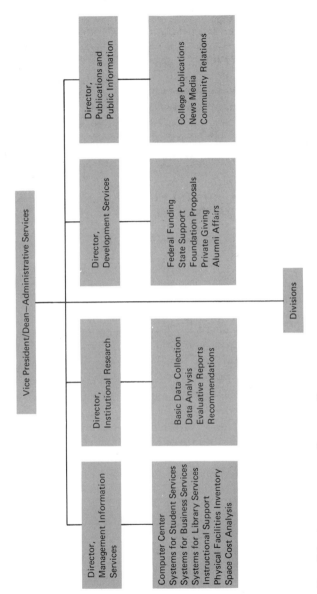

FIG. 7.1 ADMINISTRATIVE SERVICES DETAIL

The growth of management information services and institutional research have been identified by Rourke and Brooks as two of the most significant developments in recent years affecting the administration of four-year colleges and universities (6). Evidence suggests that similar developments are taking place in two-year colleges at a somewhat slower pace. Many of the services that we have grouped in this area have been considered nonessential by two-year institutions, especially during their hectic early years of formation and growth. As a period of rapid development and geometric rates of growth increasingly gives way to the period of consolidation (predicted for the 1980s by Clark Kerr), institutions will have the time to develop more sophisticated administrative services. At the same time, increasing demands upon present modes of funding is likely to force greater attention to new sources of revenue.

Director, Management Information Services, Level 3

Computers are found in increasing numbers on two-year college campuses. Institutions that cannot afford their own installations frequently purchase services. Most institutions approach computer services on one of two basic premises. The first assumes that the use of computers to provide administrative services will reduce costs. It is fair to say that this premise is seldom if ever accurate. Computers make it possible for colleges to provide improved and more accurate services in less time, but their use does not accomplish this at less cost. Contrary to assumptions that were popular in the early days of computer development, few personnel are displaced. The institution discovers new services which immediately become indispensable, and though shifts in personnel allocation occur, the net result is to increase costs. The cost of computer-based management services is only justifiable if such services are under the direction of sophisticated administrators and technical specialists.

A second basis for an institution becoming involved in a computer installation is the desire to provide instruction in computer programming and systems analysis. Federal Vocational Education Act funds are available to many colleges for the lease or purchase of computers intended primarily for instructional use. The availability of a computer then serves as a catalyst for the development of administrative systems. A common consequence of the decision to use a computer for both instructional and management services is competition for computer time. Competition also occurs among staff sections for priority access to the computer and support personnel. One reason for placing management information services in a separate area of specialization as opposed to relating them directly to the business office or instructional office is to ensure that decisions concerning priorities are resolved outside the context of specialized interests. In the absence of an office of administrative services, it is probably best to have the director of the computer center report directly to the president who would provide equitable access for all staff sections.

In addition to use as a laboratory device for instruction in data processing, computers are also being developed and used for computer-assisted and computer-managed instruction. In the former case, instructional units are developed and stored in the computer. Students complete these units as a normal part of their learning sequence or use them for special assistance determined by the instructor. In the case of computer-managed instruction, a record of the student's past achievement is maintained and examinations or learning sequences are selected by the computer based upon an analysis of student progress. Both approaches are expensive and highly experimental at this point. Contrary to popular opinion, however, such techniques do not dehumanize the learning process. Faculty members who use such approaches report increased time for individual consultation and for intensive work with students who require such assistance.

Instructional use of the computer cannot properly be regarded as a system, if by system we imply a group or complex of parts interrelated in their actions toward specific goals. Given this more rigorous definition, the first system developed by most institutions is for student accounting. Included within this area are registration, grade reporting, and the maintenance of permanent records (2:318–87). As the system develops, one objective is the establishment of a data bank which can be used to produce information for administrative and institutional research purposes. Reports are also generated and, in some instances, the system may include a billing procedure for payment of student fees. All of these components combined may be properly termed a student information system.

It is immediately apparent that data and procedures developed as a part of the student information service are interrelated with other systems. Business services may require student data for reports involving state reimbursement. Systems to support business services were the second most common use of computers in the Rourke and Brooks study and this finding would appear to be equally true for two-year colleges (6:21).

Accounting and payroll are the services that normally are first programmed for computer applications. Physical inventory is another common utilization. Purchasing frequently becomes integrated into the accounting system. Less frequently, the computer is used in budget development where it can be highly effective in providing immediate feedback concerning the consequences of each decision. The use of the computer substantially reduces clerical time in typing the budget and lessens typographical errors in revisions. By having all budget information in the computer it becomes a simple matter to analyze expenses in a variety of categories. The use of the computer as an analytical tool is almost indispensable in moving toward planning-programming-budgeting systems (PPBS). When all of the applications mentioned above are interrelated, we have a business information system.

Just as close relationships exist between certain aspects of the student and business information system, we find close relationships with two other applications. Some institutions have successfully implemented student scheduling and sectioning systems (3). The process involves the collection of student requests, and matching these requests to available facilities, staff resources, and course time requirements. The results are combined in a master schedule of course offerings. Students are then placed in sections by a procedure which in many instances takes into consideration instructor preferences and time limitations. While there are no insurmountable technical problems with respect to this application, as evidenced by the fact that many secondary schools have been implementing the process for a number of years, at the college level, the development of master schedules and the sectioning of students have encountered substantial resistance from faculty and students. In consequence, it is probably the least common application to be found.

Federal and state requirements for physical facilities information have motivated many institutions to computerize such inventories. The availability of such data, like that on student characteristics, encourages analyses of space utilization and cost. Likewise it becomes a simple matter to obtain teacher load information and to compare such data with requests for additional space or additional staff members.

Computers are also being used increasingly in connection with learning resource centers, one element of which is the library. When information concerning current holdings is placed in computer storage, new requests can be checked by determining immediately if an item is already in the collection, in process, or on order. If it is not in one of these categories, a purchase order is printed. It is also easy to print, upon request, reports related to special holdings for use by faculty and students. Less commonly, the circulation process may be managed by the computer with warning notices automatically prepared along with appropriate reports.

When the various systems previously defined are planned as a part of a total program intended to yield data for institutional decision making, forecasting, or simulation, there exists a total management information system. While most institutions do not begin with a plan for a total system, the natural interrelationships of the subsystems, if recognized and utilized, can create a significant management tool that goes far in the direction of making administration less of an art and more of a science. It is safe to say that the positive attractions of PPBS will motivate more institutions toward a total systems approach.

Director, Institutional Research, Level 3

As in the case of management information services, institutional research is in its infancy in the two-year college. It is likely that colleges have such programs more as a result of the pressures of academic fashion rather than because they have recognized research as vital to improving institutional services. Historically, two-year colleges have emphasized the teaching function and tended to dismiss or downgrade the research function as an inappropriate responsibility. For this reason, most of the research on two-year college programs has been done in universities, which have tended to concentrate quite naturally in those areas of greatest interest to their staffs as opposed to the areas that might have been of the most assistance to two-year colleges.

The new emphasis upon institutional research represents an attempt to generate evaluative data that can be useful in the decision-making process. Where effective programs have been implemented, the consequences can be observed in improved instructional practices, more consistent feedback on the effect of various programs, and a new attention to the relationship between resources expended and results achieved. As important as these effects are, there may be an even more significant result for the institution as a whole. As the institution becomes more involved in the development and exchange of evaluative information, its environment is perceptibly altered. Institutional research can become the arbitrator in such issues as productivity versus quality. It can improve the means through which objectives are increasingly refined and clarified and procedures revised. In other words, it allows the application of accountability. Of course, two-year colleges have not been noted for their use of the evaluative process in direct change. But the systematic collection of data which supplies the material necessary to gauge effectiveness can pave the way to the requisite concept of accountability.

It would be gratifying to state that institutional research is currently being used effectively in most institutions as such an agent of evaluation and change. Unfortunately, this is not the case. Institutional research has a low priority in colleges and where appropriately staffed offices do exist, it is probable that much time is spent completing routine questionnaires and performing services that, while useful, do not result in any significant change. But the possibility exists and the hope is there for the future. Institutional research can become a process through which the periodic renewal of institutional processes is effected.

Director, Development Services, Level 3

Most institutions of any size employ someone on their staff who is given the title of director of federal affairs or its equivalent. Increasing categorical federal support during the past decade accompanied by the requirements for complex reporting procedures have dictated the creation of this position. There is also ample evidence that two-year colleges do not fare well in the competition for funds that are not exclusively reserved for their purposes. While a part of this unequal distribution can be attributed to a bias on the part of the U. S. Office of Education in favor of four-year colleges and universities, it is also apparent that two-year colleges have lacked the sophistication and persistence demonstrated by their four-year counterparts in the pursuit of available funds. During most of the past decade and a half, community colleges in particular have been riding the crest of a wave of popular support that has made outside sources of funding less important to the provision of basic services.

However, the situation has now changed, and community colleges find themselves caught up in the same pressures toward fiscal insolvency that threaten the futures of institutions which in the past have been looked upon as models of affluence. Under these pressures the competition for available funds will become more intense. Unless two-year colleges give increased attention to all dimensions of the development function, they will not fare well in the competition.

The primary focus of most two-year college offices of development will continue to be the federal government and those state offices which distribute nonmandated funds. These will be the sources of most available funds. Increasingly, however, two-year colleges must organize to bring concerted influences to bear in a consistent and continuing pattern on state and federal legislators. In a similar manner, the current haphazard applications submitted by many colleges must be replaced by proposals carefully thought out by the best minds the institution can muster.

Foundations have demonstrated a growing interest in two-year colleges, and a number of institutions have put the necessary effort into the development of proposals that have resulted in substantial grants for projects such as the education of the disadvantaged. Foundations, however, do not as a general rule reserve funds for two-year colleges. Proposals receive exacting scrutiny and are subject to severe competition. An office of development with appropriate resources can assist two-year colleges to take advantage of the risk capital available from private foundations. It is probably essential that they do so if new programs are to be initiated within the restraints of limited resources.

Private giving is not an area that has received much attention from most public two-year colleges (1). In part, this has been true because the policies of many firms have precluded gifts to public institutions. At the same time, it must be recognized that the philosophy of the open-door community college has a strong appeal for many private citizens. A sufficient number of institutions have availed themselves of these sources of income to demonstrate that it can be done. Most colleges that have embarked upon campaigns to encourage private giving have found it desirable to develop a college foundation. Such an organization has at least three distinct advantages. It ensures prospective donors that contributions will be used for the purposes intended by keeping them out of the reach of state offices and governing boards. Second, it provides a visible structure within the community which is identified with the concept of private giving. Finally, it provides a means of involving influential citizens of the community in the affairs of the college through membership on the foundation board.

Few public two-year colleges have done much to explore the possibilities of alumni support. Many arguments can be advanced against the concept. Significant numbers of students transfer and prefer to identify with the baccalaureate institution. Many two-year colleges are new and alumni are not in a position to provide support. A large percentage of graduates are women who marry and contribute primarily to the institution attended by the husband. Such arguments overlook a number of equally important considerations. Many students who attend two-year colleges do develop a strong sense of identity with the institution. The fact that many continue to reside in the community after graduation provides the opportunity to strengthen that identity. Even if only a small percentage of graduates contribute, the funds can still be significant because of the numbers involved. Those who cannot contribute funds may still be willing to work to build community support for bond elections. On the balance, the arguments are persuasive for organizing and maintaining a systematic procedure for exchanging information with alumni. It may be a number of years before the system can begin to pay its own way from a financial point of view, but the possibilities of such an arrangement would seemingly more than justify its implementation.

Director, Publications and Public Information, Level 3

Closely related to development services is the publications and public information program of the college. An institution which fails to project a strong positive image is unlikely to have much success in development activities. Each publication carries information about the college in addition to its printed content; cover design, layout, and the absence or presence of errors convey different impressions to the college's constituency. The decentralization of responsibility for publications, typical of many institutions, can lead to negative results in quality, style, and content. Or, unfortunate errors in public relations may be committed, such as distribution of an apparently costly brochure during a tax campaign.

The publications program, like the management information system, can involve direct relationships with faculty and students in colleges with graphic arts programs where much of the printing is done in-house. Unlike the computer center, the graphic arts laboratory is clearly an instructional responsibility. This fact raises important questions concerning priorities and the point at which a given publication ceases to be a learning experience and becomes instead exploitation. Also of concern are the financial advantages of in-house printing contrasted with the disadvantage of potential union reactions if it appears that the level of printing activity exceeds that normally associated with a learning program.

Public information programs in many colleges have missed the emphasis that their importance would seem to warrant. While it is true that a good program will sell itself and that nothing can sell a poor program, there are certain time factors involved that are of increasing importance. Many people who help to support public institutions never come into contact with them directly, indicating a need for colleges to explain themselves and their services to the general public. In the absence of a carefully planned and methodically sustained program, institutions seem to respond only during intermittent crisis conditions. Unfavorable information in headlines results in a flurry of activity oriented to erasing the impression created (e.g., a tax issue is imminent so the public is flooded with information).

Attitudes toward institutions are formed as a part of total exposure over a long time. The best defense against the unfortunate publicity surrounding a crisis is a sustained program utilizing all media over a continuing period of time. In addition to the media, newsletters, advisory committees, community services, open houses, and a host of other activities shape public opinion. The question is not whether the institution will be interpreted to the public, but rather how. The absence of a carefully coordinated total program of public information invites a variety of impressions, many of which may be negative and may make the vital difference between success and failure in maintaining the ongoing vitality of the institution.

BUSINESS SERVICES

Vice President / Dean, Business-Services, Level 2

Business services, like the administrative services previously discussed, seem more remote from student and faculty interaction than instructional services. (See Figure 7.2.) Yet the decisions that are made in this area and the evaluation and implementation of such decisions can have a profound impact on all aspects of institutional life. It must be recognized that this is the area in which the chief executive normally has had the least experience; consequently he is likely to have the most difficulty distinguishing between specialized interests and the best interests of the total institution. Because the area of business services involves finance, which is central to the sustenance of all other activities, it is not uncommon for the business officer to exercise influence beyond that appropriate to his expertise. It is a truism that an institution can undertake only activities that can be financed; but too often, alternative solutions to problems are not explored on the excuse of lack of funds. The business officer is frequently delegated undue discretion in deciding what constitutes a legitimate expense. This problem is particularly acute in state systems, in multicampus operations, and in situations requiring a pre-audit.

The answer to these problems may be found in a series of practices which limit the scope of influence of the business officer while at the same time protecting the institution against inappropriate or illegal use of funds. As a starting point, the institution must define its educational objectives and the priorities for implementation. Based on the educational plan, operating units submit estimates of expenditures required to implement objectives. When the information has been collated, requests inevitably exceed anticipated revenues. Ideally, decisions are preceded by careful examination of expense estimates submitted by each subunit. In any case, the review process becomes the focal point for determining the institution's future. When it finally becomes necessary to postpone lower-priority programs, budgetary estimates are readjusted so that income and expenditures balance.

In addition, conflict between business services and other segments of the college occur because too many administrators and faculty do not understand that the annual operating budget is the most important single policy document written each year. An operating budget is an explicit statement of planned development and change within the institution. Because of the pervasive importance of the budget to the entire educational effort of the college there should be as broad participation as possible in its development.

Once budgets are approved, all subunits are informed of their allocations and are faced with the responsibility of living within them. The business office, on the other hand, is responsible for ensuring funds are available for expenditure requests. It need not exercise judgment on the relative importance of such requests. In a similar manner, priority determination is not the responsibility of the business office, but, rather, a shared responsibility for all of the offices concerned. In consequence, the

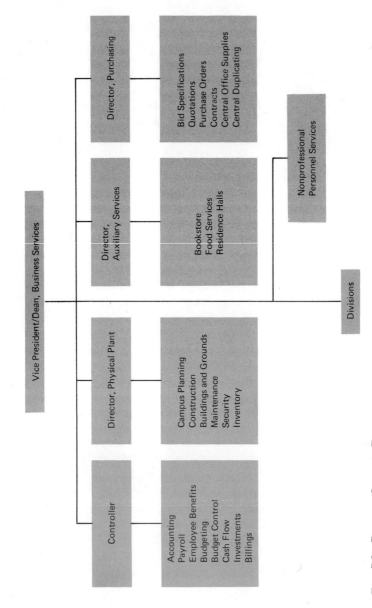

FIG. 7.2 BUSINESS SERVICES DETAIL

148

business office emerges as a service function and not as a source of educational decisions.

There is a great temptation for state systems and multicollege units which receive allocations based on projected enrollments to work this process backward. The available funds are calculated and then distributed to operating units on some kind of formula basis. This is poor practice for at least two reasons. The process of budgeting should always be preceded by a clear statement of objectives arranged according to priority. The absence of such a statement invites overfinancing of special interests or pet projects. In addition, the budgetary process is a prime source of intrainstitutional conflict. The absence of clear and acceptable bases for decision making invites suspicion of unfair practices even where none exist. Of course, it should be added that when an individual is provided with a budget which he helped to formulate and within which he is expected to operate, fiscal responsibility is promoted to a far greater extent than when this is not the case.

For a variety of reasons there is a great temptation for chief administrators and their business officers to conceal as much as possible the true financial condition of the institution. The motives are varied but include the desire to maintain confidentiality in salary matters, attempts to conceal reserves in salary negotiations, and a general lack of confidence in the ability of the institution to explain its fiscal practices to its constituencies and to the general public. These temptations need to be suppressed. If the institution is doing something wrong it will benefit from learning about it as quickly as possible. If it is not, then it ought to be able to explain its practices and status to its constituencies. As painful as the process of revelation may be, the consequences of attempting to continue a policy of secrecy are apt to be even more drastic.

Controller, Level 3

Fiscal control is the most obvious aspect of work in the business office. Central to effective decision making is the development of information which provides a clear picture of the institution's assets and liabilities. The accounting system accomplishes this through a series of steps. First of all, a chart of accounts is developed which represents a functional classification of all sources of revenue and areas of expenditure. Actual revenue and expenditures are entered periodically and compared against projections. Ideally, an encumbrance system indicates funds which have been committed but not expended. Monthly reports to each subunit head provide a continuing picture of the cash flow. Fundamental to the entire system is a procedure for ensuring that commitments are avoided unless funds have been allocated and are available.

The office of the controller is also responsible for payroll. In addition to processing salary checks, the payroll procedures must withhold amounts required by the federal and state governments. Depending upon whether or not the payroll is automated, the institution may also perform a variety of services in the form of optional withholdings and transmittals of funds for tax-sheltered annuities, United Fund, credit unions, membership dues, or savings bonds. The trend is toward more services of this sort which, in turn, creates substantial pressure for payroll automation.

While the business office may not be involved in the determination of employee benefits, particularly where collective bargaining is involved, it will most certainly be expected to develop information on the options available and the estimated costs of implementing each option. The responsibility for enrolling employees in benefit programs, for administering claims, and for providing general information must also be accomplished.

Estimating the cash flow can be an especially important activity of the controller's office. Since there is normally a period of time between the receipt of revenues and the processing of expenditures, it is frequently possible to invest surplus funds. This device can provide an important source of income to the institution.

Director, Physical Plant, Level 3

Campus planning is a vital and continuing responsibility for all institutions. While architectural firms provide essential services in this regard, it is extremely desirable to have a staff person charged with liaison between the architects and the college staff and student body. In this capacity, the director of physical plant aids in identifying the priority needs in terms of educational objectives and in interpreting these needs to the architect. He also assists in protecting the interests of the institution during the construction phase. Frequently, he may be able to handle the design and implementation of minor renovations without involving the services of an architectural firm.

The director is also responsible for coordinating complex relationships with state and federal agencies during the planning and construction of the college physical plant. These government agencies have numerous regulations concerning aesthetic requirements, interior spaces, safety, and other matters. Many state systems of community colleges have laid down explicit requirements for buildings and equipment which make necessary comprehensive and often involved technical explanations.

In addition to campus planning and construction, the proper maintenance of the college plant can reduce costs and prolong the life of equipment. The cleanliness and attractiveness of the campus will also be his concern through the custodial and grounds staff. Of considerable importance is the security of the campus. A college is vulnerable to theft and vandalism because it is easily accessible to the public. Institutions which operate evening programs and provide facilities for community services are almost compelled to develop security forces. The frequently tense social and political atmosphere on many campuses demands a trained security force capable of the judgment necessary to avoid dangerous confrontations.

The director of physical plant must be concerned with an inventory both of the physical plant and of fixed and moveable equipment. Many of the responsibilities of the physical plant director relate closely to activities of students and faculty, so both he and his staff must be sensitive to the requirements of the service function they perform and its implications for staff and student morale.

Director, Auxiliary Services, Level 3

The financial aspects of operating enterprises such as food services, the bookstore, and residence halls fall under the jurisdiction of the business office. These activities probably produce the most serious differences of opinion between students and administration. The business officer can expect to be questioned in detail by students who are concerned about the costs of books and materials sold in the student store, and about the cost and quality of food sold in the cafeteria. Unless he can provide satisfactory answers to the questions that are raised, there is always the possibility that such issues can escalate into major campus confrontations.

Because the bookstore is operated as a separate financial enterprise and may not be subject to the same accounting procedures required of the rest of the institution, undesirable practices may evolve under the supervision of an inexperienced or unscrupulous manager. The institution must guard against this possibility by establishing the same kinds of accounting procedures for the bookstore that are required of the rest of the institution. The college should also have a statement of policy with respect to the use that is made of bookstore profits. If these profits are used to support student activities such as the athletics program or the student center, there is less chance that students will object to the prices that are charged.

The same statement is true for profits from the food service activity, although, as a general rule, food services do not do much more than break even, if they provide a satisfactory level of service and acceptable quality. The institution should be particularly careful about entering into contracts with catering firms. While this is frequently a desirable method of providing food service, the institution should reserve the right to exercise control over quality and the size of portions, as well as the right to terminate the contract on reasonable notice for substandard performance. Since students very seldom distinguish between the institution and the contracting firm in expressing their dissatisfaction, the institution must be prepared to act on its own if necessary.

Residence halls are less likely to be a source of difficulty for the business office, since disciplinary problems are normally the responsibility of student personnel services. However, the business office is responsible for paying off the mortgage, and this implies a requirement for policies designed to keep residence halls fully occupied. Because court decisions have invalidated requirements for dormitory occupancy unless such occupancy can be related to the requirements of the educational program, colleges should exercise extreme care in obligating themselves for residence halls unless they are very certain that student occupancy can be assured.

Director, Purchasing, Level 3

The purchasing process is both complex and time consuming. However, purchasing procedures can result in substantial savings to the institution. Of all aspects of purchasing, the development of bid specifications is probably the most complex. Many institutions are required, either by their own regulations or by state law, to advertise such specifications on purchases exceeding a certain amount. Often this amount is unrealistically low, and the institution is compelled to invest too great an effort to obtain the needed quality and type of item.

Perhaps no area of business services arouses more faculty antagonism than the procurement of one piece of equipment when another has been requested. It is essential that the purchasing office consult with staff members on the development of specifications and the acceptance of substitutes. At the same time, however, the office must be sensitive enough to distinguish between a legitimate request for a more expensive item and a bias which is based upon nothing more substantial than the staff member's familiarity with the equipment requested.

Professional staff members are not noted for the enthusiasm with which they prepare requisitions. Nevertheless, the director of purchasing must ensure that purchase orders are issued only after proper procedures have been followed, including approval of the requisition by the appropriate budget officer, and availability of funds. Contract documents must conform to legal requirements. The director of purchasing must reconcile the need for flexibility in emergency situations with the requirement for sound business practice in an extremely sensitive area of institutional operation.

The advent of duplicating equipment has been a mixed blessing from the standpoint of business affairs. When someone can push a button and produce fifty copies of three pages of a textbook in a very short period of time, two problems arise. The most apparent of these is cost. Less apparent but equally important is the violation of copyright involved. In addition, much of the duplicating equipment is quite complex and cannot withstand occasional usage by amateurs. For these reasons, most institutions have found it preferable to set up a central duplicating service which maintains control over the duplicating equipment and also makes it unnecessary for staff members to waste time and money attempting to operate equipment with which they are unfamiliar. Central services are also frequently charged to maintain a continuing inventory of common-use items such as stationery, envelopes, index cards, and other materials that are used in all administrative operations so much that they are normally charged to the general institutional budget.

Director, Nonprofessional Personnel Services

Some office must be charged with the responsibility for maintaining records involving nonprofessional personnel. Frequently, this office will also be responsible for recruiting personnel based upon special requests. The office may also screen applicants and administer tests to candidates for clerical positions. Credit checks are performed by this office.

Once an employee has been appointed, it is necessary to maintain records of sick leave, vacation, evaluations, and eligibility for promotion or increments. The absence of well-defined personnel procedures for nonprofessional staff can cause an institution quite as much trouble as the same omission with respect to professional staff.

The growing emphasis upon negotiations for the determination of issues involving salary and fringe benefits creates the need for the collection and processing of data to serve as a basis for decision making. When collective bargaining legislation is passed, attention is normally focused on the activities of the professional staff. Less attention is given to the needs of nonprofessional staff members since their numbers are fewer and the costs involved in salary discussions are much less. At the same time, it must be recognized that one-third or more of the total staff of an institution is included within the ranks of the office and clerical workers and the custodial and maintenance staff. These individuals have the same aspirations and the same human needs as their professional counterparts. Equally important, they are as indispensable to institutional operations.

The first lesson learned by most institutions in working with the nonprofessional staff is the need for at least two organizations to represent their diverse concerns. The issues raised by the office and clerical staff are sufficiently different from those of the custodial and maintenance staff to warrant the development of separate organizations, each with its own structure, grievance procedure, and elected representative for communicating group concerns. Even in the absence of unions or collective bargaining legislation it is nonetheless important to recognize the significant contributions of the nonprofessional staff and to afford them the opportunity to express their opinions on matters that affect them.

While it is usually necessary to have separate organizations for the two major divisions of the nonprofessional staff, it is desirable to develop a single set of personnel policies for both groups. The complexities of personnel administration for the nonprofessional staff dictate a high priority for the development of a unified personnel service. In a society where the voice of the individual is heard primarily through the organizations to which he belongs, administrators must assume that staff members will form organizations to represent their interests regardless of institutional posture on the desirability of such organizations. The probability of group action suggests serious and continuing problems for the college that lets each office handle its own personnel matters.

SUMMARY

Administrative specialization develops within organizations as a means of encouraging the development of expertise through limiting the scope of activities. While the activities of some areas of specialization impinge less directly than others upon faculty and student concerns, the degree of impingement is not a measure of the importance of the activities. In this chapter, we have considered the two areas of specialization which have the least direct contact with faculty and students. At the same time, we have suggested that these offices require direct communication with faculty and students which can be achieved through deliberate violation of the principle of unity of command. While such an action would be dysfunctional for authoritarian models of governance, it is a contributing factor to the effectiveness of the participational model.

Administrative services represent a relatively new category of administrative specialization. As a consequence, the functions we have grouped within this category may be distributed among other areas of specialization in many institutions. Included among the major dimensions of administrative services are management information, institutional research, development, and publications and public information. The institution's need for more comprehensive and timely data is provided through the development of computer systems in the areas of student accounting, business services, and other areas. Institutional research provides the medium through which the quality of response can be evaluated. Properly used, it can serve as the basis for change. Development services are concerned with seeking new sources of financial support under increasingly difficult circumstances. The public information program is the key to interpreting the institution to its external constituencies for continuing support.

Business services deal with the management of fiscal resources, maintenance and security of the physical plant, the development of new facilities, the supervision of auxiliary enterprises, and personnel services for the nonprofessional staff. The budget document is the most important planning instrument generated each year by the institution. While careful attention must be given to the tenets of good fiscal management, it is imperative that educational decisions be made by educators and not by business officers. In addition to coping with the problems of fiscal management, the business officer must also give consideration to the management of human resources as represented by the nonprofessional staff.

REFERENCES

1. BLOCKER, CLYDE E., FLOYD S. ELKINS, and FRED BREMER, *Philanthropy for American Junior Colleges.* Washington, D.C.: American Association of Junior Colleges, 1965.

2. BROWN, WARREN, "Systems, Boundaries and Information Flow," *Academy of Management Journal,* 9:318–87 (December 1966) .

3. FLINT, LANNING L., "Switch." Sectioning with Instructor and Time Choice. Unpublished document, Bakersfield College, 1966.

4. LIKERT, RENSIS, *The Human Organization.* New York: McGraw-Hill, 1967.

5. MEDSKER, LELAND L. and DALE TILLERY, *Breaking the Access Barriers: A Profile of Two-Year Colleges.* New York: Carnegie Foundation for the Advancement of Teaching, 1971.

6. ROURKE, FRANCIS E. and GLENN E. BROOKS, *The Managerial Revolution in Higher Education.* Baltimore: Johns Hopkins, 1966.

7. SIMON, HERBERT A., *Administrative Behavior,* 2nd ed. New York: Free Press, 1965.

eight

Administrative Specialization: Instructional and Student Personnel Services

The major impact of the transition from an authoritarian to a participational structure of governance is generally experienced by administrators in the middle levels of management. Because the activities of instructional and student service administrators are carried out primarily through faculty and students, any role redefinition involving these constituencies will be felt most acutely by these two groups. Traditionally it has been assumed that the chief instructional officer exercised authority over the faculty while the chief student personnel administrator maintained a similar relationship with the students. The development of faculty and student organizations with the objective of representing their respective constituents in direct discussions with the president and with the trustees has undermined these traditional assumptions through establishing alternate channels of communication and through confronting the authority of position with the threat of collective action.

The role of the chief executive officer, while obviously altered by the participational structure, still retains significant influence because of centrality within the communications net and because of the continuing responsibilities for relating the needs of internal constituents to the board of control and to the larger community. The same statement cannot be made about middle level administrators who may be bypassed whenever issues of serious consequence arise. Threatened by what they perceive as loss of status and authority, instructional and student personnel administrators have in a number of states created their own organizations designed to strengthen influence through joint action under the guise of professional improvement.

While we would not argue against the desirability of organizations for administrators as one approach to coping with the insecurities resulting from role redefinition, there are other steps of a more constructive nature which can be taken. Historically we have tended to define the responsibilities of middle level administrators in terms of the constraints they were expected to enforce in their respective areas of influence. Supervision, evaluation, and discipline were central processes. The participational model shifts much of the responsibility for these areas to the individual and to faculty and student organizations. While there is still a need for administrators to maintain accountability, the shift in emphasis provides an opportunity for more leadership through example and facilitative services and less requirement for efforts intended to support the observance of minimal standards. It has always been possible to lead people further than they can be pushed so the net consequence of role redefinition can easily be positive if viewed in the proper context.

New roles create a demand for new responses. Our purpose in considering instructional and student personnel services in some detail is to suggest adaptations of existing concepts and configurations that may prove constructive in implementing new forms of administration.

INSTRUCTIONAL SERVICES

Vice President / Dean, Instructional Services, Level 2

The most important function of instructional services administration involves the establishment of the educational goals of the institution and leadership in the management of resources to implement those goals. The office of instruction must serve to identify needs through examination of the societal context within which the institution functions, through interrelationships with other staff offices, and with students and members of the faculty through the committee structure. After confirming the existence of needs the institution implements the learning process through curricula, courses, seminars, and workshops.

The fulfillment of this primary function depends upon the ability of the office to gather evaluative information from a variety of sources. Increasingly, the role of the office is not so much to perform the evaluation as to stimulate faculty and students to work together in the development of evaluation procedures that generate the information required, while at the same time maintaining accountability.

In addition to the leadership role relative to the instructional program and the resources that support it, the office also performs important coordinating functions. Included among these functions are the class schedule, examination schedules, course outlines, and the selection of instructional materials. It must be noted again that it is not the function of the office of instruction to dictate which materials shall be used or which classes will be taught, although it is sometimes necessary to exert a mediating function in these areas. Rather, it is the responsibility of the office in a consultative capacity to ensure that proper inputs are received at appropriate times in order to coordinate a flow of information to those who procure instructional materials or develop registration procedures, and to others active in the work of coordinating the instructional program.

Instructional administration normally takes the initiative in matters involving personnel administration for the professional staff. This requires the development of personnel files, as well as routines for maintaining application materials, teaching credentials, evaluation reports, eligibility for promotion, sick leave, and similar matters. In exercising its responsibility for personnel matters, the instructional office is in a particularly sensitive relationship with members of a professional staff. We will deal with this relationship at greater length in a later part of the book.

In some institutions, responsibility for the instructional program is divided among a variety of offices carrying such titles as Dean of Liberal Arts and Sciences, Dean of Career Programs, and Dean of the Evening School. Where these titles are combined with a line relationship to the instructional staff we would consider this arrangement unsatisfactory, because it tends to fragment the instructional program and to create unnecessary divisions among the staff. It is preferable that the responsibilities for the total program of instruction center in a single office with sufficient staff assistance to ensure appropriate attention to each of the various functional divisions.

Figure 8.1 represents one approach to dividing the responsibilities of the office of instruction. It differs from the more common approach in that two of the staff offices provide services to the entire instructional program and to the personnel who serve in it, while the other two staff offices have responsibilities for specific programs. More commonly, the responsibility for services and programs are combined in a single staff office. The division of responsibility between an Associate Dean for

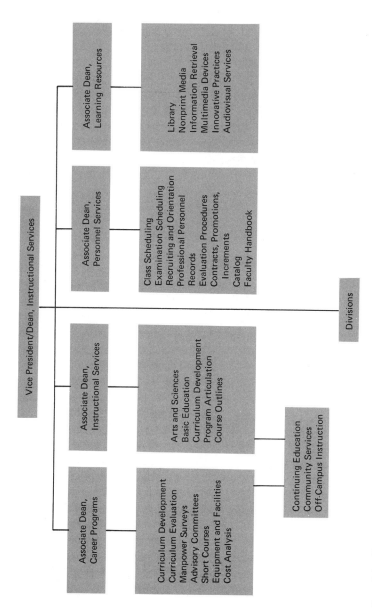

FIG. 8.1 INSTRUCTIONAL SERVICES DETAIL

Career Programs and an Associate Dean for Instructional Services is also open to question. Our rationale for this division is that the development and maintenance of career programs requires far more time than college parallel programs, or even developmental programs. Although more staff members usually teach in college parallel programs, the existence of one staff office to provide personnel services for all programs eliminates the necessity for having a separate Associate Dean of Arts and Sciences. Further, it is probable that this arrangement reflects the order of priorities that should be given by community colleges to the various programs which they offer in terms of staff support.

Associate Dean, Career Programs, Level 3

Certainly one of the greatest challenges facing the instructional office of any institution is the development of career programs. The first stage in such development involves conducting periodic manpower surveys to determine the needs of the area that is served. Frequently, some of this information can be obtained from the state employment service, but seldom is the information sufficiently complete to serve as a basis for program development. The trend toward improved coordination at state levels increasingly requires a review of manpower requirements and training on a wider-than-area basis.

Upon completion of manpower surveys and the necessary coordination, advisory committees must be appointed to assist in program development. The search for persons who should be invited to serve on such committees, while in part a function of the manpower survey, is nonetheless time consuming and essential to the future success of the program. If properly utilized, advisory committees will be most active during the developmental stages of the curriculum in subcommittees and as a committee of the whole. The administration should devote as much time as possible to the coordination and direction of such committees.

The implementation of career programs also requires careful study of the requirements for equipment and facilities. Not the least important aspect of this survey is a cost analysis in order to determine the probable costs of starting the program as well as the per student cost after the program is in operation.

In the development of career programs, it is important to make realistic projections of student enrollments. A determination of the minimum average of enrollees in each program necessary to keep it financially feasible permits a projection of the number of career programs that the institution can afford at each stage of its development. Without sound projections, a college may develop too many programs too quickly, producing low enrollments and inordinately high per student costs. Since most institutions operate on some kind of a formula which does not consider differences in cost of operating career programs as compared to the less expensive college parallel programs, cost analysis becomes an important consideration.

Once a career program has been developed, it must be evaluated on a continuing basis. Both the advisory committee and data obtained from employers and employees contribute to this evaluation. As part of the development, implementation, and evaluation cycle for career programs, the office of instruction will become aware of programs that can be offered for adults in the evenings or on the weekends. Indeed, some programs designed for the inservice education of those already employed are initiated on a part-time basis in the evenings and later become offerings for full-time day students. The interaction of college and community which grows out of interviews with employers, advisory committees, and through other contacts can provide many opportunities for developing community service programs. Frequently, it may prove desirable to offer instruction at an off-campus location in order to better serve the needs of this group of students.

Associate Dean, Instructional Services, Level 3

The college parallel program normally enrolls the highest percentage of students at most two-year colleges. In the past, the assumption has been made that such programs correspond to a considerable degree to the offerings of the four-year institutions to which students transfer, and hence little can be done of a creative nature without their approval. However, the effects of growing student bodies at community colleges, and student attacks on the relevancy of the baccalaureate curriculum have presented two-year colleges with a chance for increased flexibility in this area of curriculum.

There is admittedly a need for periodic articulation conferences between four- and two-year institutions to ascertain what competencies required at the junior level are taught in the community college. But ultimately, less administrative time is normally spent on the college parallel program because it is less specialized and because faculty are more familiar with its requisites and are more likely to initiate curriculum development and evaluation.

The periodic review of graduate performance in each discipline at four-year institutions can provide an important basis for needed program revision. In one sense, course outlines represent a coordinating function since these are clearly developed by the faculty members concerned and not by the office of instruction. But course outlines should be regarded as a general guide to the objectives of a given sequence of instruction rather than as a means for controlling instruction.

Two-year colleges are most frequently open-door institutions. Even those which exercise some degree of selectivity admit students who would not be considered qualified by traditional standards. This implies the need for a strong program of basic education oriented toward helping students to remove deficiencies. It is particularly important that the program of basic education be individualized since the range of deficiencies presented by learners at the college level is too diverse to lend itself satisfactorily to group instruction.

There is no area that is more important to the success of a nonselective institution than its program of basic education. There is also no area which offers more formidable obstacles to its successful achievement. Nevertheless, it is imperative that functional programs be developed and that they be carefully related to advanced course offerings and to counseling programs of the institution.

As in the case of career program development, opportunities for continuing education, community services, and off-campus instruction must be given full consideration in relation to offerings in the college's parallel and basic education areas.

Associate Dean, Personnel Services, Level 3

A number of functions must be performed by the office of instruction to provide coordinating services for the professional staff. In a traditional organization, the tendency is to combine these functions with responsibilities for specific programs. In other words, the dean responsible for the arts and sciences program is also responsible for personnel services for the faculty who teach in this program. From our point of view, there are advantages to be gained in separating personnel services from instructional leadership, since it is apparent that the traditional relationships to administrative authority either no longer exist or have been greatly modified by the development of faculty organizations.

The development of the class schedule has important implications for both faculty and students. It is also important to growing two-year colleges, most of which have space problems and cannot operate on a convenient nine-to-two timetable. If faculty are to have some choice of when they teach, and if students are to be able to have something to say about the faculty members who teach them, the class schedule must be developed as soon as possible after registration for the preceding semester. Institutions that continue to require final examinations can also save themselves much difficulty if these examination schedules are published as a part of the class schedule.

The recruitment and selection of new faculty is the most important single factor in the success of any organization. Those programs that work best seem to be the ones which emphasize the greatest amount of faculty involvement in the selection process. Whenever possible, an effort should be made to recruit from as wide a geographic area as possible, and candidates should not be appointed prior to a personal interview and, preferably, a visit to the campus. The responsibility of the office of instruction for the recruiting process again should probably be primarily that of coordination. It is important that information concerning position vacancies be properly distributed as early as possible in the recruiting year. It is also helpful to coordinate the flow of materials that passes between candidates and the college. Ideally, the individual divisions become the most active elements in the search for new faculty. The office of instruction should restrict itself to providing supportive services and a monitoring function in the recruitment process.

Candidates should be given as much information as possible about the institution and its expectations prior to the employment offer. In this regard, the office of instruction can develop a statement which specifies clearly expectations of all new faculty with respect to teaching load, service on committees, responsibility for evening services if required as part of the normal teaching load, and similar information. The office of instruction should also give careful attention to the development of an orientation program to induct new staff members effectively into the ongoing program. It makes little sense to condemn each new faculty member to repeat the mistakes of his predecessors. In the development of orientation programs it is particularly important to avoid subjecting returning faculty to many of the programs that are designed for new staff members. Still, returning faculty have an important function to perform in the induction of new staff members, and they need to be vitally involved in the orientation process. The use of constant evaluation and significant faculty participation in planning can make the orientation program a major factor in shaping institutional growth.

The office of instruction commonly oversees professional personnel records. Controversy in this sensitive task is likely, especially if evaluative information is kept on file without the faculty's knowledge, or records are not open to faculty inspection. In the past, evaluation of those who performed teaching services has been viewed as a major function of the office of instruction. In order to perform this function, the office has defined minimum standards and then has sought, through a variety of approaches, including class visitations, student observations, and faculty self-reports, to determine whether or not minimum standards were being met. The results of the evaluation were then used in making decisions concerning increments, promotion, and contract renewal. It must be emphasized again that our view of human behavior is markedly different from that of the traditional organization. It is our view that evaluation of the professional staff should be shifted, insofar as possible, from the office of instruction to the individual faculty member. If the primary function of evaluation is improvement, then such improvement is far more likely to take place if the faculty member defines his own objectives and collects the information necessary to determine to what extent these objectives have been met. It is far more difficult to rationalize one's own findings than it is to rationalize someone else's. Under this arrangement, the office of instruction becomes concerned primarily with maintaining faculty accountability to students and the administration, and is forced to devote extensive attention only to the very small percentage of faculty who emerge in each institution as unresponsive to the self-evaluation approach.

The faculty handbook is an important orientation device. Ideally, such a document should contain all of the policies and procedures of the institution that relate to faculty members in a concise and easy-to-use format. Emphasis should be upon the kind of supportive services that are available to help faculty members accomplish their objectives rather than upon prescribed behavior. The office of instruction also normally has responsibility for that part of the catalog which relates to the curriculum and course offerings.

Associate Dean, Learning Resources, Level 3

If the college is to take advantage of educational technology in its instructional program, it follows that an office needs to be given the responsibility for coordinating the various media and for assisting faculty to use such media effectively. It has been said that the library is the core of the instructional program, and this statement undoubtedly continues to be true. Increasingly, however, more reliance is being placed upon nonprint media, especially since such media seems to provide a more effective means for reaching certain categories of students.

It is important that the use of media grow out of program requirements rather than being superimposed as an institutional fad. Learning continues to be a highly individualized experience, both for the teacher and the individual taught. Not all approaches will work equally well for all students or for all faculty. Some instructors can defy many of the best principles of teaching as these are normally defined and still be more effective with their students than other faculty members who meticulously observe such principles. It must also be recognized that faculty members resent what they regard as administrative pressures to reform their teaching practices. For this reason, if for no other, a supportive role rather than a prescriptive role is particularly appropriate in the use of instructional media.

The best approach to utilizing the wide array of new media now available seems to be to provide information concerning such media and to make them available on a trial basis to those faculty members who are interested. As faculty members begin using equipment, some of their colleagues are quick to note the advantages and applicability to their own disciplines. It is essential that technical assistance be provided both to maintain equipment and to provide assistance in its use. An institution should recognize that providing equipment without supportive services is an extremely precarious investment.

The college should also be especially careful about investing in expensive systems which tend to be inflexible. Technology in education, as in other areas, advances at a rapid pace. Many of the functions which could once be performed effectively only through the use of costly dial acccess systems can now be provided through inexpensive cassettes and playback units. Several of the functions of the centralized television distribution system can be achieved less expensively through portable videotape recorders and monitors. A college which commits itself to a sizeable expenditure for certain kinds of equipment is making some guesses about its instructional program which may or may not be borne out in practice. The less costly a given approach, the more quickly it can be discarded in the event that new approaches or new techniques seem to make this desirable.

Innovation is an elusive term. What represents an innovation for one institution may be standard practice in another. Equally important, not all innovations are good, nor are they all effective. Nevertheless, it is possible for an institution to develop an environment which encourages faculty members to try new ways of improving their teaching and to evaluate the effectiveness of these new methods in relation to their cost. This is innovation of the very best type, and it can be fostered through the kinds of services and relationships provided by the office of instruction.

STUDENT PERSONNEL SERVICES

Vice President / Dean, Student Personnel Services, Level 2

The development of Student Personnel Services has been a recent phenomenon among institutions of higher education in general and within two-year colleges in particular. Shaffer and Martinson show the role of student personnel services to be a twentieth-century event, but the Raines' report asserts that three-fourths of the community colleges surveyed in the early 1960s had less than adequate programs (6:4).

Included among the deficiencies identified by the Raines's group were lack of coordination, evaluation and inservice training, absence of career information, lack of professional leadership and inadequate staff (4).

Spurred by the Raines's report, there has been a discernible improvement in student personnel services on many campuses during the last five years. The rapid development of a highly professional staff in most institutions has not been accomplished without a certain amount of institutional stress and some undesirable consequences. Chief among the latter has been the tendency to fragment student life into academic and nonacademic components. Even within the nonacademic component, additional specialization without concurrent coordination has created problems for the student who cannot always be sure which professional staff member has the answer to his problem. As with much contemporary medical treatment, there has been a tendency to refer the student from office to office while the original complaint is further complicated by the delay in receiving attention.

The growth of centralized student personnel services has been interpreted by many teaching faculty as a justification for limiting their own activity in advising students. Not infrequently counselors have added to this tendency by limiting general faculty access to certain types of information and by discouraging them from carrying out the advisory activities that have traditionally been a part of a faculty member's role. The gradual accretion of the number of specialized persons in student services has tended to make these activities more remote from the day-to-day concerns of teaching faculty. As remoteness has increased, there has been a tendency to ignore or discourage faculty participation and to employ even more specialists who hopefully will provide the required services.

A major undesirable concomitant of the growth of student personnel services has been the assumption that such functions could be centralized and carried out by a special staff. Many administrators have not understood the necessity for student personnel services to constitute a pervasive part of the responsibility of all members of the staff or, if the need for total involvement has been understood, the structure of our institutions has been so arranged as to make it extremely difficult to insure that student services are accorded the appropriate level of emphasis and the necessary degree of coordination among the entire staff (2:585–89).

By placing all teaching faculty within a framework which has emphasized their instructional responsibilities, the ability of the student personnel officer to exercise influence and leadership among staff members has been seriously impaired. The consequence has been artificial distinctions in the provision of professional services, lack of lateral communication, and reliance upon different specialists operating in partial isolation to provide services that could be more effectively offered under conditions which would foster coordination and integration.

Student personnel services can best be organized into three mutually dependent and somewhat overlapping levels of service. The first of these may be defined as divisional services and requires limited specialization to implement. This level of service is accomplished primarily by members of the instructional staff and includes faculty advising and the sponsorship of student activities. As the staff members most closely in contact with individual students, a vigorous faculty advising system and interested faculty sponsors are basic to the implementation of a comprehensive and coordinated program of student personnel services.

The second level of student services can be thought of as those functions suitably provided by a counselor with specialization at the master's degree level. Such services are likely to be more intensive and will involve a broader range of activities than those provided by the teaching faculty member. Examples of second-level services include individual and group counseling, related to vocational, educational, or social problems as well as psychological testing and interpretation. Second-level services are attuned to the reduction of emotional tensions and, when necessary, culminate in a referral process.

The third level of services includes activities which are sufficiently specialized to require assignment to a staff member whose preparation is different from or more advanced than that normally possessed by those providing second-level services. Examples of third-level services would include admissions and record keeping, health services, and financial aid. The arrangement of student personnel services in this way has been more completely described by two of the authors elsewhere under the heading of a trilevel concept (5:126–30).

If the student personnel officer is to exercise responsibilities on the broader scale envisioned by this kind of organization, his relationship to the divisions, and hence to the faculty, must be the same as that defined for the instructional officer.

If a division is to be held accountable for student personnel services as well as for instruction, its staff must include specialists who have a dual responsibility: to division chairmen who provide leadership to divisional personnel, and to appropriate members of the student personnel staff for communication and for the quality of divisional student personnel services.

Decentralization of student personnel services represents an attempt to integrate student personnel staff more thoroughly into the normal operation of the institution and to strengthen their relationship to faculty and students through the medium of physical proximity. While decentralization of services can alleviate some of the undesirable aspects of traditional organization, it will not achieve maximal effectiveness unless it is accompanied by procedures which make all members of the professional staff feel responsible for all aspects of the students' learning experience. The merging of institutional resources to stimulate maximum development of students will be realized only if faculty members accept and understand their roles in effective learning.

All the concepts described above are incorporated in Figure 8.2 which is one approach to organizing student personnel services. In this pattern, the Dean of Students and the Dean of Instruction have similar relationships to the divisions within the college. The assignment of a specific function to a given office is not intended to imply that that same function may not be implemented at the division level. Rather, the definition of function implies coordination and communication. The principles of administering student personnel services do not differ significantly from those which apply to other staff functions. The purpose of the proposed organization is to reduce the dichotomy that currently exists in many institutions between student personnel services and instruction. The gap which can develop between student personnel workers and members of the instructional staff must be avoided if the student personnel office is to be successful in involving the total staff in initial planning and in subsequent inservice education.

Associate Dean, Admissions and Records, Level 3

The admissions service is the point of initial contact for most individuals with the college. Consequently, the implications of this service for the image of the institution are substantial. In addition, the program is also an important determinant in the success of the various programs offered by the college. Not infrequently the failure of a new career program to attract a satisfactory number of applicants can be traced to poor communication between those who develop the program and the admissions office, resulting in a lack of accurate information for potential students.

Most admissions programs do a good job of conveying information to feeder schools and in establishing good relationships with the counselors of these institutions. Less frequently, the admissions service recognizes its responsibility to reach out into areas of the community that may not be accessible through feeder schools. Adults who work in factories or businesses can be contacted more effectively through the public media and through the personnel offices of their companies. Low income and minority group residents may not respond well to the efforts of high school counselors or they may be high school drop-outs. An admissions service needs to be as comprehensive as the institution it serves. In the case of the community college, this implies well defined approaches for all potential students within the entire community.

Prior to the advent of student information systems and computerized records, the collection of information from applicants and the mainte-

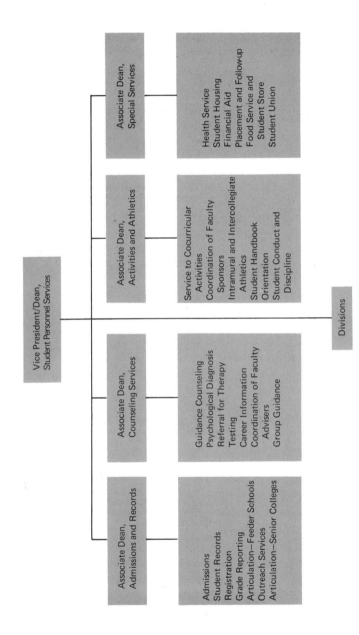

FIG. 8.2 STUDENT PERSONNEL SERVICES DETAIL

169

nance of records of student achievement represented a time-consuming and arduous task. While the compilation and maintenance of student records continues to be a task requiring care and precision, the level of supervision in an institution that has computerized its operations is substantially less than in the traditional setting. This development affords an institution the opportunity to make the process of record keeping more a service and less a constraint. Through careful design of the process of record keeping and reporting, important information concerning student characteristics can be generated and distributed to those who need it. The process of registration and grade reporting can be operated with less clerical demands upon the professional staff.

Of course, technological advances carry with them built-in hazards. Some institutions have been accused of using computers to limit student choice of hours of instruction and instructor. Despite the need in many instances to accommodate student enrollments exceeding all normal measures of physical plant capacity, it is usually possible to order priorities within the admissions and records office to ensure that student needs are given primary attention. The phenomenon of the walk-in student who visits the college for the first time on the last day of late registration provides the admissions office with its greatest test of philosophy and endurance. While the programs arranged for late registrants may be far from ideal, it is essential that the college, insofar as possible, provide the same services to these students as it does to those who follow more standard schedules. Many late registrants are nontraditional students, and their initial attitudes toward the institution are often directly reflected in their subsequent achievement.

It is apparent that the admissions and records service is a third-level service and as such it will be carried out primarily by highly specialized personnel operating in a centralized location. By the same token it is important to recognize that the objectives of the office cannot be implemented without close working relationships with other areas of the institution. Computerized grade reporting requires an understanding by all faculty of the importance of submitting grades by a specified deadline. The process of articulation with feeder schools can be significantly improved if it has the advantage of faculty support. The extent to which the faculty view the admissions and records office as service oriented will determine the level of cooperation and support which they will be willing to provide.

Associate Dean, Counseling Services, Level 3

The trilevel concept of student services applies particularly to counseling services. If such services are to be extended to all students through the use of faculty advisers, it is important to understand that not all such individuals will be equally adept at carrying out all of the responsibilities of the advisory program. For this reason it is essential that some selectivity be exercised by the student personnel office in requesting faculty members to undertake certain kinds of assignments. In addition to selecting advisors carefully, there is a need for inservice education and complete and accurate information in an easily accessible format.

Some writers have suggested that only those faculty members who have a significant commitment to student advising and the willingness to participate in inservice programs ought to be involved. It is our contention, to the contrary, that the environment of the institution should place substantial emphasis upon the responsibility of all staff members to contribute to the out-of-class development of students. It is certainly true that the student personnel office may choose not to ask all faculty members to assist in the formal program of helping students to select their course programs since some faculty members do not adapt well to such responsibilities. A decision not to involve a specific faculty member in the formal program of educational advising should not lead, however, to the conclusion that such a faculty member has no responsibilities for students outside the classroom setting. Many faculty members who exercise substantial and lasting influence over their students lack the ability or the inclination to provide assistance in course selection. This does not limit their effectiveness in providing other significant services to students.

We have suggested that a second and more intensive level of counseling should also be available within the division through the placement of a counseling specialist who would have administrative responsibility both to the division chairman and to the student personnel office. The decentralization of second-level counseling services requires a high level of coordination from the office of counseling services. Any student personnel program to be effective relies to a considerable degree upon the referral process which is designed to identify the nature and complexity of student problems and to ensure prompt attention from appropriate specialists. The referral process is significantly improved by a close relationship between first- and second-level services. At the same time, noncounseling specialists can be given assistance in identifying students who can benefit from services available.

Counseling services are also a part of the third-level program. Within the counseling center, arrangements must exist to diagnose individuals who give evidence of having deep-seated disorders which may be harmful to themselves or to others. While most two-year colleges have rejected the role of providing long-term therapeutic assistance, they cannot avoid the requirement of being able to identify such disorders and to refer individuals to appropriate clinical assistance.

One major trend in providing counseling services involves the development of specially structured groups. In some instances, encounter techniques are used in working with the groups. While encounter groups do not constitute an alternative to individualized counseling, they do provide an opportunity to extend counseling services more broadly and more intensively than has been possible in the past. At the same time, they bring some of the strength offered by group interaction to the human development process. The use of group guidance approaches has in some institutions evolved into courses of instruction for which academic credit is given. Under such circumstances, relationships between the instructional program and the program of student services are further strengthened.

The testing service in most two-year institutions provides the basis for placement in specific courses such as English or math as well as the criteria for admission to programs such as nursing or drafting and design technology. Tests are not normally used to determine admissibility to the college. The low correlations that have been observed between many standardized tests and subsequent student achievement has created doubt in many minds of the effectiveness of testing programs, particularly when such programs are used with nontraditional students. The trend is away from conventional testing programs toward broader methods of evaluating student potential for success in specific programs. While testing will continue to play a role in the counseling program, it will receive much less emphasis than in the past.

A large percentage of students who attend two-year colleges have poorly defined or no career objectives. A major responsibility of the counseling service is to correct this deficiency through vocational guidance. This cannot be accomplished without adequate reference materials which provide not only detailed information about the characteristics of various occupations, but also the employment outlook, both local and statewide. Since many of the students attending two-year colleges will enter employment unrelated to their academic work at college and prior to completion of a college program, counseling services must insure the availability in a centralized location of up-to-date and comprehensive information related to career guidance. Certain references such as the *Occupational Outlook Handbook* and the *Occupational Outlook Quarterly* will need to be available at each of the centers where second level counseling services are provided.

Associate Dean, Activities and Athletics, Level 3

Student activities and athletics, like counseling services, require the effective involvement of faculty. Most institutions endorse the policy of relating the development of student activities to student needs. Presumably this implies that activities should disappear when the needs that gave rise to them no longer exist.

The cycle of development, growth and demise creates a number of problems with which the faculty advisor and the student personnel service must contend. The human tendency to perpetuate existing modes of activity is very strong. It is difficult to determine that point at which an activity results more from the interest of the institution or the faculty advisor than from student needs. In recent years, intercollegiate athletics have come to the fore as one example of a student activity which may have outlived the needs that originally led to its development.

One effective method of control is to place responsibility for the use of student activity funds with the student government and to abide by the decisions that they make. Under such circumstances, if an activity really meets student needs, then funds will be appropriated for its support. If, on the other hand, the activity is primarily related to the interests of faculty members, the activity may not be funded.

A second method for ensuring that student activities are based upon student needs involves a careful definition of the role of the faculty advisor combined with effective mediation by the student personnel office in instances of dispute. Ideally, the role of the advisor should be such that he is not able to dominate the activity. By the same token, students involved in the activity should not be able to proceed without coordinating their plans with the advisor. The equal distribution of power through a system of checks and balances between the faculty advisor and the student organization probably represents the most effective way of ensuring that student activities will be responsive to the needs of students without ignoring institutional requirements.

While it is desirable for student organizations to exercise control over their own funds, the procedures for using such funds should correspond to the normal fiscal policies of the institution. The college should make every effort to avoid yielding to the temptation to use fiscal policies as an instrument for the control of student activities. The best defense against this temptation is the development of policies which clearly spell out rights, responsibilities, and the procedure for resolving differences of opinion.

The effectiveness of the traditional orientation program of informational meetings has been questioned by both students and faculty. In place of such programs, encounter groups organized to help students learn more about themselves and how they are perceived by others can function throughout the semester under the direction of the counseling service. Preregistration orientation may be handled through either counseling services or admissions and records.

The development of a student handbook, organized around student needs and with student involvement, can provide assistance during the first weeks of school. Social activities can also be planned around the theme of integrating new students into the ongoing life of the institution.

Some commuter institutions, for example, sponsor a freshman weekend where interested new students have an opportunity to become acquainted with each other and with returning students in an informal and relaxed atmosphere. Ideally, orientation activities, like all other facets of the college program, should relate to the development of individuals within the context of the ongoing programs of the institution.

Since it is generally accepted that the institution no longer functions in loco parentis to the student, the college's role with respect to conduct and discipline has changed drastically. For the most part, there is little need for a separate code of conduct for students. If those activities which are really regarded as detrimental to the best interests of the college community are carefully defined, it can be observed immediately that such activities would be equally offensive if undertaken by faculty or administrators. It is no longer safe to assume that only students are likely to engage in such activities as disruptive behavior. Consequently, it is best to suggest that with faculty and student involvement, some minimum standards of behavior for the institution as a whole be developed along with the guarantee of due process in dealing with individuals who are accused of violating such regulations.

Associate Dean, Special Services, Level 3

Unless an institution is very large, and has residence halls, it is unlikely to have a division of special services staffed by an associate dean. We have used this functional area as a miscellaneous category for activities which in most institutions would be assigned to one of the three areas previously defined or which might report directly to the dean of student personnel services.

The health service can and should be an important asset to the entire institution. Health counseling may range from questions involving drug usage to contraception or venereal disease. Physical abnormalities which have implications for the instructional program should be identified and reported to appropriate staff members. Preventive health services can be provided both to staff members and to students. Athletes require physical examinations and, in some instances, corrective treatment.

Most commuter institutions do not provide housing services. At the same time, student surveys reveal that from fifteen to twenty-five percent would like to receive services in this area. It is probable that most two-year institutions of any size require some attention to this service even in the absence of residence halls. Where residence halls do exist, the college has a responsibility to ensure that the method of organization and the patterns of interaction make a positive contribution to the total learning experience for each resident student.

Financial aid services have become very complex as a result of the wide variety of state and federal funding sources available. Each program has its own reporting procedure and accounting requirements can become burdensome. Most programs of financial aid emphasize a package arrangement including some type of grant, a loan, and a job. Even institutions that charge little or no tuition must recognize the total expenses involved in college attendance. Current federal estimates indicate that even for an institution charging no tuition, the cost, not including income forgone, would be in the vicinity of $1,500 per year for a student.

Financial aid is closely related to the admissions service with which it is sometimes combined. At the same time, it must have a close relationship with the business office. While institutions in the past have designated financial aid as a responsibility of a counselor, this is a poor way of handling the service. A far better approach is to appoint someone to serve specifically in this area, then provide him the necessary training to insure the objectives of the financial aid program are properly related to the objectives of the college.

Job placement and follow-up, like housing, is one of the more neglected services in two-year colleges. Because so many of the students entering express their intentions to transfer, placement may be downgraded. In the past, there has also been a tendency for business and industry to concentrate exclusively on recruiting the baccalaureate graduate. A good placement service can not only be answerable for ensuring that the graduates of career programs and those who do not graduate at all find employment, but it can also provide important information to assist in the evaluation and improvement of the college's program of instruction.

It is inevitable that the faculty of career programs will assume responsibility for some of the placement activity that is carried out by the institution. At the same time there is need for a centralized service to maintain continuing records of graduates who are placed so that such hiring companies can be contacted by future employment seekers. An aggressive placement office will also be responsible for identifying new sources of employment that faculty members who concentrate their efforts on a seasonal or part-time basis may not recognize. The placement office can also serve as an important adjunct to the financial aid program by developing information about part-time jobs and making this information available to students.

As mentioned previously, food service and the student store are two sensitive points with respect to student-institutional relationships. Student services can provide material assistance to the business officer through the development of advisory committees which monitor these activities and which provide regular evaluative information to assist the college in correcting conditions promptly. Such committees can also interpret problems involving these services to the rest of the student body.

The student union is the center for cocurricular activities. As such, programming will be an important consideration for the student personnel office. In the absence of an associate dean for special services, the student union might well be subsumed within the office of activities and athletics. Properly utilized, the student union should be much more than a lounging area where students play cards or converse during breaks between classes. Ideally, it should offer a wide range of activities designed to foster student identification with the institution and to contribute to the objectives of the college.

INSTRUCTIONAL AND PERSONNEL SERVICES

Division Organization, Level 4

When we use the term division we are referring to the operating unit organized to provide professional services to the student. Divisions ordinarily represent groupings of related disciplines although in some instances, for example the house plan, they may be organized on some other basis. Large institutions may choose to have subunits within the division which are most frequently called departments but may be designated by other titles. Most of what we say about divisions applies equally to departments. Leadership normally is provided to the division by a chairman who also does some teaching. Much less frequently, the division may be headed by a full-time administrator who is regarded as a staff member of the office of instruction. We consider the latter arrangement less desirable (1:9–12).

In many respects, the division is a transitional unit within the structure of administration. While the division bears many of the characteristics of Level 2 administrative offices with respect to its organization for communication and maintaining accountability, the faculty of the division exercise substantial autonomy in the performance of their professional responsibilities and normally have a decisive voice in the selection of division leadership. The faculty also exercise great influence through the governance structure; consequently they cannot be regarded as operating within a hierarchical relationship to the rest of the institution except in areas where agreement exists concerning responsibilities and procedures. Division chairmen represent the focal point for stress between the administrative structure and the governance structure. Where relationships are not carefully specified or where an institution is undergoing a period of stress such as in the case of organizing for collective bargaining, division chairmen may be forced to renounce their normal ambivalence and make a clear choice between administration and faculty. This is seldom a happy experience either for the institution or the individual.

In many institutions divisions may be specialized along functional as well as subject matter lines. Counselors may be organized within one division, while faculty providing instruction for college parallel courses are placed in a second, and faculty teaching in career programs in yet a third. We regard such specialization as undesirable and believe that it is a part of the root cause of the communication lapses which can sometimes be observed between counselors and instructors and between the college parallel and career program staff. The organization of staff members in this way is a natural consequence of attempting to follow the principles of the bureaucratic model by making the structure within the division correspond to the areas of specialization that are found at Level 2. If division chairmen report to more than a single vice president, there is no real need for specialization to occur along lines suggested by the second level administrative structure and some very good reasons why it should not.

We believe that a division should have as its primary objective human development, and that this objective can be implemented most effectively through comprehensive services which relate to more than one area of administrative specialization. The professional staff within a given division should include faculty who teach in career programs, college parallel programs, and basic education programs. Whenever possible, faculty should teach in more than a single program. In addition, counselors should be a part of each division to provide leadership in carrying out student personnel responsibilities. Whether the instructional staff within a division are members of related disciplines as is normally the case or are deliberately mixed as occurs within the cluster-college concept, the important characteristic should be comprehensiveness, and the focus should be the total student, not the academic student.

Figure 8.3 represents the detail of a typical division. While only one program or department is shown, a division might typically have from five to eight of these units. Depending upon the size of the program or the department, as well as the preferences of those who belong to it, there is a possibility that no coordinator or chairman would be appointed. We use the term program coordinator in addition to the more traditional title of department chairman to indicate that institutions may find it desirable to have a broader base for organizing disciplines below the division level than the traditional department. Programs may cut across division lines as well as across subject matter disciplines. As noted previously, the participational concept of organization finds nothing wrong

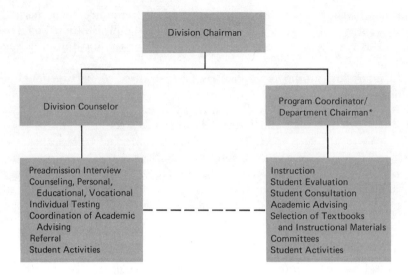

*Replicated as many times as necessary.

FIG. 8.3   DIVISION DETAIL

with having one individual report to more than one other individual, provided that the nature of his relationships to each are clearly defined, and one is given the responsibility for initiating personnel actions.

In addition to the responsibilities indicated in Figure 8.3, a division would normally be expected to carry out the following activities:

1. To initiate, review, and recommend revisions to curricula and new courses.
2. To review and evaluate course outlines and syllabi.
3. To participate in the selection of new staff members.
4. To develop and coordinate the class schedule and assignment of instructors.
5. To maintain a continuing inventory of physical property assigned to the division.
6. To develop and improve library and other instructional resources required by the division.
7. To participate in the development and administration of the division budget.

The division chairman is both an administrator and a teacher. If he is to carry out his responsibilities properly, he must have adequate released time and clerical assistance. While there is no formula that will prove equally satisfactory for all institutions, the recommendation of the American Association of University Professors that a division chairman determine his own schedule seems an appropriate way of determining what constitutes sufficient released time. Many institutions make a practice of providing additional remuneration to those who assume the responsibilities of division chairmen. Unless this remuneration is in compensation for a lengthened work year, it carries with it a clear implication that administration is more important than teaching.

O'Grady has suggested that department chairmen should be given the title of associate dean. In making this recommendation, O'Grady obviously considers the department chairman analagous to our definition of the division chairman (3:36). We would disagree with O'Grady's recommendation even for the division chairman, because such a designation would impair a division chairman's ability to function effectively as an interpreter of the administration to the faculty and vice versa. It might also make it more difficult to continue the principle of rotation of division leadership which is important if both the administration and faculty are to have an opportunity of periodically reviewing the accountability of the division chairman.

Division Counselor, Level 5–6

The division counselor is the student personnel specialist for the division. In addition to his relationship with the division chairman, he will also report to the associate dean for counseling services. The knowledge of division programs gained as a consequence of his close relationship to the teaching faculty can be of significant value in explaining divisional programs to new students and in helping them make satisfactory course choices.

In the course of the preadmission interview, the counselor is in a position to determine whether the student should be assigned to a faculty advisor. In addition to coordinating the assignment of students to faculty advisors, the counselor must also assume responsibility for ensuring that advisors receive the necessary information and inservice education to do a satisfactory job of advising. The counselor supports the faculty advisory system to ensure that students are referred when referral is needed.

The division counselor is located in an area that is frequented by students who come for faculty assistance. Consequently, it is as natural to be in his office as it is to be in the office of any other member of the faculty. The combination of faculty-counselor interaction and counselor accessibility acts to encourage student self-referrals as well as faculty referrals. Individual testing may be used to supplement the counseling program where indicated. A division counselor must also be alert to ensure that students who requires services that can be more effectively provided by central staff reach the appropriate office with a minimum amount of confusion.

Program Coordinator / Department Chairman, Level 5—6

The program or department is the basic unit for instruction. As such, it has responsibility for the initiation of course outlines and the development of evaluation procedures to ensure that instructional objectives are being met. While the division is a transitional unit, exhibiting characteristics of both administrative and faculty organizations, the program or department is clearly a faculty unit.

Most of the activity that goes on within the department is not supervised or directed in the conventional sense. Each faculty member is responsible for selecting his own text and supplementary instructional materials. Members of a program or department using the same course outline may select diverse methods of instruction and achieve significantly different results. While it is essential that some objectives be held in common, there is also a need for substantial flexibility to encourage innovation and experimentation.

Ideally, the program or department views its role as more than just providing instruction in its area of specialization. Departments which demonstrate their concern for the total welfare of the student through sponsoring appropriate activities and through their involvement in student planned events will find that student response will enhance the effectiveness of the learning environment.

SUMMARY

In the last two chapters we have set forth a proposal for organizing the structure of administration for two-year colleges. We have done so in full recognition of the need for variation based upon such considerations as size, relative priorities, and method of control. To avoid being prescriptive, we have purposely discussed administration in general terms. The structure we have defined has served the purpose of facilitating the communication of ideas concerning administrative aspects of organizational life.

Obviously, it is not entirely accurate to speak of the structure we have defined as participational. In order to implement a participational form of governance, two other essential elements must be present. The first of these is a defined structure for the renorming or governance process which encourages the legitimate involvement of all constituencies of the institution. This aspect of the organization will be discussed in the next chapter. A second requirement for the participational model involves procedures through which the administrative structure and the governance structure interact and induce redefinition of individual attitudes, institutional structures, and procedures as a part of the process. This aspect of organization will be considered under the heading of "The Dynamics of Interaction," in Chapter 10.

Our objective in describing the administrative structure has been to define a series of relationships and responsibilities which has the potential for effective interaction with the governance model that will be postulated. The postbureaucratic conceptualization of administrative organization presented deliberately violates such traditional principles as unity of command and span of control in order to achieve flexibility and to destroy bureaucratic attitudes concerning authority and inclusiveness, which are inconsistent with a system of governance meeting the requirements of the concepts expressed in Chapters 4 and 5.

The organization of instructional services should reflect the priorities of the institution. By the same token care should be taken to avoid the fragmentation of personnel or programs. These objectives can best be accomplished by centralizing the responsibility for the instructional program under a single office. Staff personnel in the areas of career programs, college parallel programs, and basic education can provide the necessary support for each of these areas. Since the office of instruction normally has responsibility for a significant number of personnel and coordinating functions, it seems advisable to have a designated staff member assume responsibilities in these areas. The advent of technology and the need to apply new techniques and equipment to the instructional processes implies the requirement to provide support for this area of the program as well as to coordinate the use of print and nonprint media.

It is desirable for the chief student personnel officer to have the same relationship to division chairmen as designated for his instructional counterpart. Student personnel services, to be effective, must become the responsibility of all staff members. In this regard, it is desirable to decentralize services to the furthest extent possible while still retaining a close relationship among student personnel staff. A logical organization of student services involves a trilevel concept with faculty constituting the first level, division counselors the second, and a highly specialized central staff the third. The key to effective service is a referral system ensuring that student problems receive prompt attention from appropriate staff members. Combining first and second level services through physical proximity is an asset to the referral system.

For purposes of implementing the instructional and student personnel programs, faculty are organized into divisions and departments or programs. We favor comprehensive divisions offering a combination of career, college parallel, and basic education as well as student personnel services. The division chairman is a transitional figure with close ties both to the faculty and to the administrative structure. The ambivalence of the position is intensified under conditions of faculty-administrative conflict. Ideally the transitional role should be maintained through faculty selection subject to administrative approval, the possibility of rotation of the chairmanship, and avoiding additional compensation for administrative duties.

REFERENCES

1. BLOCKER, CLYDE E. and WILLIAM A. KOEHNLINE, "The Division Chairman in the Community College," *Junior College Journal,* 40:9–12 (February 1970).

2. KIRK, BARBARA A., "Guidelines for University and College Counseling Services," *American Psychologist,* 26:585–89 (June 1971).

3. O'GRADY, JAMES P., JR., "The Role of the Departmental Chairman," *Junior College Journal,* 41:35–36 (February 1971).

4. RAINES, MAX R., *Junior College Student Personnel Programs: Appraisal and Development.* A Report to the Carnegie Corporation, November 1965.

5. RICHARDSON, RICHARD C., JR. and CLYDE E. BLOCKER, "A Tri-Level Concept of Personnel Services in Two-Year Colleges," *The Journal of College Student Personnel,* 9:126–30 (March 1968).

6. SHAFFER, ROBERT H. and WILLIAM D. MARTINSON, *Student Personnel Services of Higher Education.* New York: Center for Applied Research in Education, Inc., 1966.

nine

Structure

of

Governance

Just as there is within each institution a structure of administration, so too should there be a structure of governance. Writers in the field of higher education have long noted what they termed a dual procedure for making decisions (1:34-35). While the administration has concerned itself with matters involving long-range planning, allocation of resources, fund raising and similar areas, the control of the educational program has been firmly in the hands of the faculty in most universities. A careful examination of two-year colleges reveals an absence of these parallel structures for decision making accompanied by pervasive administrative dominance (5:40–42).

It should be noted that the concept of the dual structure, while useful from a historical point of view, has not been instrumental in preventing or solving the problems related to the distribution of power. The weakness of the dual decision-making process has been the tendency of each segment to operate in splendid isolation from the other. The administration has exercised complete authority in its domain while the faculty has maintained similar power in its traditional areas. The students have been systematically excluded by both groups, creating what Talcott Parsons has referred to as "the layered society" (4:493).

The existence and continued health of the layered society was completely dependent upon the willingness of each group to recognize and respect the autonomy of the other groups. Unfortunately, this structure was not very responsive to change, and by the end of the sixties it was almost completely out of touch with reality except in remote backwaters of American higher education. As soon as faculties began to insist that they had a right to be involved in making some of administrator's decision making, the structure was endangered. When students demanded a voice in the total process of governance and followed their demands with action, the entire obsolete structure began to disintegrate.

We can identify, then, two distinct patterns of governance which served higher education in the past, but which were no longer relevant to the requirements of contemporary institutions by the early seventies. The dual structure of the university, by fostering isolation among its constituencies, had lost the ability to adapt to change in order to maintain relevancy. The administratively dominated structure of the two-year college and less prestigious four-year institutions of higher education was generally based upon an unrealistic assumption concerning the nature of authority and, consequently, was equally under attack by students and faculty demanding an appropriate share in the decision-making process. The bureaucratic society is proving more vulnerable than the layered society of the university simply because there is only one major constituency, the administration, interested in maintaining the former; while both faculty and administration have at least some vested interest in maintaining the latter.

A major aspect of the problem involves the probable direction of change. The university, with its history of strong faculty involvement and dominance over some segments of its decision-making process, is in a better position to move creatively in seeking solutions to the need for new patterns of governance. The bureaucratic pattern of the two-year college has inhibited the opportunity for anyone other than administrators to gain significant experience with the decision-making process. As a result, the institution must draw primarily upon external influences in altering current imbalances of power. The most obvious model is the labor-management relationship developed within industry. Consequently, there is a strong move in this direction frequently aided by laws passed with labor union support and based upon their experience. The adversary relationship created by such developments does encourage the redistribution of power, but it has certain undesirable concomitants for the practicing professional.

A professional, by the nature of his responsibilities, must exercise judgment and enjoy a reasonable amount of freedom in this process. The labor union pattern secures this freedom in the form of concessions from the employer which are formally defined in the contract. Of course the process of securing concessions is not a one-way street, and the employer seeks to impose as many constraints as possible in return for the guarantees he is forced to make. In the process, the initiative for individuals to seek out new and better ways of doing things is sacrificed in order to obtain certain minimum standards of performance. Furthermore, changes to the contract are negotiated by a limited number of representatives at specified periods and again must represent the mediocrity of the majority at best.

There is an additional problem. The collective-bargaining process is a layered-society approach which assumes the absence or indifference of students when faculty and adminstration agree on how the institution shall be run for the ensuing contract period. The assumption behind this exclusion is the same assumption that proved fallacious for the university.

It is presumed that the faculty in their deliberations will keep in mind the welfare of the student. However, from our experience in comparing the decisions groups make when forced to choose between their welfare and the interests of an outside constituency, we can have little hope that the labor union model will prove any more successful than the university senate in dealing with the real concerns of students. What advocates of the labor union pattern may forget is the proximity of consumers in the two-year college.

The alternative to the bureaucratic or layered society approach to campus governance has been definitely set forth by Keeton (3:36–37). The concept of shared authority depends not so much upon a particular arrangement of campus governing bodies as it does upon a redistribution of power among campus constituencies accompanied by the establishment of credible procedures through which differences of opinion can be resolved equitably. The major characteristics of the concept of shared authority may be summarized as follows:

1. Campus structure should reflect a genuine desire to share power among the various constituencies.
2. The structure must provide each constituency with the opportunity to pursue its legitimate interests within a cooperative framework, while at the same time minimizing the possibility that the special interests of a specific group will exercise a controlling influence within the decision-making process.
3. Each constituency must have the opportunity of influencing action at each level where decisions are made affecting their interests.

4. Constituents of a multi-institutional system must be provided with appropriate procedures to influence decisions at the system level as well as in their local unit.
5. Procedures must exist to resolve differences of opinion among constituencies without creating the necessity for coercion or conflict.
6. The structure of governance must be flexible in order to accommodate rapidly changing conditions.

While we placed emphasis upon the need for flexibility and responsiveness in administrative structure, this consideration becomes even more critical when we talk about patterns of governance. In a sense, the attempt to establish a structure for governance is an effort to institutionalize the informal organization so that it can be used to promote the renorming process and to maintain the attitudes and values of the constituencies to the extent necessary for goal realization.

This point requires further elaboration. Earlier we suggested that colleges have experienced difficulty to the extent that common attitudes concerning the appropriate role of campus constituencies have disappeared. Trustees and administrators have attempted to perpetuate traditional roles through the leverage afforded by a bureaucratic structure, while faculty and students have established formal and informal affiliations to significantly modify the power structure. Because of these very fundamental differences of opinion, no modification in the administrative structure, no matter how well intentioned, can change attitudes without additional procedures for significantly involving all the constituencies in the decision-making process.

By the same token, the renorming process itself cannot occur without a framework wherein values and attitudes may be examined and altered. The administrative structure is not adequate for this task because faculty and students do not view themselves as a part of this structure. If they do, they do not agree with the role that has been assigned to them by those who control the structure. Obviously there must be a common meeting ground outside the administrative structure if adversary relationships between competing bureaucracies established by boards and faculties are not to be the determining factor in institutional decision making. The governance structure can provide this common meeting ground if the tenets of shared authority can be implemented.

We have suggested that the pattern of competing bureaucracies locked in an adversary relationship, as reflected in the collective bargaining process, is a singularly unpromising development for the two-year college. However, institutions which are currently managing relationships between constituencies in this way may also benefit from the concept of participational governance. The existence of a faculty union or an association strongly organized for collective bargaining will impose certain restraints on the procedures through which the institution organizes for governance. By the same token, however, no form of organization is immune to change when it can be demonstrated that the legitimate interests of all are involved. Too often the process of sharing authority has been regarded, in Keeton's words, as "a zero-sum game" in which the gains of one constituency must be precisely reflected in the losses of another (3:123). Faculty members organized in a union or association to force delegation of power from a reluctant board still carry with them professional concerns about the welfare of students and of the institution. Boards faced with the necessity of engaging in collective bargaining are anxious to keep negotiations on a local level whenever possible.

The interests of trustees and faculty may coincide in a number of areas. An examination of the positive aspects of dealing with faculty or students through representative bodies, rather than on an individual basis, may lead to the conclusion that sharing authority may become a positive-sum game, or even a nongame (3:123–24). In the former, each gains because of enlightened mutual self-interest; in the latter, those involved are willing to sacrifice some of their own interests because of mutual concern for each other or a third party, in this case the student. In the nongame situation, the student can become a catalyst through which some self-interests are submerged in the name of a common good, rather than the far more typical situation where the student becomes a device through which other constituencies seek to promote selfish interests.

It would be desirable to assume that the third alternative, the nongame situation described above, will occur as a natural consequence of faculty and administrative concern and values. The history of mass movements, along with the inability of groups to divest themselves of concern for their own welfare, suggests that student welfare will not become a primary concern in the absence of compelling forces in that direction. If more evidence is needed, examination of institutions of higher education in the early 1970s reveals that research, scholarly activities, budgetary interests of conservative boards of trustees, and pecuniary interests of the faculty all seem to have higher priorities than student needs, at least in the absence of campus disruption.

The lesson is clear. Unless students are organized to promote their own self-interests, it is unlikely that anyone else will take these interests very seriously. A failure to provide for legitimate student influence in the decision-making process encourages lack of consideration for student rights, which in turn creates the conditions under which students may feel compelled to turn to extralegal recourse. Accordingly, effective organization of the student body becomes a significant element of the governance process.

An organization of the faculty becomes a second key element in the governance structure, enabling this group to assert its legitimate interests.

In the past it has been possible for administrators to be a part of this organization, and in many instances to control it. This pattern of organization seems destined for an early demise. Where presidents still chair meetings of the general faculty, separate faculty associations often exist to act as escape valves when decisions are reached that run contrary to the perceived interests of nonadministrative personnel.

In the future, faculty organizations which exclude administrators are likely to become the rule rather than the exception. Administrators and trustees will be unable to exercise control over the membership, purposes, or activities of such organizations. Thus the goal becomes an adaptive one, taking advantage of the positive aspects of such organizations while avoiding the possibility of unilateral power over aspects of institutional decision-making by any one constituency. A major purpose of this chapter is to suggest alternatives for the integration of faculty associations within a governance structure, rather than dealing with them as an external constituency on an adversary basis.

The third internal constituency that must be considered within the governance process is administration. In the absence of careful effort to ensure administrative involvement at all levels it is very possible that the president may find himself dealing directly with faculty and student leadership under circumstances which promote isolation of the midlevels of administration. The administrative structure, by itself, is inadequate to serve as the basis for representing administrative interests. Since the hierarchical structure of administration is suspect, faculty and students will seek to go outside it to solve important problems. The option for administration is the creation of transitional bodies where administrators, faculty, and students may meet on neutral ground to hammer out solutions to issues of joint concern.

COMPARISON OF BUREAUCRATIC AND PARTICIPATIONAL MODELS

Just as we were able to identify two approaches to administrative structure based upon organizational premises and objectives, so, too, can we identify contrasting approaches to the structure of governance. Previously we have suggested that in many two-year colleges governance is subsumed within the administrative organization. Faculty and student concern about involvement in the decision-making process has forced institutions to consider the development of a governance structure distinct from the structure of administration. The arrangement that most commonly results when a bureaucratic organization responds to the need for greater involvement may be referred to as a separate jurisdictions approach. Fun-

damentally, the institution applies the principles of bureaucratic organization to establish for each constituency distinct areas of responsibility
and imputed competency. The reader will recognize in this approach the
characteristics of the layered society which have proven dysfunctional for
the university.

Figure 9.1 represents a separate jurisdictions approach to college governance. This type of structure would relate to the bureaucratic model
of administration described in Chapter 7. Deegan, Drexel, Collins, and
Kearney have correctly identified the limitations of this model (2:18–19).
The student organization is isolated from the mainstream of institutional
decision-making. Its influence is limited to suggestions or proposals
to the faculty and indirect influence on the administrative structure, normally through the student personnel officer. There is no
provision for joint consideration of issues which may affect all constituencies when legitimate differences of opinion exist. The decision-making
process is fragmented with no central integrating mechanism other than
the administrative structure. This has its own vested interests and may
lack credibility as an impartial arbitrator in the eyes of the other two constituencies. It is apparent that the students' position in the separate jurisdictions model, as in the bureaucratic structure, is at the bottom.
Students find it difficult to secure responsiveness from either faculty or
administration, and this generates frustration and the probability of confrontation as the only viable alternative to passivity.

In contrast to the separate jurisdictions model, Figure 9.2 represents
the essential elements of a participational model of college governance.
This structure would fit well within the circular conceptualization of the
internal environment presented in Chapter 5. It also relates to the participational structure of administration previously discussed. While the
model presented is one alternative among many, it can serve to guide our
discussion of the structure of governance. The precise organization of a
specific institution, the number of committees, and the nature of the central forum may change, but the major concepts are essentially similar.

In our model we have identified three internal constituencies: administration, faculty, and students, each having separate interests which at
times may coincide with the interests of other constituencies while in
other instances be in opposition to them. Each constituency must have
a structure through which its legitimate interests (which are likely to be
self-defined) are identified, formalized, and vigorously represented in
relationships with other constituencies and the board. Such a statement
does not assume that all members of a constituency will be in agreement
about either the nature or direction of their concerns, but does assume
the existence of internal mechanisms to define majority views.

Each constituency, depending upon its numerical size and internal co-

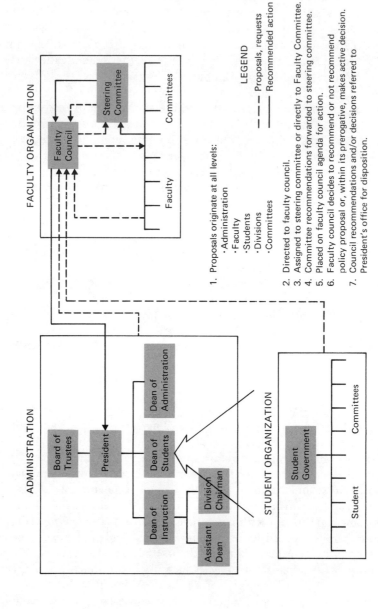

FACULTY ORGANIZATION

Steering Committee

Faculty Council

Faculty   Committees

LEGEND

- - - Proposals, requests
——— Recommended action

1. Proposals originate at all levels:
   · Administration
   · Faculty
   · Students
   · Divisions
   · Committees

2. Directed to faculty council.
3. Assigned to steering committee or directly to Faculty Committee.
4. Committee recommendations forwarded to steering committee.
5. Placed on faculty council agenda for action.
6. Faculty council decides to recommend or not recommend policy proposal or, within its prerogative, makes active decision.
7. Council recommendations and/or decisions referred to President's office for disposition.

ADMINISTRATION

Board of Trustees

President

Dean of Administration

Dean of Students

Dean of Instruction

Division Chairman

Assistant Dean

STUDENT ORGANIZATION

Student Government

Student   Committees

Fig. 9.1   College Governance: A Separate Jurisdictions Model

190

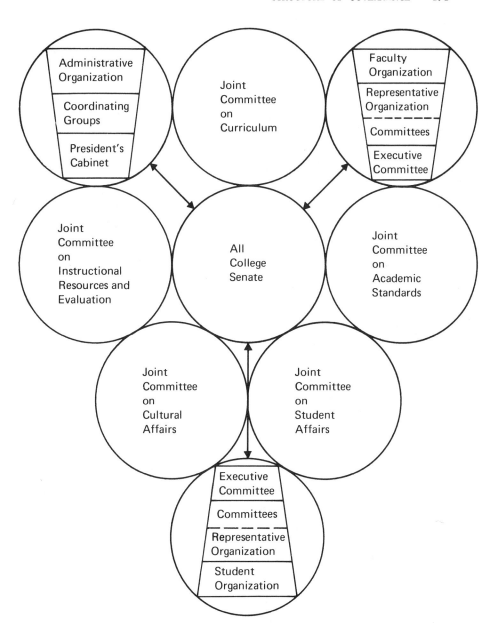

FIG. 9.2   COLLEGE GOVERNANCE: A PARTICIPATIVE MODEL

hesiveness, will utilize several distinct structures. There must first of all be some general agreement on the membership of the constituency which will become formalized in an organization of the whole. Issues such as full-time versus part-time student status or teaching faculty versus non-teaching faculty give rise to definitions of who is eligible to belong to the student or faculty organizations, establishing the boundaries between internal constituencies. While we can and will state our preferences with respect to the composition of these bodies, it is important to recognize that administrative preferences are unlikely to be the decisive factor in the definition of boundaries between constituencies.

Once a constituency has been defined, it must decide whether it will function as an organization of the whole or develop a representative body to serve as the spokesman for the total membership. The numbers involved are likely to be a major determinant in this decision, although the level of participation and interest of individual members will also be a significant factor. Thus in even very small student bodies, a representative organization is the rule while some rather large faculty groups may continue to operate as organizations of the whole.

Whether or not a representative body evolves, there will be developed an executive committee to act on behalf of the constituency in its regular relationships with other constituencies. The executive committee provides the administrative structure necessary to carry out planning and to implement objectives for the constituency.

Each constituency will also develop its own committees to provide a medium through which the total membership may give focus to its major concerns and propose solutions that may be advanced for consideration. Such committees may report their findings and recommendations to either an organization of the whole or a representative organization where such exists. Upon endorsement of committee proposals, the executive committee is in a position to implement them if they do not involve other constituencies, or to press for their adoption by the institution if the interests of other constituencies are involved.

In order to provide for the resolution of proposals which require the concurrence of other constituencies, the institution must establish joint committees. The membership of joint committees is representative of the legitimate interests of the constituencies involved. Such a committee as one dealing with student affairs should have a majority of student members and be chaired by a student. On the other hand, the curriculum committee would have predominantly faculty membership and a faculty chairman. Administrators are assigned to such committees on the basis of their functional specialization in order to provide administrative input and to ensure that the activities of the committee are coordinated with the offices and organizations to which they report. Clerical support is also furnished to the joint committee through administrative assignment. Thus, we would expect that the vice president / dean of instruction would be a member of the curriculum committee while the vice president / dean of student personnel services would serve on the student affairs committee.

In addition to a defined organization for each constituency combined with joint committees to consider issues which involve the interests of more than a single constituency, there must also be an organization which has sufficiently broad representation to serve as the decision-making body for the total college community. While joint committees can recommend solutions to specific problems, if their membership is sufficiently limited to enable them to function effectively, they will not include enough of the individuals who will be affected by a decision to achieve the attitudinal change that may be required for a decision to be successfully implemented. Furthermore, joint committees must report their recommendations to some agency. If they report to separate bodies, the institution may still end up without a majority viewpoint on a specific issue.

The answer to this need is the all-college senate, composed of representatives selected by each constituency. The college senate is not a substitute for organizations of the various constituencies, nor should it attempt to become an organization which defines solutions to specific problems in general session. It can best serve as a central forum reviewing and effecting compromises for all proposals that affect more than a single constituency. Equally important, the all-college senate must be sufficiently visible and vital to influence the attitudes of all constituencies so that compromises endorsed can be accepted and used to guide institutional direction.

Before discussing each element of a participatory model in greater detail, let us consider briefly some implications of the preceding discussion for the multi-institution district.

MULTI-INSTITUTION DISTRICTS

We have defined a participatory model of governance intended to apply to a single-campus college. Given the trend toward multi-institution districts identified in Chapter 6, we need to consider ways in which the concept can be applied to these systems. The starting point is the individual unit. The organizational characteristics suitable for the single campus college will also apply to the units of a system. At the same time, however, relationships within the multi-institutional district are far more complex than for the single-campus college. Consideration must be given not only to problem solution and policy formulation within the unit, but also to the reaction of a central administration as well as the impact of individual actions on other units of the system.

The most common and least effective approach to this problem is to funnel all recommendations originating on the campus through the chief administrator. There are two principal weaknesses to this solution. Decisions pertaining to the individual unit are dependent upon a single communication channel, which in turn relies upon the influence of the campus administrator among his colleagues and with the central office. As previously noted, the bureaucratic structure is much more effective at coordination than it is at solving problems. Consequently, we can expect that the central office will be much less likely to recognize the need for change where the need is made manifest only through the channel primarily used to effect coordination.

The second major weakness of dependence upon the chief campus administrator is the development of a credibility gap, real or imagined. The chief administrator is frequently tempted to use his key position in the communication network to ensure that his decisions are the ones that prevail. He can advise his campus constituency that a decision is mandated by the central administration, and at the same time misinterpret or distort the concerns of the campus constituencies. Even if he does not succumb to these temptations he will soon be suspected of doing so by other groups.

The alternative to routing all campus policy recommendations through the chief administrator is to establish separate channels for policy formulation. The central administration can establish district representative bodies for each of the distinct campus constituencies. Policy recommendations received through administrative channels can also be received through an organization selected by the faculty members of each unit. A similar process can be established for the students. These steps ensure that each campus constituency receives a full and fair hearing at the central administration and board level.

The use of district-wide organizations to formulate policy for faculty, students, or administrators does not negate the need for a campus system, although it will impose some restraints on the functions of such bodies. Obviously, the board and central administration will negotiate with the district faculty organization in matters involving salaries and working conditions. There are many other matters, however, which can and should be left to the discretion of each unit. While alternate channels must exist, if for no other reason than to lend credibility to campus procedures, care can be exercised by central administration to discourage the use of such channels to solve problems that are better left to campus governance procedures.

The question might be raised concerning the desirability of a system forum where the various district representative organizations could come together to review matters of importance to the entire system. Because of the lack of practical evidence, we would prefer to suspend judgment on the feasibility of this approach at present. Representative governance seems to work most effectively when the policy formulators are chosen directly by the constituency, and where there is involvement of a substantial percentage of the constituency being represented. It works less well when the representatives choose representatives, although this may be necessary under some conditions. The best procedure would seem to place the responsibility for making the decisions which affect a specific campus as close as possible to those who are a part of that campus community.

At the same time, system organizations for each constituency can provide a process of checks and balances to ensure that power remains distributed, and to prevent individuals in key positions from manipulating governance procedures to serve their own ends. Ideally, the recommendations carried forward to district organizations will originate with and receive the endorsement of campus constituencies. The possibilities of responsiveness and flexibility are much enhanced when three distinct channels tell the same story to the central office. It is one thing for the central office to counter the recommendations of a chief campus administrator; it is quite another to overcome recommendations endorsed by district organizations composed of faculty, students, and administrators. Finally, even if the answer is negative, the chief campus administrator benefits from having some assistance in explaining this decision to his campus constituency. The central administration will benefit, too, by gaining a better understanding of the full impact of any decisions it may make.

A clear delineation of the limits of campus autonomy is essential to participational governance in a multi-institution district. These limits will of course vary for each system and will be related to the structure of administration. We can make one nonprescriptive observation in this area: there is likely to be a direct relationship between the amount of autonomy accorded the unit of a system and the level of tension that results. To the extent that a campus of a multi-institutional district is described as an independent college and staffed accordingly, it is encouraged to function as if the central administration and other campuses of the system were not significant constraints. Since it is apparent that the unit of a system must inevitably be regulated by and in turn contribute to the regulation of other units, it is essential that descriptions of campus governance stress interdependency between units at least as strongly as autonomy. The failure to achieve recognition of this interdependency in the structuring of governance units for the system contributes to the development of competition, resentment, and frustration among units and among constituencies. Size is just as much a mixed blessing for two-year colleges as it is for the university. It demands a considerable degree of sophistication and accommodation in the practices of each.

Having identified considerations related to the implementation of a system of participational governance for the multi-institution district, we can now examine in greater detail the characteristics of three levels of governance: the central forum, joint committees, and organizations of the constituencies. While our frame of reference has been the single-college district, what we have said about joint committee structures and organizations applies, within our previously defined limits, to the multi-institutional district.

The All-College Senate

The all-college senate provides a forum to discuss and resolve issues of concern to the entire college community. It is the focal point for proposals developed among the various constituencies which affect other members of the college community, and hence depend upon their concurrence for effective implementation. The all-college senate is the key decision-making body which determines the number, composition, and responsibilities of joint committees, and serves as the agency to which they report their findings and recommendations. In an important sense, the all-college senate legitimates the actions of the joint committees by providing an opportunity for representatives of all members of the college community to debate the actions of such committees, and to participate in deciding whether to accept, reject, or modify their actions. Institutions which lack an all-college senate have substantial difficulty in encouraging student participation on joint committees, since it is apparent that committee recommendations are then taken to bodies where students are systematically excluded, and where recommendations are decided away from direct student involvement.

As important as the preceding purposes are, the communication and improved understanding among constituencies resulting from the existence of a college senate may have even greater significance. Administrators, faculty members, and students form perceptions of each other based upon what they want to believe or what suits their convenience. The two-year college can best convey a distinct identity and a sense of philosophy to the members of its community through vigorous open debate of all the issues. Faculty members who would immediately ignore any administratively sponsored authority on two-year college philosophy will listen intently to discussions of philosophy, when they understand that at the termination of the discussion they will be expected to vote on an issue that will affect their future. Thus, the all-college senate becomes an important device for inservice education, stimulating people to examine and reshape their attitudes.

It must be noted, however, that any attempt to manipulate the activities of the all-college senate to accomplish the specific purposes of any one constituency will destroy its usefulness. It is only when renorming emerges as a natural consequence of involvement in the decision-making process that it becomes effective as an inservice device. Neither should the all-college senate be used for exchanging verbal announcements which could just as easily be transmitted in writing. The all-college senate is a deliberative body. The advantages of enhanced understanding and improved communication flow from the visible actions of the body serving in this capacity, and not from a conscious effort to achieve these results.

If the all-college senate is to convey an appropriate sense of equality among constituent groups, it is important that certain principles be observed in determining its composition. Perhaps most important is the concept of parity between students and faculty. Arguments to include more faculty than students are: the greater continuity of the former, the relative importance of professional as contrasted with student judgments, and extended implications of decisions for faculty compared with short range impact on students. Counter arguments include: the greater number of students, their central position in the educational process, and the contribution they make to paying the bills. The opposing arguments can only lead to stalemate, and the ultimate conclusion that, in the absence of any definitive evidence to the contrary, a better argument can be made for equal numbers of students and faculty than for either of the alternatives.

Administrative representation is an area where there is likely to be much more agreement—at least between faculty and students. Both groups will seek to limit administrative representation because of the past history of dominance by this group. While the answer to this issue will have to be negotiated by each campus, two general guidelines can be cited. Administrators in key decision-making roles need to be included both because of the information they can contribute and because of the need for their cooperation in the process of implementation. It must also be possible for administrators to serve at some time on the senate so that they do not feel victims of discriminatory practice.

The conditions defined above suggest the need for two categories of voting membership on the all-college senate, ex officio and elective. One possible distribution would include as ex officio members the president of the college, the vice-presidents, the president of the faculty association, a faculty representative to the board of trustees, the president of the student association and student representative to the board, the chairmen of all joint committees, and the chairmen of the associations of nonprofessional staff. We include representatives from the nonprofessional staff to recognize their contribution to the total college community. The elective membership of the all-college senate would include a sufficient number of students and faculty to balance ex officio assignments, as well as a limited number of vacancies that could be filled on a rotating basis by administrators not included in the ex officio category.

There is no simple answer to the question of size. While small groups function more effectively they are less representative. Each campus must determine its optimal arrangement. We would suggest not less than thirty nor more than fifty members. The choice of representatives must be left to constituent bodies. Student representatives should be chosen by the student senate and faculty representatives by the faculty association. Any attempt by one constituency to influence the choice of representatives by another will inevitably raise questions concerning the credibility of the body as an impartial agency for conflict resolution.

The functions of the all-college senate should be clearly defined and approved by board action. The bylaws of the senate should make it clear that decisions of this body will be reported to the board of trustees, whether or not such decisions have the concurrence of the president of the college. This does not mean that the president must be bound by these decisions; only that in instances where he chooses to act contrary to the will of the senate, the difference of opinion must be reported to the board with a full and fair review of the rationale supporting each position. The functions of the college senate should be sufficiently broad to include the entire range of institutional operation which might serve as a basis for controversy or conflict. The following list of responsibilities is representative of the functions that an all-college senate might assume:

1. Curricula addition, revision, or deletion
2. Admission standards for curricula
3. Requirements for degrees and certificates
4. Class size
5. Alterations in the academic calendar
6. Attendance policies
7. Provision of services to the community
8. The administrative structure of the college
9. Student affairs and activities
10. Evaluation procedures for administration, faculty, and students
11. Allocation of funds
12. Physical facilities
13. Establishment and responsibilities of joint committees
14. Periodic review of responsibilities and function of all-college senate.

It should be noted that the responsibilities of the senate in these areas is policy formulation and conflict resolution and not administration. Most matters related to policy implementation or interpretation will be resolved within the administrative structure of the college. It is only as significant differences of opinion arise or as new policies must be formulated that the college senate becomes involved. The listing of responsibilities is not intended to imply that the senate will be continuously involved in decision making in all of these areas. Rather, it is an attempt to define areas which have the potential for affecting the total college community. It also is intended to imply that policy additions or revisions for any of these areas will not be recommended to the board prior to review by the senate, and that the senate's decisions will always be made known to the board and will serve as a significant factor in its deliberations.

Joint Committees

A second element of the governance process is the network of joint committees which serve as working bodies to develop policies for consideration by the all-college senate. Such committees also serve in an advisory capacity to administrative offices to assist in making decisions in areas such as scholarship awards, admission criteria, and similar situations where it is desirable to have faculty and student input. The purpose of joint committees, then, is to investigate, advise, and recommend to the college senate and to appropriate administrative officers topics dealing with their assigned areas of responsibility.

It is important that all members of the college community be eligible to serve on all ad hoc and standing committees with full voting privileges. Those committees which deal with matters predominantly related to student concerns should have a majority of student members and a student chairman. Those committees dealing with issues of primary concern to the faculty should have a majority of faculty members and a faculty chairman. We would suggest that administrative representatives to these committees be appointed by the president of the college. Such representatives should be chosen so that committees related to a specific area of administrative concern have included among their membership the administrator who provides services for that area. The size of the committees should probably not exceed ten to fifteen. A defined process of rotation can ensure that all faculty members take their turn serving on college committees. This prevents some staff members from becoming overworked, while at the same time avoids the entrenched committee that becomes a barrier to change.

As in the case of the all-college senate, committee members should be selected by their respective constituencies. Committees should receive input through the administrative structure of the college, not serve as an alternative to administrative leadership. Arrangements should be made so that policy recommendations developed by a specific committee are circulated to members of the college senate well in advance of the date on which they are expected to take action. Committee meetings should be open to all members of the college community and the agenda of such committees should be published sufficiently far in advance so that any individual who has a specific interest in an issue can be given appropriate consideration. It goes without saying that minutes should be kept of all committee deliberations, and these minutes should receive the widest possible circulation. It is helpful if each committee is required to provide a written report on an annual basis summarizing its efforts for the preceding year. Not only do these annual reports require a certain amount of self-examination, but they also provide guidance to future committees.

In a previous section of this chapter, we suggested an arrangement that would include five joint standing committees of the college. In general, we would favor keeping the number of committees small. In many institutions, committees proliferate to the point where faculty members may be serving on two or three or more. A small number of committees with specifically defined responsibilities provides much more effective involvement in the governance process than a larger number of committees, some of which do not function at all. While it is our continuing desire to avoid being prescriptive, it may be helpful to illustrate the way in which joint committees function if we provide a review of the membership and functions of the five committee arrangement previously described.

Curriculum Committee

Composition: A representative of each division, a member of the student personnel staff, a member of the Learning Resources Center staff, a member of the allied health program staff, and three students. The president of the college may designate an additional member. The chairman shall be a faculty member.

Functions

1. To recommend new policies or courses of action as needed.
2. To concern itself generally with the educational policies governing the programs of the college and with their appropriateness as means to the realization of the educational objectives of the college.
3. To review new curricula, programs, departments, and courses, or changes, and to report its recommendations to the college senate for action.
4. To review the existing curricula, programs, departments, and courses, and to make such recommendations as seem desirable.
5. To review and evaluate the number, descriptions, credit hours, contract hours, and prerequisites of courses.

Instructional Resources Committee

Composition: Five faculty members, Director of Learning Resources Center, and three student members. The chairman shall be a faculty member. The president of the college may designate an additional member.

Functions

1. To review new developments in educational technology and to provide information to the faculty concerning such developments. To arrange for demonstrations when this may be appropriate.
2. To develop and recommend to the faculty, procedures for ensuring the

acquisition, availability, and use of a well-balanced collection of books, periodicals, and other instructional materials.

3. To stimulate proposals for innovative approaches to the educational objectives of the college, and to review proposals involving requests for released time. Recommendations concerning such proposals shall be made available to division chairmen and administrators for their guidance.

4. To study and recommend to the college senate methods of collecting information for the evaluation of instruction.

5. To recommend to the college senate revisions of existing policy or developments of new policy to facilitate implementation of the above described responsibilities.

Academic Standards Committee

Composition: Five faculty members and five student members. The president of the college may designate an additional member. The chairman shall be a faculty member.

Functions

1. To concern itself with all questions pertaining to high academic standards, criteria for admission to career and transfer curricula, development of policies for the evaluation of transfer credit, the awarding of honors and academic probation.

2. To act as a board of review for petitions by students or faculty requesting modification of graduation requirements, by students seeking readmission, and by students requesting a reevaluation of transfer of credit.

3. To act as a policy-making body for the allocation of financial aid. To recommend policies for the allocation of scholarship funds, grants in aid and long-term loan funds.

4. To make recommendations to the college senate in connection with policies concerning the foregoing responsibilities.

5. To assume responsibility for the formulation of policies and guidelines concerning the commencement program.

6. To prepare and recommend to the college senate the annual academic calendar.

Student Affairs Committee

Composition: Five student members and four faculty members. The president of the college may designate an additional member. The chairman shall be a student member.

Functions

1. To consider requests for recognition by campus student organizations and to make recommendations to the student senate concerning the type of recognition to be granted.

2. To review the activities of student organizations annually and make recommendations for the withdrawal of recognition on the basis of inactivity or failure to observe the conditions of their bylaws.

3. To serve as an advisory board to the student newspaper. In this capacity, the committee shall endeavor to encourage journalistic responsibility. In the event that an editor fails to exercise responsibility, the committee may take steps to impeach or remove him after holding hearings and according due process rights.

Recommendations involving removal of a student editor shall be provided at the request of the faculty advisor to the student newspaper or the president of the college.

4. To serve as a review board with respect to choice of speakers. The names of individuals to be invited to speak on campus for other than classroom situations shall be provided to the dean of student personnel services prior to the time that any invitation is isued. In the event that the choice of speaker is questioned, the matter shall be referred to this committee. The recommendations of the committee will be reported to the president of the college for final disposition.

5. To make recommendations to the college senate regarding policies and their implementation in the cocurricular affairs of students. The committee may also consider and make recommendations concerning problems and practices, new services or such other matters related to cocurricular activities as may be brought before it by members of the student association, faculty, or administration.

6. To serve as a review board for requests for the replacement of faculty advisors. The recommendations of the committee will be reported to the president of the college for final disposition.

Cultural Affairs Committee

Composition: Six student members and three faculty members with provision that the president of the college may designate an additional member. The chairman may be either a faculty or a student member.

Functions

1. To outline the annual calendar of cultural events for the ensuing academic year.

2. To coordinate and recommend to the college senate all cultural activities that are to be held on or off the campus on a college scale including films, lectures, seminars, and art exhibits.

3. To work closely with the social activities committee in planning a well-balanced program of events for the academic year.

It is apparent that the joint committees, serving as an interface between separate constituencies and the all-college senate, hold administrative and policy-formulating responsibilities. Serving in this dual capacity, the committees receive input from all constituencies as well as from individuals within those constituencies. In addition, each committee may initiate a review of its own functions, or may in exercising its investigatory powers define a need for policy revision and initiate a response to that need from among its own membership. The institution must recognize, however, that college administration cannot be accomplished through committees, and such bodies should not be regarded as an alternative to normal administrative structure.

Organizations of Constituencies

FACULTY ORGANIZATION. Our basic premise provides for an organization of faculty which will exclude administrators. Administrators are defined as those individuals who supervise and evaluate the work of other professionals. Thus instructors, counselors, librarians, and other specialists on the professional staff will be included. It is of paramount importance that the faculty organization include as broad a representation as possible. Institutions which seek to prevent the development of separate faculty organizations may retard their development temporarily; however, when the organization does come into existence, it may well develop abrasive relationships with the administration because of its experience during the formative period. If administrators sought to use power to prevent the development of a faculty organization, then that organization will seek to use the power of numbers and the power of legislation in its relationship with administration. If, on the other hand, administration has served in a facilitative role during the development of the faculty organization, the basis may exist for future cooperation in other areas.

From our point of view, it is less important whether the organization of the faculty be an independent faculty organization, a faculty union, or an affiliate of the National Education Association. Despite the title of the group, its first concern is likely to be the welfare and security of its membership. To the extent that this welfare and security can be guaranteed without the need to resort to outside agencies on the part of either the association or the board, the relationships that are involved will be much less complex and probably will provide more satisfactory answers for the college community.

The organization should also be concerned with the professional interests and general welfare of its members, and with the dissemination of information that will enhance the faculty members' awareness and their ability to participate meaningfully in the governance process. As an aspect of security, the organization can be expected to represent its members in any difference of opinion that may develop concerning salary increments, grievances, or dismissals. The association will also seek an active role in negotiations involving salaries, fringe benefits, and working conditions.

It is interesting to note that the strongest and most obstructive faculty organizations have invariably developed in situations where boards have been the most reluctant to share their authority with members of the faculty, and where administrators have persisted in authoritarian behavior. Faculties have sought outside help from union organizations and from NEA affiliates to combat conditions created by the actions of boards and administrators. Faculty organizations will continue to rely upon outside agencies to the extent that this is made necessary by the actions of the boards themselves.

Once developed, there are two basic roles that a faculty organization may take in relation to the administraton and the board. The first, and most common, is an adversary role. The adversary relationship rests upon the assumption that decision making within the institution is a zero-sum game, that whatever the faculty gains represents a loss for the administration and vice versa. There is little question that faculty organizations in most institutions are in an adversary position. We should like to theorize, however, that while this is the most common course of action, it is not an inevitable one.

It is possible for a faculty organization to be integrated within the governance structure of the institution. Such an organization can assume all of the normal functions of any faculty organization including security and welfare, while at the same time becoming a significant force for encouraging professional responsibility. The same committee of the faculty association that serves to support faculty members in their grievances against administration under an adversary relationship can also serve to support administrators in their grievances against faculty under a participatory approach. We would distinguish, then, between the adversary relationship, which is a natural consequence of the bureaucratic relationships within an institution, and the interdependent relationships that can develop between a faculty association and the other constituencies of the institution when the tenets of participatory governance are followed.

There is nothing particularly mysterious about integrating a faculty association within the governance structure of an institution. One starts with an analysis of all the points that the faculty might win if they resorted to an external agency such as a faculty union or an NEA affiliate. If these rights can be won through external affiliation, then the institution should be able to develop a procedure to grant these rights through internal decision making. A faculty that can achieve the ends which it considers important within the governance structure of an institution will have no motivation to go outside that structure. Furthermore, the absence of external influence in the area of internal governance, combined with a reduction in the adversary nature of the development of a faculty organization, can have a positive effect on the entire governance process. This is not to say that differences of opinion will not develop, will not be hotly debated, and will not erupt in attempts by constituencies to bring every influence they have to bear on a specific decision. It is to say that given appropriate internal procedures, these differences of opinion can be resolved by those who are most directly affected rather than by external agencies which may lack necessary information to determine the best approach to the institution.

We believe that a college should take every possible step to avoid the development of adversary relationships between internal constituencies. The solution is obviously not the development of company unions. This policy will be no more successful in education than it has proven in industry. Rather, trustees and administrators must delegate to a faculty association, whose membership and responsibilities are defined by the faculty themselves, the responsibilities and authority that faculty unions have been successful in winning for faculty members in two-year colleges across the country. The process of contributing to the realization of faculty objectives rather than attempting to stifle them can create the kind of relationship between the administration and the faculty that will make it possible for them to interact on a positive and continuing basis for effective policy formulation and implementation.

STUDENT ORGANIZATION. We have talked of the organization of the faculty and suggested that administration should adopt a facilitative role with respect to such organizations and create conditions whereby administration and faculty can work together in a mutually dependent relationship. We have also suggested that the faculty organization be given encouragement and assistance in its development in order to obviate the necessity of an appeal for external assistance. The development of strong student organizations is not inevitable by any means, and if such organizations are to develop, particularly within the context of the two-year college, strong administrative leadership will be required. From our point of view, it is even more important to assist the students to organize for participation in governance than it is to assist the faculty.

Because faculty organizations will develop and come to exercise great power, the question that must be answered is, "How can student rights be protected?" In the bureaucratic structure, the answer to this question was, "The administration and the board will make certain that the objectives of the organization are responsive to student needs." Given the possibility of administrative and faculty structures cast in an adversary role, the absence of a strong and viable student organization implies issues will be resolved on the basis of administrative and faculty concessions and priorities rather than on student needs. There is a strong possibility that the college may become even less responsive to student interests and needs where adversary relationships exist between faculty and administration than in the least flexible bureaucratic structures of the faculty preorganization era.

We may conclude, then, that providing students with a strong and viable organization is indispensable to a respect for their rights within the context of the participational model which we have postulated. It is apparent that the majority of students will have neither the inclination nor the time to become involved extensively in institutional governance. Consequently, we shall need to rely upon some type of representative structure. One of the criticisms most commonly leveled against student governments is that they are not representative. Certainly one answer to this problem is contained in the report of the Study Commission for the University of California at Berkeley (7). The composition of the representative student body must be based upon defined constituencies. The at-large elections of student representatives which are so typical of most two-year colleges fail to take into consideration the need to have an individual responsible to the needs of subgroups within the college.

The student senate should be so organized as to occupy a position within the college governance structure parallel to that occupied by the faculty association. While it is possible to define the areas of responsibility which should be accorded students—and this has been done—it should be noted that students may exhibit little concern for many of the areas where theoretically they should have substantial interest, and a great deal of concern about other areas where theoretically they should have little or no involvement (6:36). The safest answer to a definition of areas in which students should be involved is to assert that they have a right to be involved in any area which affects them. The immediately cited reference article suggests that faculty appointment, reappointment, promotion to higher rank, termination, and tenure should be the exclusive concern of the administrative officers and faculty committees. Since then, student demonstrations have occurred specifically directed toward these issues.

In addition to a concern with those areas of responsibility previously defined for the all-college senate, the student senate, must, therefore, have a right to determine its own affairs, insofar as these do not conflict with the interests of other college constituencies. This implies that the student senate should have the right to fix the activity fee and to approve the allocation of this fee subject only to the principles of sound financial management. It also implies that the student senate should have significant responsibility with respect to the regulation of conduct, and that administration and faculty should not become involved in student discipline unless there is a need to hold student organizations accountable for a failure to deal satisfactorily with significant problems.

Thus it can be seen that the student senate, like the faculty association, must inevitably become something of a welfare and security organization for its membership. It will also serve to focus attention upon student concerns and can provide the means through which student interests are protected in deliberations involving them.

The test of effectiveness of student participation is not the number of students who participate in the routine decision-making procedures of the institution; students are notorious for their absence from deliberations considered of no significant concern to their perceived interests. The real test involves how students respond when they feel that their legitimate interests are being threatened. If the structures that exist are utilized, then there is evidence of faith on the part of students in their ability to induce change through legitimate channels. If, on the other hand, it becomes necessary for students to go outside of established channels, then the institution can safely assume that students lack confidence in the degree of access that has been afforded to them in the decision-making process.

ADMINISTRATIVE ORGANIZATION. We have discussed previously the structure of administration. It may seem odd that there is a requirement for a corresponding governance structure within the organization itself, unless the reader understands that we are discussing an interface between the structure of administration and the structure of governance. This interface, which will be discussed in greater detail in the next chapter, requires a different kind of organization from that which serves the purposes of administration.

There is a need for three kinds of coordinating and policy-formulating bodies within the administrative staff. The first of these we may designate administrative staff, or, alternatively, the president's cabinet. The administrative staff exchanges information and resolves internal differences that may impair efficient staff functioning. In a sense, the administrative staff serves as the executive committee of administration. If we understand that administration is no longer dependent upon individual personalities, but rather represents a group process, then it is apparent that a central coordinating structure must exist to keep administrators informed of the activities of other administrators and to provide general direction for administrators in relating to both internal and external constituencies. Membership on the administrative staff may range from a number as limited as the president and his second echelon staff to a much larger group involving all of the major administrators of the college. Under either arrangement, the administrative staff can provide key advisory services to the president and influence the professional growth and development of its membership.

A second type of administrative body may be termed the administrative council. It is normally the purpose of the administrative council to formulate and review policies pertaining to the administration of the college. The membership of the administrative council is broader than that of the administrative staff, and usually includes division chairmen as well as representatives from the faculty association and the student association. Because of the broad representation on the administrative council there may be a temptation for this body to engage in decision-making that should more appropriately be left to the all-college senate, and care must be exercised in defining the responsibilities of the council to limit this possibility.

It should be noted also that the administrative council should not serve as a funnel through which the recommendations of the various committees are sent to the all-college senate. While the council may provide a monitoring function by ensuring that matters referred to committees do not get lost, the council, insofar as it is possible, should stay away from any attempt to reach decisions in areas that have been delegated to organizations such as the faculty association, the student senate, or the combination of these in the all-college senate.

A description of the responsibilities of an administrative council might include the following:

1. The development and periodic review of institutional objectives.
2. The determination of priorities as they relate to the allocation of institutional resources.
3. The planning to achieve institutional objectives.
4. The review of proposed administrative structure, policy, and procedures.
5. The evaluation of the effectiveness of existing administrative structure, policies, and procedures.
6. The allocation of financial resources.
7. The development of physical facilities.
8. The relationship of the college to its constituencies.
9. The resolution of problems involving the coordination of staff organization.

It is apparent that one of the most important functions of the administrative council is to provide staff members who do not normally have direct access to the president with an opportunity to influence his position on matters involving policy formulation. It is important that the administrative council take minutes and distribute or make them available to all members of the college community. A failure to disseminate widely the activities and actions of the administrative council will inevitably lead to distrust and suspicion from faculty and students.

The final type of administrative grouping is one that we choose to call the council of deans and division chairmen. This group functions with respect to the administrative council as the joint committees of the college function with respect to the all-college senate. It is an implementing body rather than a policy-formulating body, although it will inevitably develop policy recommendations as a part of its attempt to coordinate administrative activities in all areas of college functioning. The council of deans and division chairmen normally includes among its membership the second echelon administrators, appropriate representatives from their staff, and division chairmen.

The council of deans and division chairmen, operating within the framework of policies approved by appropriate bodies, would consider and take action in the following areas:

1. College publications, public information, and advertising.
2. The recruitment of professional staff members.

3. Recommendations concerning employment, advancement, retention, or changes in work load for professional staff members.
4. Programs of orientation and professional development.
5. Class schedules and final examination schedules.
6. The annual budget.
7. Evaluation of curricula and recommendations for new curricula.
8. Proposal for support from state, federal, or private agencies.
9. Institutional research and computer services.
10. Student services.

The council of deans and division chairmen is a working body concerned with the coordination, articulation, and communication necessary to the efficient operation of the administrative structure of the college. When discussion reveals the existence of differences of opinion that cannot be resolved to the mutual satisfaction of those concerned, or when such discussion reveals a need for a review of existing, or the development of new policy guidelines, the items concerned are normally referred to the administrative council. As in the case of the administrative council, it is extremely important that the council of deans and division chairmen keep minutes, and that these minutes be given wide dissemination among those affected. This enables other constituencies whose interest may be involved to review such activities and raise questions when the need arises.

NONPROFESSIONAL STAFF ORGANIZATION. The recognition of the right for specific college constituencies to participate in the governance process seems to be an evolving process. Historically, the initial assumption was that the governance process of the institution should be under the direction of the board of trustees and the administration. More recently, we have come to the conclusion that faculty members have an appropriate role in governance. Subsequent to the recognition of the faculty role, we have become concerned with the involvement of students. To this point, there has been little attention given to those members of the college community who do not fit into one of the three major constituencies.

All institutions have a significant group of staff members employed to provide support in clerical services, maintenance, custodial services, and business services. These staff members are as indispensable to the operation of the institution as any of the groups about whom we have previously written. Yet it does not seem at this point that much attention has been given to how they may be included in the process of governance. For the sake of convenience we shall term those employees of the college not considered members of the professional administrative staff as classified employees.

As soon as a college employs any significant number of classified staff members, it can expect that attempts will be made to unionize the staff members by categories. One of the first groups to organize under normal conditions is the custodial staff. It is much less common for white-collar employees and members of the clerical staff to become unionized, although there is a good chance, in an institution that is undergoing the throes of organization among faculty and student constituencies, for such staff members to seek their own organization.

We would consider it most desirable for the classified staff to have their own associations. Whether the association becomes affiliated with external agencies may be of less importance than the kind of relationship that exists between the associations and the administration of the college. The most common pattern with respect to classified staff is administration by crisis. The major attention of the institution is focused upon faculty and students, with the result that little attention is given to the needs of the custodial or clerical staffs until severe problems have developed to threaten the morale, and hence the continued effectiveness, of this part of the college community.

Associations of the classified staff can help to focus attention upon impending problems so that solutions are reached before the development of crises. Associations which are given formal recognition help staff members develop a sense of their importance as viewed by the rest of the college community. While the concerns of the classified staff do not normally coincide with the major issues that must be resolved between faculty, students, and administration, there is still a need for communication. Consequently, we would recommend representation of the classified staff associations on the all-college senate primarily for purposes of communication and recognition.

There is seldom a need for representatives of the classified staff to serve on joint committees of the college, although in some instances they can and do make significant contributions. It is apparent that this area of governance is evolving, and that it may well become the next major area of concern after problems involving faculty and students are brought to some level of control. We would argue that the classified staff deserves far more attention and involvement in the governance process than they have received to this point.

SUMMARY

In this chapter, we have suggested the need for a process that parallels the structure of administration. We have given this process the title "governance." We have attempted to show that the governance process has a structure quite as distinct as that defined for administration.

The components of the structure of governance include an all-college senate, joint standing committees of the college, and an organization representing each of the various constituencies of the college. We have suggested that the three major constituencies of the college are administration, faculty, and students. Each of these constituencies will define the boundaries for membership and its own internal organization. The internal organization for faculty and administration is likely to be an organization of the whole, although matters involving relationships with other constituencies and planning will be done by an executive committee.

The student constituency, both because of its size and because of the diversity of interests represented, will normally utilize a representative organization. The process of developing this organization to a point of parity with the structures for governance of the faculty and the administration requires significant administrative leadership. By the same token a failure to develop strong patterns of student involvement may leave institutions without the means of responding to legitimate student interests.

While most of our attention was focused upon the three major constituencies of the college, the need for providing an appropriate organization for the involvement of employees other than professional administrators and faculty in the governance process was suggested as an emerging concern.

While it is probable that most institutions will move in the direction of adversary relationships between the various constituencies, this is by no means an inevitable or irreversible process. Proper attention to the structure of governance and the establishment of credible decision-making bodies can turn the concern for involvement on the part of students, faculty, and classified staff into a powerful force for institutional adaptation to societal change.

REFERENCES

1. CORSON, JOHN J., *Governance of Colleges and Universities.* New York: McGraw-Hill, 1960.

2. DEEGAN, WILLIAM L., KARL O. DREXEL, JOHN K. COLLINS, and DOROTHY KEARNEY, "Student Participation in Governance," *Junior College Journal,* 41:14–22 (November 1970).

3. KEETON, MORRIS, *Shared Authority on Campus.* Washington, D. C.: Association for Higher Education, 1971.

4. PARSONS, TALCOTT, "The Strange Case of Academic Organization," *Journal of Higher Education,* 42:486–95 (June 1971).

5. RICHARDSON, RICHARD C., JR., "Policy Formulation in the Two-Year College: Renaissance or Revolution?" *Junior College Journal,* 37:40–42 (March 1967).

6. RICHARDSON, RICHARD C., JR., "Recommendations on Student Rights and Freedoms," *Junior College Journal,* 39:34–44 (February 1969).

7. *The Culture of the University Governance in Education,* Report of the Study Commission on University Governance. Berkeley: University of California Press, 1968.

ten

The Dynamics
of
Interaction

The administrative structure exists to provide the means whereby an institution may achieve certain types of objectives. The nature of administrative organization provides for specialization, coordination, communication, and control. The administrative structure is responsible for long-range planning and for the implementation of programs through the allocation of resources. Administrative decisions provide direction, establish constraints, and contribute to the definition of roles for all who belong to the organization. In the process of carrying out these and other functions, tensions are created which, if not equitably resolved, can ultimately set in motion forces that may seriously attenuate or even destroy the effectiveness of institutional endeavor.

To deal with the forces set in motion by the administrative structure, institutions develop a system of governance which has as its principle function the sharing of authority among the internal constituents, establishing a system of checks and balances which will prevent the administrative structure from dominating the decision-making process. Ideally, the components of the college governance system will not function in an adversary role, but will be integrated through the decision-making process.

It is possible to understand the subdivisions of an organization without having an awareness of how these entities function in relation to one another, or how their individual contributions become a part of the larger totality. In this concluding chapter we will address ourselves to this problem by examining several areas of interaction, identifying policies that protect the interests of those affected, and also provide for the orderly resolution of differences.

In the discussion which follows, it is important to recognize that institutional processes can never be defined in such a way as to make them exclusively the province of administration or of the governance structures. It is the effectiveness with which the two structures interact that determines the quality of institutional response both to its environment and to the needs of its constituencies.

ESTABLISHING GOALS AND EVALUATING OUTCOMES

Most two-year colleges develop a general set of objectives growing out of a basic philosophy of education at an early point in their history. Henceforth, such objectives receive little attention except in relation to visits from regional accrediting associations, when an attempt is made to relate them to descriptive data collected after the fact to demonstrate that objectives are indeed being met. Unfortunately, the objectives normally are not defined in such a way as to make them effective in guiding institutional development. Neither do they receive the regular review and evaluation by all constituencies that could make them a vital force in the renorming process.

Each institution needs to establish performance objectives which can become a source of direction for staff efforts as well as the basis for determining the effectiveness with which resources are used. It is not enough for a college to commit itself to offering career programs. Ideally, this objective should be phrased in terms of the total percentage of enrollment to be served by such programs, the relationship of these programs to the manpower needs of the community, and the actual number of positions to be filled by program graduates. In a similar fashion, an objective concerning guidance services should identify the kinds of problems to which counselors will address themselves, as well as the anticipated results. Obviously, the preparation of objectives which lend themselves to this type of evaluation will not be easy for many areas, but the effort must be made if objectives are to serve as a yardstick for evaluation and improvement.

The sources of institutional objectives include both external and internal constituencies. Enabling legislation normally defines minimum services and general mission. Regional accrediting associations have expectations for each type of institution and thus establish guidelines for performance in a variety of areas as well as providing constraining influences based on the biases of those who provide consulting services and who are members of evaluation teams. The professional associations, through influence of literature and position statements, also provide inputs. Expectations of the local community as reflected by boards, advisory committees, and informal contacts also play a significant role.

In addition to influences from external constituencies, the attitudes and expectations of administrators, faculty, and students make a significant contribution to goal definition. Just as the quality of institutional life is a function of the effectiveness of interaction between internal structures, the quality of institutional objectives depends upon the effectiveness with which the needs and expectations of external constituencies are related to the attitudes and resources of internal constituencies. Once again, the focus of the process must be upon mediation, with information flowing in both directions to contribute to attitudinal change.

The development, periodic review, and revision of objectives at the institutional level is only the starting point. Each functional level within the administrative structure must also define specific objectives to guide the employment of resources and to provide a means for evaluation. This is the point which most institutions fail to grasp, and it leads to a number of undesirable consequences. A failure to develop clear and attainable objectives at each operating level permits staff offices to pursue different and in some instances conflicting priorities. It contributes to an emphasis upon the personality of role incumbents rather than the needs served by the office. It makes evaluation difficult or impossible, and it creates the environment for innumerable intrainstitutional conflicts.

The requirement that each operating level extending to and including the individual faculty member develop objectives expressed in behavioral terms leads to at least two significant refinements in management practices. The first involves the opportunity to review the objectives and priorities at each level, ensuring that they are consistent with the objectives and priorities of the total institution. The second refinement has been referred to as management by objectives. Once a staff function has established quantifiable objectives which have been reviewed and endorsed by appropriate constituencies, the objectives become a form of contract between the office and the institution and can be used to measure contribution and effectiveness. Some schemes for management by objectives relate a system of rewards to goal achievement, but this practice is not essential to the use of the concept.

Job descriptions have sometimes been equated with objectives for a specific office or individual. Obviously, traditional job descriptions bear the same relationship to operational objectives that traditional statements of institutional philosophy and objectives bear to the type of guidelines used to direct the deployment of institutional resources and evaluate effectiveness. Job descriptions lack precision and are not normally defined in terms of anticipated consequences. In the effort to be inclusive, they fail to provide a sense of institutional priorities. Odiorne identifies three types of objectives which can be defined in behavioral terms (8). He describes routine objectives as those recurring daily. Problem-solving objectives are those which depend upon the identification of specific areas of difficulty and which establish priorities for the employment of resources. Innovative objectives are designed to focus the attention of the office or individual on the need for adaptation, and also serve as a continuing impetus for change.

PROCESS OF GOAL DEFINITION, IMPLEMENTATION, AND EVALUATION

Our primary concern rests with the process by which goals are defined, since this provides an opportunity to demonstrate interaction between the dual structures. The first step involves a study of designated offices within the administrative structure, including community needs as well as constraints that may be imposed by budgetary considerations. Prominent in the review of available data is evaluative information concerning past performance and institutional strengths and weaknesses. From the study of available data, new objectives and priorities are formulated on a tentative basis. Such objectives are then prepared for review by the total administrative structure through the administrative council. Once approved by this body, objectives are transmitted through council representatives to the faculty and student organizations for review.

The proposed objectives now move to the central forum where an opportunity is afforded for interpretation and compromise. Following appropriate discussion, objectives are formally adopted for transmittal to the board of trustees. While the objectives of the institution seldom become the cause of much controversy, review and formal adoption force consideration of institutional objectives by the faculty and student constituencies, and in the process create an awareness that would not otherwise exist. Moreover, if institutional objectives are defined to make priorities clearly evident, they may, in the context of limited resources, become the focus of meaningful discussion.

The process by which the governing board reviews institutional objectives provides an opportunity for input from the external community.

Equally important, the periodic review of objectives can be instrumental in focusing the attention of the trustees on the purposes for which the institution exists. Once trustees commit themselves to a specific set of priorities for institutional resources, they are less likely to respond hastily to external influences which may develop intense pressures for brief periods. Clearly defined objectives become a contract between trustees and the college, representing consensus on what the institution should be directing the greatest emphasis.

The contract remains in effect for a limited period of time, and revisions are made with the same involvement that characterized the initial definition. The flow of information and proposals between the administrative organization, the structure of governance, and the controlling body creates a series of opportunities for error correction, compromise, and attitudinal change.

Performance objectives must also be identified for each major subdivision of the institution. Such objectives are reviewed both at the level to which the subdivision reports and by the constituency which it serves. In this way, multidirectional accountability and expectations are communicated and enhanced. For example, the objectives of the office of instruction need the the review of both the chief executive and the instructional staff. The objectives of the teaching division need input from the office of instruction as well as from faculty and students. The development and review of objectives for operating units is primarily a function of the administrative structure, with involvement of the governance structure reserved for issues involving priorities or resource allocation.

A central part of goal definition is the development of criteria that will serve to determine the extent to which goals have been achieved. In addition, attention must be paid to the nature of data that will be collected to support criteria, as well as to the means for collecting, reporting, and interpreting such data. Advance agreement on procedures for evaluation makes two essential contributions to the improvement of institutional effectiveness. It insures against the practice of collecting data after the fact to support biases; at the same time it sets the goal definition and evaluation cycle on a continuing basis (3:107-25).

Evaluative data is the only reliable source for establishing new goals. As information concerning the consequences of employing certain resources becomes available, it is shared with the governance structure and with the board. New objectives are formulated and serve to confirm or revise institutional direction. The development of management information systems should have great impact on the process of management by objectives. Obviously, new decisions can only be as effective as the quality and comprehensiveness of the data upon which they are based. The use of the computer to summarize and report complete parameters of institutional performance should constitute a significant management tool in the seventies and beyond.

Individual Goals

In the preceding discussion, our attention has been focused on the development of objectives for the institution, its major subdivisions, and the concept that management by objectives must pervade the entire organization. In order to complete the last quadrant of the circle, we must now look at the individual. The discussions of human behavior in Chapter 4, and the principle of administration by integration and self-control in Chapter 5, make it clear that the process of defining objectives is applicable to the guidance and evaluation of individual performance.

A procedure for evaluation, if it is to promote maximum professional growth, must place upon the individual the major responsibility for establishing objectives and assessing the extent to which these objectives are achieved. It is the responsibility of the office to which the individual reports to maintain interaction between individual and institution to insure consistency of goals. The governance structure, in rare instances, may be required to mediate differences between the individual and the administration, but most of the responsibility for the evaluation procedure rests within the administrative structure. The following minimum requirements of a satisfactory evaluation procedure are:

1. Performance objectives must be established. Each individual must define what he intends to do so that it is possible to determine whether or not objectives are attained.
2. The determination of the degree to which objectives are achieved must be based upon both external evidence and intrinsic satisfaction. External evidence is required in order to determine the degree to which service has been rendered to others, while intrinsic satisfaction is an indicator of needs satisfaction for the professional.
3. The system of evaluation must contain built-in procedures to identify outstanding practitioners, and to protect the institution and its constituents against unethical or incompetent practitioners.

Criteria for Faculty Evaluation

In order to develop a system of evaluation which places the responsibility for both goal determination and performance evaluation on the individual, guidelines must exist to assist the individual in developing objectives and evaluating performance within the context of institutional goals. In this way, guidelines and evaluative criteria encourage compatibility between the objectives of the institution and those of the individual. Possible criteria along with potential performance measures for a member of the teaching faculty might include the following:

1. Client satisfaction (students)
   a. Use of anonymous rating questionnaire
   b. Interviews
   c. ˙Retention rate
   d. Willingness to enroll in other courses taught by the instructor
2. Effectiveness in the Learning Process
   a. Objective evidence of measurable growth by students toward predetermined objectives
   b. Use of effective innovation in the learning process
   c. Use of anonymous student rating questionnaire
   d. Use of classroom visitations by qualified members of the professional staff
3. Effectiveness in Advising Students
   a. Number of hours available for individual assistance
   b. Number of students seeking individual assistance
   c. Student perceptions of the value of the assistance received
   d. Statement from student personnel services on quality of advising
4. Productivity
   a. Student contact hours
   b. Student credit hours
   c. Number of preparations
   d. New courses developed
5. Contribution to Student Life
   a. Student activities, organized or sponsored
   b. Advisor or representative to student government
   c. Participation or planning assistance to student sponsored events
6. Contribution to College Service
   a. Committee membership
   b. Participation in college senate meetings or activities
   c. Administrative responsibilities
7. Community Service
   a. Participation in community activities or organizations
   b. Presentations to community groups
   c. Assistance to the community service program
8. Professional Growth
   a. Membership in professional organizations
   b. Attendance at workshops, conferences, or seminars
   c. Advanced graduate work
   d. Special recognition or honors

Procedure for Faculty Evaluation

The following procedure can be used to guide the evaluation process.

1. *Developing Objectives*
   Prior to the beginning of an evaluation period, an individual defines his objectives for that period. Objectives are developed in accordance with criteria previously specified and should be stated so that a determination can be made concerning the extent to which they are achieved.
2. *Establishing Priorities*
   Some objectives will be more important than others. Accordingly, the second step involves grouping objectives according to priorities so that in

the event it becomes apparent that not all can be accomplished within a given period, a basis exists for choosing the objectives to be emphasized.

3. *Planning and Organizing*

The individual must develop a strategy for the accomplishment of his objectives. The essential elements of the strategy include planning and organization. Planning refers to the development of a series of intermediate steps which, if successfully implemented, will lead to the ultimate achievement of objectives. Organization involves the determination of how the resources of the individual will be deployed at each stage of the process.

4. *Preliminary Review*

After objectives have been stated, priorities assigned, and a strategy for the achievement of objectives devised, the next step involves a review of objectives, priorities, and planning with the division chairman. This is accomplished by filing a statement followed by a personal interview. Essentially, the purpose of the interview is to enable the faculty member and the division chairman to determine the answers to the following questions:

a. Are the objectives realistic? Ideally, goals should be sufficiently high to require growth but not so high as to be impossible to accomplish.

b. Have the objectives been stated in such a way that a determination can be made concerning the extent to which they are accomplished? Have satisfactory procedures for evaluation of goal achievement been defined?

c. Are the priorities established consistent with the needs of the institution and designed to promote the growth of the individual?

5. *Implementation*

Once the division chairman and the faculty member have reached agreement on objectives, priorities, and methods of evaluation, the statement becomes an agreement between the institution and the faculty member clearly defining the institution's expectations of the staff member and the basis for determining the extent to which expectations are carried out.

6. *Evaluation*

The responsibility for collecting and interpreting evaluative data rests primarily with the faculty member. Using the procedures previously agreed upon, he makes a determination of the level at which objectives have been achieved. The statement of goal achievement along with supporting data is forwarded to the division chairman at an appropriate date.

7. *Final Review*

The division chairman reviews the statement of goal achievement and supporting data. Then an interview is scheduled for a review of the materials submitted and to provide the division chairman with an opportunity to raise questions or to provide feedback. This interview may also serve the purpose of stimulating thought about new objectives for the subsequent period.

8. *Reporting*

The division chairman prepares a concurring or dissenting statement, a copy of which is given to the faculty member. The statement, along with the report and supporting data from the faculty member, is forwarded to the appropriate administrator.

The outcome of the evaluation procedure, in addition to promoting professional and personal growth through the periodic intensive assessment of strengths and weaknesses, serves along with other information to provide the basis for making equitable decisions about salary adjustments, promotion, retention, and tenure. The procedure defined above, with the insertion of appropriate terms, can serve as the evaluation procedure for members of the administrative staff as well as nonteaching professionals. In our judgment, the system is valid whether or not it is linked directly to an arrangement involving material rewards. In fact, an overemphasis upon relationships between specific goals, such as productivity and material rewards, as advocated by some proponents of the systems approach, can result in negligence to higher human needs while stimulating internal conflict and retarding professional development.

MAINTAINING STABILITY AND PROVIDING FOR CHANGE

An institution is a dynamic entity in a constant state of interaction with its environment. Writers who stress the difficulties of inducing change are usually speaking of a specific change which is desirable according to some frame of reference, but which may be resisted because of conflicting frames of reference held by those who are a part of the internal or external constituencies. Because an organization is not static, change is constantly occurring, although the increments of change may be so small as to render measurement difficult. Viewed in this context, the problem is not primarily one of either inducing the change process or of promoting stability. Both of these forces are constantly at work. Rather the need is to manage change and stability so that a sense of direction can be maintained and limited resources can be employed most effectively to attain defined objectives.

The process by which the forces of change and stability interact is the decision-making or policy-formulation process. While individuals in the administrative structure may perceive the need for change and may formulate the procedures, it is the structure of governance which provides the necessary dissemination of information to create an institutional awareness, as well as providing the forum within which alternative institutional responses can be identified, discussed, and ultimately reconciled with the need for institutional stability (2:1–25).

The change process begins with the realization that there is a need to formalize or standardize a procedure, or more commonly with a generalized awareness of the existence of a problem that does not seem to lend itself to solution by existing policies or procedures. The stage of awareness occurs most frequently as a response to problem identification, although it may also occur in anticipation of the development of a problem. Ideally, problem solving in the policy-formulating process is initiated in reasonably close proximity to the developing problem. If the process is initiated too early, many will fail to see the relevancy of the solution proposed and, indeed, by the time the situation does occur, conditions may have altered the validity of the predetermined solution. By the same token, failing to deal with an actual problem promptly may result in rising tensions and a general complication of the policy-formulating process.

In addition to awareness, McClelland defines four other steps in relating the change process to the adoption of an innovation (5:18). Figure 10.1 is the paradigm he suggests. The illustration shows the complexity of the change process. Note that there are two separate inputs, one involving the characteristics of the change agent and the other involving the characteristics of the individual that are to be changed. From awareness, the process proceeds through the stages of interest, evaluation, trial, and decision. A change may be rejected as well as adopted, but neither rejection nor adoption constitutes the final step in the process. In both instances there are additional steps which, in turn, provide evaluative feedback to the change agent.

Rogers' definitions of the perceived characteristics of innovation relate directly to the attitudes of those involved in institutional decision making. He defines "relative advantage" as the degree to which a change is seen as an improvement. Economics, prestige, or convenience may all contribute to this factor. Compatibility refers to the congruence between the proposed change and the past experience of the individual. Complexity involves the difficulty required to implement change. The failure of many institutions to use expensive equipment purchased by administrative innovators is an example of change being defeated by complexity. Divisibility refers to the degree that a specific change may be broken down into stages which can be adopted successively. An indivisible change would have to be adopted in its entirety (10:67–77).

Organizations are composed of individuals at varying levels of attitudinal development, with differing capacities to cope with new situations. Thus, the process of change for an organization is like the process of change for an individual raised to the nth power, with n representing the number of individuals within the organization. It can be seen that the complexity of coordinating policy formulation will vary directly with the size of the organization that is involved. The process may be viewed as a six-step sequence:

1. The college studies its environment on a continuing basis to detect changes that may call for new responses. This is similar to the awareness stage for the individual.
2. The identification of actual or impending changes in the environment requires a review of existing response patterns to determine if the need for change exists. This may be the most difficult part of the process since value

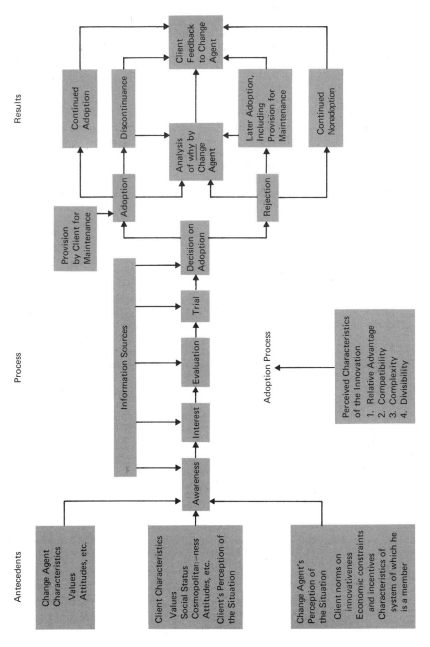

Fig. 10.1 Paradigm for Adoption of an Innovation by an Individual (after Rogers)

223

reorientation is frequently a requirement. A failure to encourage change and experimentation at previous stages in the institution's development can constitute a serious barrier to a willingness on the part of staff to consider alternative institutional responses.

3. Once there is general agreement that change is necessary, its direction must be chosen through the analysis of alternatives and their probable consequences. This is the evaluation stage. Because of the centrality of the administrative structure in the decision-making process, it is frequently the constituency that first perceives the need for change. The administrative structure may then become the agent of change. The administration's failure to understand the dynamics of institutional change may lead to an attempt to proceed directly from a realization of the need for change to the determination of the nature of that change. This is done through the exclusion of faculty and students during this stage of the decision-making process. As a consequence, administrators may find themselves in the untenable position of attempting to alert other constituencies to the need for change, while at the same time prescribing what that change should be. Attempting to proceed from awareness to a decision on adoption without appropriate involvement of those who will be affected by the change creates the possibility of alienating other constituencies and inducing an opposite and equal reaction culminating in a stalemate.

4. The evaluation stage produces a decision on the selection of a specific alternative. Faculty and student involvement in the evaluation process provides a natural entry to the next stage, which is implementation. Since the degree of success experienced during the implementation phase will most certainly be dependent upon the attitudes of all who are involved, it is worth noting that an alternative which does not appear feasible from an administrative point of view may become the most effective solution if it receives enthusiastic acceptance from other constituencies.

5. Finally, the alternative selected for implementation must be evaluated and the results integrated into the policy-formulation process so that the experience gained can serve as a guide to future decisions.

Thus, it can be seen that the process of policy formulation and change, like the process of establishing objectives, is sequential and ongoing. Each decision provides the basis for an evaluation which in turn contributes to new decisions in an unending chain. Institutions regarded as resistant to change commonly fail to provide for the systematic collection of evaluative data, and as a consequence must rely upon tradition. Since tradition does not change in relation to an institution's environment, it cannot serve as the basis for value reorientation, which is an indispensable part of the change process (4:3–6).

Perhaps no aspect of institutional functioning provides a better illustration of interdependencies than the process of change. The administrative structure, organizations of the various constituencies, committees, and the central forum must act with each other and with the external environment in order to create and sustain an effective level of response to the varied demands of the societal contest. Those who urge stronger administrative control to facilitate responsiveness and change along the lines of the bureaucratic structure, overlook two important points. First, to whom should interdependent administrative bodies be responsive? Second, what is the relative importance of getting something done as compared with ensuring that what does get done has lasting effect? The interdependent relationships mandated by the participational model of governance ensure the consideration of the broadest possible range of interests, combined with an emphasis upon the renorming process through broad involvement in policy formulation.

Professional Negotiations

Reaching decisions relative to such considerations as salary, fringe benefits, and working conditions must be regarded as a special application of the policy-formation process outlined above. Because of the tensions that frequently develop in this situation and the potential for disruption of institutional processes, professional negotiations merit special consideration (6:57–85). Boards of trustees are presently compelled to negotiate with faculty in a limited number of states, but the evidence suggests that this emerging trend will ultimately affect virtually all institutions, including those within the private sector. Even in the absence of state laws compelling professional negotiations, institutions must recognize the practice as one facet of the participational model of governance. As such, it represents nothing more than an equitable arrangement for resolving differences of opinion in economic areas in a manner similar to the procedures which have prevailed in educational areas. The procedures that we suggest are equally applicable to institutions functioning with or without the constraints of formal legislation. Obviously, refinements will be required in some instances to conform to the legislative mandates of specific states.

The point of departure for the development of procedures to resolve issues related to economic factors and working conditions must be the analysis of existing legislation. In this regard two extremes need to be avoided. In many states, the absence of laws compelling professional negotiations has been interpreted by trustees and administrators as a mandate to exclude faculty from involvement in discussions related to economic welfare. This narrow interpretation of board powers can only enhance the efforts of labor-related organizations to secure the passage of legislation which may go far beyond that needed to ensure a balance of power between board and faculty interests. The opposite extreme occurs much less frequently when trustees and faculty enter into negotiation agreements without adequately considering the safeguards which should be observed. For these reasons, faculty organizations, trustees, and their administrative representatives should probably review procedures and limits established by states having legislation before defining their own agreements (9).

Most institutions that initiate bargaining procedures in the absence of legislation seek to do so through existing structures which frequently include faculty and administrators in the same organization. While this approach is desirable in theory, it does not seem to work well in practice, and if professional negotiations are to have real meaning the faculty must be able to represent their own interests. There are two additional reasons for separating administrators and faculty in the bargaining process. The first involves public sensitivity to any implication that their interests are being undermined through administrative collusion in the bargaining process. The second involves the need to be able to define bargaining units under formal legislation in such a way that supervisory personnel are not included.

Professional negotiations must provide an equitable procedure for resolving differences of opinion among internal constituencies, and between internal and external constituencies in the economic sphere, just as procedures must exist for resolving differences of opinion in other areas. The process of bargaining primarily involves the structure of governance, since its goal is the establishment of general policies that will apply to certain major constituencies. In the absence of legislative requirements, boards and administrators are motivated to engage in professional negotiations by the advantages of keeping the bargaining process within the internal structure. They avoid submitting by default to the intervention of external agencies in the form of professional unions and labor negotiators. Those institutions which have lacked a credible internal procedure for professional negotiations have been the first to experience organization by outside agencies after the passage of enabling legislation.

One immediate goal of trustees, after experiencing organization of their faculty and contending with external influences in the form of professional organizations, is the return of negotiations to the local level. It is far more difficult to correct past actions which have caused the faculty to doubt the credibility of the administrators, trustees, and the organizational hierarchy, than it is to anticipate the need for, and to assume leadership in, establishing a structure for professional negotiations. We submit then that administrators and trustees, even in the absence, or perhaps, *especially in the absence of legislation compelling collective bargaining,* should move to establish the procedures defined below. Trustees and faculty alike stand to save substantial sums of money in the form of fees paid to professional negotiators and dues paid to professional organizations, if they are successful in defining procedures that will enable them to solve their own problems in this area. The alternative lies in appealing to external influences and thus setting the stage for lengthy, frequently bitter, and always costly power struggles.

The first step in developing procedures for professional negotiations is to define the scope of the bargaining unit. It is essential that clear distinctions be drawn between those who will be involved in administering the policies that are negotiated in a supervisory capacity and those who will not. The involvement of the former as a part of the bargaining unit creates a clear conflict of interest, because the same people in other circumstances represent both the faculty and the administration. It is in the best interests of the faculty association to include program coordinators and division chairmen as a part of the bargaining unit, since by doing this they gain additional leverage both in the bargaining process and subsequently in the administration of negotiated policies. Frequently, division chairmen and program coordinators prefer inclusion, since this resolves some of the normal ambivalence of their roles.

If the bargaining process is to be equitable, however, division chairmen must be excluded from the bargaining unit. The decision to exclude program coordinators is more open to question. If the role of a program coordinator includes responsibility for making recommendations relative to employment, dismissal, and salary increments, then the position should be excluded from the bargaining unit. The issue of who is eligible for membership in the bargaining unit, where laws compelling professional negotiations exist, must frequently be resolved by appeal to a state level labor relations board, with each party presenting evidence to support its position. Since a decision will normally depend upon evidence concerning the presence or absence of the responsibilities mentioned above, it is important for an institution to have job descriptions available to all staff members, clearly excluding supervisors from the bargaining unit.

The exclusion of supervisory personnel from the bargaining unit does not imply that the trustees have no responsibility for discussing economic issues with management personnel, nor does it necessarily mean that there can be no relationship between agreements reached with the bargaining unit and benefits extended to the supervisory staff. Ideally, the president or his representative will meet with, and discuss the concerns and recommendations of, midlevel administrators. The morale of both faculty and administrators must be considered in establishing a definite relationship between the agreements accorded to each constituency. A failure to give proper consideration to the total spectrum of administrative personnel needs in the process of organizing and implementing professional negotiations can encourage the same breakdown of internal communications with this group that the process of collective bargaining seeks to avoid in relation to the faculty.

After defining the scope of the bargaining unit, the next step is to reach agreement on the issues that are to be negotiated. The objective of administration is to keep the range of issues as restricted as possible, preferably limiting discussions to salaries and fringe benefits. The objectives of the bargaining unit will be to broaden negotiations as much as possible to include under the general heading of working conditions every possible consideration that could impinge upon the individual faculty member. The prototype agreement suggested by the higher education affiliate of the National Education Association includes increases in salaries and fringe benefits, limitations on hours of availability for meetings or other responsibilities, limitations on class size, reductions in contact hours, and a complete set of policies which, if adopted, would create confusion concerning administrative or faculty responsibility for administration. Of course, the prototype agreement is intended to represent one extreme, in the expectation that the position of the board will represent the other extreme; each side will therefore have something to give up in order to achieve its primary goals.

The process described above is an adversary relationship that need not develop if an institution has a structure of governance that recognizes the right of the faculty to be involved in the formulation of all policies that affect them. Under such circumstances, there is no need to bargain for this right. If the faculty association is so defined that it constitutes an appropriate unit for professional negotiations from the point of view of both the faculty and the administration, then the process becomes one of recognizing the special considerations that are a part of economic issues, and creating a structure and a procedure to resolve such issues equitably.

With respect to defining the issues that would be appropriate for negotiation with a bargaining unit under the bureaucratic model, and which might be assigned to a special committee of the faculty association under the participational model, the preferred approach is to confine discussions to those issues which have economic implications. Obviously, a primary concern of trustees is with costs that will be generated by any agreements that may be reached. Faculty have strong concerns about their economic welfare. By separating issues that have no economic implications from those that do, the process of professional negotiations can be simplified, and improved decision making may result in both the economic and noneconomic spheres. When the two issues are combined, there is great temptation on the part of both groups to use important noneconomic issues to force economic concessions. This confusion of goals and priorities may ultimately lead to making decisions about educational priorities on the basis of the wrong set of considerations. In addition to salaries and fringe benefits, issues having economic implications are faculty load, class size, and the use of paraprofessional personnel.

After defining the issues to be considered in professional negotiations, it must be determined who bargains. Where the faculty association affiliates with an external agency for the purpose of receiving assistance in the bargaining process, it is essential that the trustees obtain similar assistance, preferably by employing and training a staff member to function in this capacity. The trustees should not be directly involved in the bargaining process other than through the establishment of general guidelines for the negotiator. Such guidelines must provide sufficient flexibility to enable the negotiator to work with the faculty association in a meaningful way. Trustees must also preserve unity during the process of negotiations, and must avoid making commitments that would compromise the position of their representatives. While negotiations should be carried out under the supervision of the office of the president, he should not be involved directly, thus retaining the ability to reunite the institution after the bargaining process is concluded.

It is essential that the team which represents the faculty in the bargaining process be selected by those for whom they are bargaining, and through formal procedures that are acceptable to all. Where laws exist, procedures have been defined to ensure legitimation of the bargaining unit and its representatives. In the absence of such laws, procedures must be developed so that the acceptability of the unit and of its representatives are confirmed by a vote of those being represented.

When a faculty association is integrated into the governance structure of an institution and does not choose to affiliate with a faculty union, the committee approach can be used as an alternative to formal collective bargaining procedures. The committee approach involves the selection of administrative representatives who meet with an appropriate committee of the faculty association to collect and analyze data, in order to formulate a joint proposal to the board of trustees. It should be noted that administrators represent the interest of the board and the external constituency in this process, while the faculty committee represents the interests of an internal constituency. The assumption is made that an optimal solution exists for both external and internal constituencies, and that the job of both administrators and faculty is to seek out this optimal solution. This is preferable to confrontation in adversary roles where each seeks to maximize his own position at the expense of the other. The formal process of collective bargaining is normally a zero-sum game, while the committee approach may be a positive-sum game or even a nongame.

The committee approach, then, as distinct from the collective bargaining approach, involves the use of shared information in a cooperative attempt to reconcile the needs of the staff with the financial capabilities of the institution. The committee approach neither precludes the presen-

tation and vigorous defense of differing points of view, nor assumes that
the search for an optimal solution precludes the possibility of impasse or
the assistance of external mediators. For this reason, procedures used in
the committee approach parallel closely the procedures applicable to collective bargaining. The major difference involves the absence of extreme
postures assumed for bargaining leverage, and the emphasis placed upon
the welfare of the institution as well as the interests of the different constituencies. The following procedures represent one method of implementing a committee approach to professional negotiations.

1. The faculty association designates a specific committee to represent them
   in developing a proposal concerning salary increments, salary ranges, and
   fringe benefits to be presented to the board of trustees.
2. The board of trustees authorizes the president or his designated representative to meet with the committee to participate in the development of the
   proposal.
3. It is agreed by both constituencies that during the process of negotiation,
   discussion of the proposal will be limited to those who are directly involved.
   It is apparent that various positions may be taken during the discussion
   phase. If either the board or the faculty becomes committed to a position
   early in the process, the flexibility of discussions will be severely limited.
   Premature exposure of initial positions may also cause unnecessary tensions
   among those who will be affected by the decision reached.
4. Agreement is reached on the information to be collected and used to
   formulate and support the proposal. Normally such information will include: changes in the cost of living index, comparable figures for other
   institutions as reported by government agencies, professional associations,
   or compiled from special surveys, and projected income available for the
   support of college programs. An individual acceptable to both faculty and
   administration is given responsibility for compiling data. It is essential that
   both constituencies have access to the same data if they are to have maximum probability of reaching agreement. Accordingly, the office of the president must make available all requested data concerning the financial status
   of the college.
5. No proposal is presented to the trustees or to the faculty until one of the
   two following conditions has been fulfilled:
   a. An agreement is reached concerning the proposal to be presented to the
      trustees.
   b. A decision is made by either the president or the committee that agree-
      ment cannot be reached following normal procedures within a mutually
      agreed upon period of time.
6. The president may communicate informally with the board to advise them
   of developments with respect to the salary and fringe benefits proposal. By
   the same token, the committee may communicate with the staff at such
   times and in such ways as it considers appropriate. However, no attempt
   should be made by either the president or the committee to use their respective constituencies to place improper pressure on the discussion process.
7. If an agreement is reached between the president and the committee, the
   following steps are initiated:

    a. The president, with the assistance of the committee, presents the pro-
       posal to the board.
    b. If the proposal is approved by the board, the committee submits the
       proposal to the faculty for ratification at a faculty association meeting.
    c. If the proposal is not approved by the board, the procedures outlined
       below are implemented.
8. If an agreement cannot be reached between the president and the board
   and the committee, an attempt should be made to reconcile as many points
   as possible. When the areas of disagreement have been fully identified, a
   meeting is arranged with the board. At that meeting, the parties present
   their separate points of view in terms of areas of disagreement, as well as
   their recommendations in areas of agreement. Subsequent to this meeting,
   a final proposal is prepared by the president in coordination with the
   board. This proposal is presented to the committee and, through this committee, to the faculty association.
9. If the faculty association rejects the final offer of the board, those areas of
   disagreement are taken to mediation by a third party who must be acceptable to both groups. In the event that mediation proves unsuccessful, fact
   finding and binding arbitration are invoked. The process of mediation,
   fact finding, and arbitration can be carried out at board expense or shared
   between the board and the faculty association.

The committee approach facilitates the attainment of a common objective. Unresolved disputes, even in the absence of legislation authoriz-
ing strikes by public employees, are extremely undesirable in terms of
their consequences for the educational environment. The collective bargaining approach would follow a very similar sequence to that outlined
for the committee approach, with the exception that it would be somewhat more formal and would involve proposals and counter proposals.
Either arrangement requires that there be agreed upon procedures, a
defined time schedule, provision for reaching agreement, ratification,
and impasse procedures. It is suggested that under both approaches, the
separate parties agree in advance to submit an impasse to binding arbitration to ensure against the complete deterioration of institutional
processes. In the final analysis, neither the committee approach nor the
collective bargaining approach can succeed in the absence of good faith.
As a corollary, it is probable that either approach can be successful where
good faith is evidenced, although the implications of the two methods in
terms of the quality of a probable solution should be evident.

Professional negotiations in the multi-institutional system must be
carried out at the system level. For this reason the implications of our
recommendations for system organizations for each of the constituencies
in Chapter 9 should be evident. The existence of a credible system-wide
faculty organization is indispensable to the implementation of a committee approach to professional negotiations. Equally important, it can
make the transition to collective bargaining much less painful than

might otherwise be the case. If multi-institutional systems wish to confine professional negotiations to economic issues, they, like their single-campus counterparts, must establish effective channels for faculty participation in all issues in advance of the development of compulsory collective bargaining.

PERSONNEL CONFLICT. Even within a participational model, decisions that have significant impact upon one individual must be made by other individuals. While there are no procedures that can provide absolute protection against poor judgment or the unwise exercise of administrative or faculty prerogatives, there are policies which provide maximum protection against these consequences by establishing a proper balance between the rights of individuals and the common welfare of the college community.

Contractual Arrangements and Terminations

The advent of collective bargaining brought with it demands for the repeal of tenure legislation. Despite the new interest in academic tenure, it seems safe to predict that most institutions of higher education will continue to function under some variation of the principles set forth by The American Association of University Professors (1:192–93). Essentially this statement divides the professional staff into two categories: those who hold provisional appointments which may be terminated at the conclusion of an annual contract with few or no procedural safeguards, and those who hold tenured appointments who may be terminated only for proven incompetency, neglect of duty, physical or mental incompetency, or moral turpitude. In practice, appointments of the former group have been terminated without adequate cause, while tenured staff have even more frequently been retained without sufficient reason.

The wave of faculty militancy has occasioned a review of the principles of tenure, with the consequence that such groups as AAUP are now recommending due process in the termination of nontenured staff members. The courts have, in a number of instances, upheld the right of nontenured faculty to be advised in writing of the reasons for nonrenewal of an annual contract, as well as the right to a hearing in the event that they wish to contest the validity of the reasons. A serious problem is developing because parties to this dispute have chosen to define the alternatives as instant tenure versus no tenure. Neither of these two alternatives is likely to prove acceptable to both internal and external constituencies.

A viable compromise is the redefinition of contractual agreements to insure all faculty the right to procedural due process whenever a decision has been reached not to renew a contract for reasons other than retrenchment or mandatory retirement. Reasons for dismissal or nonrenewal of a contract should be extended to include unsatisfactory service. In this way, some of the protection traditionally reserved for tenured staff would be extended to new faculty, while a measure of the accountability and responsiveness traditionally reserved for probationary staff would be extended to tenured faculty. At the same time, the prevailing requirements for notification of nonrenewals would be retained so that more experienced staff would be given early notification of nonrenewal.

In order to secure faculty acceptance of such a standard contract, offered to all members of the professional staff on an annual basis without regard to length of service, certain requirements would have to be met. Among these would be written notification of intent not to renew by an agreed upon date. The written notice should specify cause, and should indicate the right of the individual to appeal such notification in accordance with an established and acceptable grievance procedure. In addition to these procedural arrangements, the key issue is a satisfactory definition of just causes for termination of service. The following are offered as representative causes which include certain necessary procedural safeguards:

1. *Unsatisfactory service.*
   Unsatisfactory service is defined as performance of responsibilities in a manner that is clearly below acceptable standards for the professional staff of the college. Evidence of unsatisfactory service may include student evaluation, colleague evaluations administrative evaluations, and other factors as may be relevant to the determination of the quality of an individual's contribution to the institution. Where unsatisfactory service is cited as the cause for termination, evidence must be presented indicating that:
   a. The unsatisfactory service occurred repeatedly over a period of not less than one semester.
   b. The unsatisfactory service was identified to the individual concerned in writing by an appropriate administrator at least three months prior to the date on which action was taken to initiate termination.
   c. Suitable assistance was provided to correct the condition of unsatisfactory service.
   d. A sufficient time period elapsed between the provision of assistance and the determination that the individual had not improved sufficiently to justify retention.
2. *Neglect of Duty*
   Neglect of duty is defined as failure to carry out defined responsibilities in the absence of justifiable reasons. Where neglect of duty is cited as a cause for termination, evidence must be presented indicating that:
   a. The acts identified as failure to carry out defined responsibilities occurred sufficiently often over a period of time to constitute a pattern of behavior.
   b. The individual was notified in writing of his actions and was given specific guidance in the correction of the problem.

   c. The individual persisted in the pattern of behavior despite the notification and subsequent guidance.
3. *Physical or Mental Incapacity*
   Physical or mental incapacity refers to a temporary or permanent condition which would prevent an individual from carrying out his normal responsibilities. In situations where the seriousness or nature of the condition is contested by the staff member, the opinions of at least two medical specialists, one chosen by the staff member concerned, should be obtained and submitted as evidence. If the incapacity should cause an absence of one year or less, the staff member should be granted a leave of absence.
4. *Violation of Professional Ethics*
   Professional ethics are defined as standards of behavior which are necessary to sustain effective working relationships with students and among colleagues. Evidence of conviction on charges of a felony or a misdemeanor involving behavior that would interfere with the staff member's performance of his duties may be cited as just cause for termination.

The following procedural standards should govern all nonrenewals or dismissals. The faculty member should be notified in writing of the complaints against him, and upon request should be accorded a full hearing before an appropriate committee of the faculty association within an agreed upon period of time. If a hearing is requested, the staff member should be entitled to be present, to be represented by a person of his own choosing, to confront and question witnesses against him, and to present evidence in his own behalf. A verbatim transcript of the hearing should be preserved.

Subsequent to the hearing, the normal process for all grievances as subsequently discussed should be followed. As in the case of economic disputes, we would suggest that both parties agree to submit to binding arbitration any differences of opinion not resolved by board action. A brief review of recent court cases establishes the right of an individual to appeal a dismissal to the courts. An agreement to submit such issues to binding arbitration is simply a recognition of the desirability of avoiding court trials. Acceptable arbitration proceedings do not encounter the result of long delays, and the undesirable publicity to both sides.

Grievance Procedures

Closely related to the resolution of termination disputes is the procedure for resolving differences of opinion that inevitably develop in other areas of personnel administration. Promotion, the granting of salary increments, workload, and other decisions made by supervisory personnel all have the potential for creating conflict. Every institution should have a clearly defined grievance procedure to prevent individual problems from affecting the morale of the entire institution. The following grievance procedure contains the essential requirements for conflict resolution.

1. In the event that a professional staff member (or group of staff members) believes he has a basis for a grievance, he shall first informally discuss the grievance with the appropriate program coordinator, division chairman, and administrative officers.

2. If, as a result of these informal discussions, a grievance still exists, the grievant may invoke the formal grievance procedure by submitting, in writing, a statement of his grievance and the remedy requested. The grievant shall file two copies of the grievance with the president of the college.

3. Within seven days from the date of filing, the president shall meet the grievant in an effort to resolve the grievance. Depending upon the wishes of the grievant, the conference may be private or the grievant may be accompanied by a representative of his choice. In the event that the grievant requests the presence of a representative, the president may also have another person present. At this stage, it is assumed that legal negotiations are not involved, and that the emphasis is upon resolving the grievance within the governance structure. The president shall attempt to mediate the grievance and indicate his recommendations in writing within ten working days of the conference.

4. If the grievant is not satisfied with the recommendations of the president, or if no recommendation has been made within the specified time, the grievant has the right to present his case to the appropriate committee of the faculty association. The committee, upon hearing and recording evidence presented by all parties to the dispute, shall declare its findings and make specific recommendations to the parties of the grievance and to the president within two working days. The president, after hearing the evidence and reviewing the findings and recommendations of the committee, shall, within one week, make his disposition known to all parties to the dispute and to the committee.

5. If the grievant is not satisfied with the action taken by the president of the college, he may, within one week, request that the grievance be submitted to the board of trustees by filing notification of such intention in writing with the president. Upon receipt of this request, the president shall be required to submit the following information to the board of trustees:

   a. The written statement of the original complaint.

   b. A summary of action taken in an effort to resolve the grievance informally.

   c. The complete transcript of the evidence received by the faculty association committee and their findings.

   d. A report of the action taken after receiving the recommendations of the committee.

   A representative chosen by the grievant shall attend and may present any additional statement in support of, or opposition to, the findings of the committee. The board of trustees shall, within thirty days of the date of receiving information, either resolve the grievance or hold a hearing with the grievant. No later than thirty days thereafter, the board of trustees shall indicate its disposition of the grievance in writing to the grievant, with a copy to the faculty association committee.

6. If the grievant is not satisfied with the disposition by the board of trustees, or if no disposition has been made within the prescribed period, the grievance may be submitted to arbitration before an impartial arbitrator who shall be bound by the rules and procedures of the American Arbitra-

tion Association. If the parties cannot agree on an arbitrator, he shall be selected pursuant to the rules and procedures of the AAA whose rules shall likewise govern the arbitration proceedings. The board and the grievant shall not be permitted to assert in such arbitration proceedings any ground or to rely on any evidence not previously disclosed to the other party. The arbitrators shall have no power to alter, add to, or subtract from the terms of the agreement. Both parties agree to be bound by the word of the arbitrator, and agree that the judgment thereon may be entered in any court of competent jurisdiction.

7. The fees and expenses of the arbitrator shall be shared by the board of trustees and by the grievant as determined by the arbitrator.
8. No reprisals of any kind shall be taken against any professional staff member for participating in any grievance proceeding.
9. The number of days indicated at each level should be considered as maximum, and every effort should be made to expedite the process. However, the time limits may be extended by mutual written consent.
10. All documents, communications, and records dealing with a grievance shall be filed separately in the personnel files of the participants. Committee hearings and deliberations shall be released only by written consent of the grievant, and then, only at the discretion of the committee. Committee recommendations may be made public at the discretion of the committee with the consent of the grievant. The grievant shall be furnished with all relevant information in the possession of the board of trustees, including an official transcript of the hearing before the board for the processing of any grievance or complaint.
11. A grievance may be withdrawn at any level by the grievant.

In the preceding discussion of administrative relationships among constituencies and governance procedures for resolving differences, we have tended to concentrate upon faculty, administration, and trustees. It is important to recognize that relationships with the student body and procedures for resolving student grievances deserve equal consideration. In this regard it may be important to note that our concern for the academic freedom of faculty has a long history. Our concern for the academic freedom of students is of much more recent origin, and received major emphasis only with the publication of the AAUP and National Student Association *Joint Statement on Rights of Freedoms of Students.* The same due process that is recommended for faculty members in disputes involving dismissal or other grievances should be accorded to students. The same attention that is given to defining working conditions and behavioral standards for faculty should likewise apply to students. Significant guidelines for establishing appropriate standards are available (7).

SUMMARY

The existence of dual structures for administration and governance within our institutions inevitably gives rise to questions involving jurisdictional boundaries. For each discussion an institution faces, the choice must be made as to the appropriate level of involvement for each constituency. There are no firm guidelines that can provide definitive answers to when a matter should be considered by the governance structure, and when it can satisfactorily be delegated to administration. The safest rule is to develop communication procedures which ensure that decisions reached at any point in the organization will be brought promptly to the attention of all who will be affected. When this approach is combined with assurance of a prompt review of the decision in the event it is questioned, the maximum protection against conflict is afforded, being combined with the minimum amount of procedural difficulty in administrative functioning.

Because decision making through group processes can be time consuming, the temptation is always present to circumvent agreed upon procedures in the interests of expediency. It is not solely administrators who are tempted to permit the structure of governance to fall into disuse. Many of the decisions commonly made by administrators become controversial only under exceptional circumstances. In the absence of crisis, faculty members are likely to abdicate responsibility for involvement, failing to recognize that it is the experience and mutual confidence acquired as a part of dealing with the routine that forms the basis for constructive interaction under crisis conditions. Of course, the widely noted propensity of students to stay away from decision-making situations that are not a source of immediate and vital concern has been identified previously and requires no further elaboration.

Earlier we suggested that authority delegated to the administrative structure can serve as a basis for guiding behavior only in the absence of disagreement over objectives, means of achieving objectives, and individual responsibilities. Where differences of opinion exist in any of these areas, mediation must occur, based upon an appropriate understanding of the interdependent nature of relationships among constituencies. While the administrative structure is very effective in implementing programs in the absence of conflict, the governance structure plays the major role in conflict resolution since it provides the only forum which can guarantee equitable representation of the differing interests which are a part of a dispute. It is imperative to understand that interdependent behavior is learned behavior. It cannot be switched on or off depending upon the intensity of the interests affected by a specific decision. If an institution is to preserve the capability of responding effectively to conflict, it must practice the procedures of conflict resolution in the absence of crisis.

While it is extremely desirable for an institution to be able to resolve conflict effectively, it is even more important to prevent the development of conflict initially. Routine use of the governance structure for consultation and review in the decision-making process can reduce the likelihood that a particular response will become a source of controversy. The governance structure also provides the means for communicating undesirable conditions with which the institution must live, as well as suggesting adaptations to minimize dissatisfaction.

As important as it is to prevent conflict or to resolve conflict, the interaction of administrative and governance structures may have a still more important role. The ability of an institution to use its resources effectively for goal attainment depends upon the existence of a satisfactory degree of congruence between the objectives of the institution and the attitudes of its constituencies. The involvement of all constituencies in goal identification, program planning, and evaluation can be a powerful force in shaping such congruence.

REFERENCES

1. "Academic Freedom and Tenure, 1940 Statement of Principles," *AAUP Bulletin*, 49:192–93 (June 1963).

2. CLARK, TERRY N., "Institutionalization of Innovations in Higher Education: Four Conceptual Models," *Administrative Science Quarterly*, 13:1–25 (June 1968).

3. HUGHES, CHARLES L., *Goal Setting: Key to Individual and Organizational Effectiveness*. New York: American Management Association, 1965.

4. LON HEFFERLIN, JB, "Reform and Resistance," *Research Report No. 7*. Washington, D. C.: American Council for Higher Education, June 1, 1971.

5. MCCLELLAND, WILLIAM A., *The Process of Effecting Change*, Professional Paper 32–68. Washington, D. C.: Human Resources Office, George Washington University, October 1968.

6. MCCONNELL, T. R., "Faculty Interests in Value Change and Power Conflict," in *Value Change and Power Conflict,* eds. W. John Minter and Patricia O. Snyder. Boulder, Colo.: Western Interstate Commission for Higher Education, October 1969.

7. *Model Code for Student Rights, Responsibilities and Conduct*. Chicago: Committee on Student Rights and Responsibilities, Law Student Division, American Bar Association, 1969.

8. ODIORNE, GEORGE S., *Management Decisions by Objectives*. Englewood Cliffs, N. J.: Prentice-Hall, 1969.

9. ROBERTSON, NEVILLE L., *Teacher-School Board Negotiations: A Bibliography*. Bloomington, Indiana: Phi Delta Kappa, 1968.

10. ROGERS, E. M., "The Communication of Innovations in a Complex Institution," *Educational Record,* 49:67–77 (Winter 1968).

Index

This book may be kept

FOURTEEN DAYS

A fine will be charged for each day the book is kept overtime.

GAYLORD 142   PRINTED IN U.S.A.